# From the Masses,
## to the Masses

# From the Masses,
## to the Masses

Third World Literature and Revolution

*E. San Juan, Jr.*

MEP Publications
Minneapolis

**MEP Publications**
University of Minnesota
116 Church Street S.E.
Minneapolis, MN 55455

© 1994 by E. San Juan, Jr.
All rights reserved. Published 1994
Printed in the United States of America

Library of Congress Cataloging-in-Publication Data

San Juan, E. (Epifanio), 1938–
    From the masses, to the masses : Third World literature and
revolution / E. San Juan, Jr.
        p. cm.
    Includes bibliographical references and index.
    ISBN 0-930656-63-6 : $39.95. – ISBN 0-930656-64-4 (pbk.) : $14.95
    1. Developing countries–Literatures–History and criticism.
2. Revolutionary literature–History and criticism. 3. Literature
and society. 4. Marxist criticism. I. Title.
PN849.U43S34 1994
809'.891724–dc20                                                         94-1228
                                                                                     CIP

Cover design for paperback by Robin Berry
of Tabet Berry Studio, Minneapolis

Capitalism will pass away. You'll no longer see the
                                            Stock Exchange
—Just as sure as spring follows winter. . . .
"An attempt to storm the heavens" said Lenin
Lenin no less (The Paris Commune)
        Communal and personal, without classes and without state
A new man with new chromosomes.
Easy to produce and distribute what we need on this celestial
                                            body. . . .
That was my vision that night. . . .
the whole of creation down to the hoardings groaned with pain
because of man's exploitation of man. The whole of creation was
        clamouring, clamouring in full cry for
the Revolution.
                        Ernesto Cardenal, *Cosmic Canticle*


Resolution in hardship, perseverance to the end. . . . Happiness is to take up the struggle in the midst of the raging storm and not to pluck the lute in the moonlight or recite poetry among the blossoms. In the absence of the greatest resolution, it is very easy to falter in mid-path. . . . People without great aims and ambitions rarely have the firmness of purpose that does not covet petty advantages or seek a comfortable existence. But only those who have aims and ambitions for the benefit, not of the individual, but of humankind as a whole can persevere to the end.
                        —Ding Ling, *Thoughts on March 8*

# CONTENTS

| | |
|---|---|
| Acknowledgments | 8 |
| Introduction | 9 |
| Literature and Revolution in the Third World | 19 |
| Transgression and Deliverance | 35 |
| Ngugi's *Petals of Blood:* The African Novel as a Weapon of Decolonization | 57 |
| Palestine, Incarnation of Our Desire: Texts from Fawaz Turki | 63 |
| Art against Imperialism: For the National Liberation Struggle of Third World Peoples | 77 |
| Ho Chi Minh: Writing as Praxis | 93 |
| Toward an Aesthetics of National Liberation: On Sergio Ramirez and Roque Dalton | 103 |
| Beyond Postcolonial Theorizing: The National-Popular in Philippine Writing | 119 |
| The Third World Artist in the Postmodern Age | 133 |
| Toward Socialism: In Solidarity with the Cuban Revolution | 161 |
| Afterword | 171 |
| Name Index | 193 |

# Acknowledgments

Every work is always a collaborative enterprise and presupposes solidarities cutting across boundaries in time and space. I am happy to record here my debt to the following for help in completing this project: Alan Wald, James Bennett, Sam Noumoff, Robert Dombroski, Paul Buhle, Neil Lazarus, and especially to Erwin Marquit. I should like to acknowledge the assistance of Mike McGrory, April Ane Knutson, and Doris Grieser Marquit in editing and preparing the manuscript for this volume.

Several essays originally published elsewhere (as indicated at the end of those essays) have been revised for inclusion here. I should like to express my thanks to the editors of the journals where early versions appeared: *Left Curve, Journal of Contemporary Asia, Weg und Ziel, Diliman Review, Journal of English Studies, Ariel, Parenthesis, Social Praxis, Theoretical Review,* and *Eastern Horizon*.

I also want to thank friends abroad who have contributed to my work in one way or another: Michael Wilding, Angus Calder, Daniel Henri Pageaux, Vladimir Makarenko, Wang Fengzhen, Ackbar Abbas, and Giovanna Covi. My collaborators on the home front, Delia Aguilar, as well as Karin and Eric, all deserve more credit than can be registered here. All inadequacies of this work are of course mine alone.

E. SAN JUAN, JR.

# Introduction

A 1992 article in *Newsweek* entitled "Let's Abolish the Third World" notes the obsolescence of the tripartite division of the planet with the passing of the Cold War. This fiat is more a symptom of anxiety and nostalgia—was there not one world from the time of "Manifest Destiny" to post-World War II *pax Americana*?—than an effort to align thought and reality. Citing the presence of "Third World" enclaves in the United States, the article then quotes a novelist from Trinidad: "The Third World is a form of bloodless universality that robs individuals and societies of their particularity." Here is where bourgeois ideology intrudes into the scene, mystifying the very problem of reification that its domination ineluctably generates. In trying to conceal inequalities and obscure contradictions, global capitalism imposes a universalizing practice—such as the U.S.-led war of the "United Nations" against Iraq, or the campaign against Somalian "warlords"—designed to secure its hegemony over all the plural "Others." Such hegemony, however, prevails only by reproducing, and even multiplying for greater profit-returns, those differences and singularities which precisely constitute its condition of possibility.

We still live in the ascendancy of late capitalism, in a *fin-de-siècle* display of its power and decay. An old world is dying, but the new is unable to emerge full-blown, hence all the moribund phenomena surrounding us. In his magisterial summing-up of political and cultural trends in the first half of the century, "Dialectical Materialism and the Fate of Humanity," the Caribbean thinker C. L. R. James gives us a profound analysis of the dialectics of general and particular, part and whole, old and new, so necessary in comprehending recent developments. He stresses the revolutionary process of history leading to "concrete universality," freedom and happiness for everyone. But in a world of military blackmail and commodity fetishism, this end can only be understood through mediations—ideas and practices where reality and will, structure and agency, become fused in historical action.

Written for the most part in the seventies and eighties, against the background of the heroic people's wars in Indochina, Chile, Iran, and elsewhere, the essays in this book seek to express those mediations as they materialized in specific conjunctures when imperialism—the old world order now christened anew—was being fiercely challenged and resisted by its victims. While events in the last decade have drastically reconfigured the geopolitical surface of the globe, the resistance fighters in Palestine, Central America, the Philippines, and numerous battlefields (in rural villages or urban supermalls) in Asia and Africa continue to persevere in intensifying the convulsive dying gasps of the imperial monster, the death rattle of a whole system of oppression and exploitation, even as the beast proclaims its triumph over its mirror image, "the Evil Empire," and the advent of transnational peace.

In retrospect, the central task of these essays is to register those convulsions and death rattles in the womb of transnational harmony. They endeavor to do this not by the evidence of the stench and corruption of imperialist culture suffered and endured every day by workers and peasants, but on the basis of implacable symptoms: the agonies, ordeals, vicissitudes of people of color in the center and periphery resisting the liberal, "humanistic" ideology of domination and, in the process, forging their own liberating milieu and their own collective practices of self-determination. Such a process is dialectical in essence: to destroy is also to build and rebuild. And what is being constructed can be epitomized in an ideographic rubric: "From the Masses, to the Masses." This slogan may be considered the key principle of the Cultural Revolution in China which, as a pivotal stage in the protracted decolonization process, dramatically elevated Fanon's *"les damnés de la terre"*—women, ethnic communities, workers, peasants, and intelligentsia of the developing neocolonized nations called the Third World—into the status of prime motive force in the making of world history. To use another figure: the Calibans are in revolt!

Between the death gasps at our back and the din of numerous hammers and rifles resounding around us, we may be able to reflect on the complex, intricate mediations connecting the petrified past and the enigmatic future: the present conjuncture. I believe that the dynamics, immediacy, and potential of this conjuncture are best grasped in literature conceived as a unity of opposites, a synthesis of contradictions. Since literary art both reflects and interrogates the contemporary upheavals and transformations we are living through, my task of interpreting and evaluating a selection of writers from the Third World can only be meaningful as part of a persisting collective effort of progressive intellectuals and radical scholars to reground the semantics of cultural praxis in historical specificity—that is, to find out where we came from and where we are heading. In my view, this specificity today can be summed up in the antithesis: imperialism (global capitalism) versus national-liberation struggles and popular-democratic social movements all over the Third World. Everywhere today, from South Africa to South Korea, from Haiti, Mexico, and Brazil to Timor, the Philippines, and Myanmar (Burma), the storm of world socialist revolution still rages. The law of uneven and combined development ordains lulls, setbacks, and sudden eruptions—there is no linear plot with a predetermined denouement. After the U.S. invasions of Grenada and Panama, the continuing "low-intensity" warfare in Nicaragua, the present international crisis in the Middle East, and before that the popular upsurge in Palestine which is still unfolding today amid manifold contradictions, the dynamics of class struggle on many levels is being played out once more in U.S. imperialism's backyard: El Salvador—and now Mexico. But how many academics in the United States can name even one writer from El Salvador that the high priests in the universities who establish the canon are teaching in their classrooms or discussing in the *New York Review of Books*? Throughout the Third World—as the neocolonial educational system, media, art, lifestyles, and various ideological practices will bear witness—the hegemony of Western culture persists, not in its undifferentiated totality, but in a particular monopolist reading of that global social text as it took shape with the imperialist adventures of France and England in the nineteenth century, and the United States in this century. It persists unevenly, generating its opposite on all fronts: the oppositional and insurgent voices of Rigoberta Menchu, Cardenal, Sembene, Achebe, and others. It resonates in the voice of Roque Dalton, the distinguished Salvadoran poet: "Under capitalism our heads ache/and they decapitate us.... In the struggle for the revolution the head is a time-bomb" ("On Headaches"). It reverberates in Peruvian activist Hugo Blanco's impassioned appeal to Cesar Vallejo: "The thing is, there are only great poets now, and no one writes for common people or the common struggle. / We have to assign all this to Vallejo. / Because if, after so many words, the word can't survive; if, after all the birds' wings the bird itself can't fly, the truth is you'd be better off just saying fuck it all, and we'll forget it" ("To the Poet Revolutionaries, To the Revolutionary Poets").

Allow me to reground here the dialectics of influence and autonomy in my personal case: I recall, back in the late fifties, at the height of the McCarthyite repression of the nationalist and radical forces in the Philippines, how together with thousands of other young students I was plunged in the discipline of memorizing William Empson's *Seven Types of Ambiguity*, quoting Eliot, Pound, T. E. Hulme, and, under the tutelage of some Fulbright professors from the United States in the University of the Philippines, was gradually initiated into the mysteries of the New Criticism as practiced by Ransom, Tate, Brooks, Warren, and their ilk. This droll story has no surprise ending. Subsequently, five years of graduate work at Harvard University served only to reinforce the domination (by consent, let us not forget) of colonialist/bourgeois ideology in my theoretical practice. And so it took me two decades of physical exile to return with halts and detours to my origins, thanks to the popular struggles in this country and around the world against the Indochina war, for the rights of women and people of color, and also the mounting resistance of the New People's Army in the homeland. It was in 1980, after years of assigning Joyce, Eliot, Yeats, and Pound, that I began a discussion with my class in "The Short Story" on the fictional craft of Third World writers—the Bengali Rabindranath Tagore, the Indonesian dissident Achdiat Mihardja, the Chinese Lu Hsun, and others—together with their allegorical and didactic enactment of class, race, and gender contradictions; a conversation which, I must confess, is not exactly "edifying" nor about "the best polity actualized so far," to quote a well-known U.S. philosopher of postmodern pragmatism.

For Third World artists, the imperative of political commitment, the vocation for responsibility to truth via the pursuit of beauty, coincides with their reason for existence. This is their singular fate. The dilemma of choosing the road of species-becoming (to use Marx's terms) traverses a space of permanent contestation, a borderland of ruptures, paradoxes, aporias, ironies, and bizarre dissonance. The Chinese communist-feminist Ding Ling (just to cite one example) wrestled with this problem throughout her rich exemplary life. The classic discrepancy between the subjective moment when the writer or intellectual becomes class-conscious and the objective structures and pressures may be illustrated in the context of the Cuban revolution in the writings and lives of revolutionary protagonists like Che Guevara, Amilcar Cabral, C. L. R. James, and many others. Or it can be found succinctly addressed in the following passage from the Cuban poet Nicolas Guillen's essay "Culture—From Where and for Whom?"

> During the time of republican life in Cuba, that is, in the fifty-odd years of fake independence, Yankee imperialism not only attacked our economy, exploiting us to our marrow. It also imposed language on us that was corroded with barbarisms in place of the pure words and criollo expressions that belong to our way of life, to our culture.

Well, we decided to complement our political independence with cultural independence, to rid ourselves of these oppressive hangovers. Just as our ideological profile is different from what it was before the revolution, we are also ready to create our own art and literature to follow this ideology and genuinely express our way of life, our real problems, our struggles, our conflicts and hopes. . . .

Recently, I visited Camaguey, where I was born, and I went to the city library. I looked at old newspapers, and among them I found one a hundred years old which published an announcement by some protectors of a poet slave, asking for public help to print and sell his verses so he could buy his liberty. I did not find out what the result was because the file of this newspaper was incomplete. But it made me think of the many talents, maybe even geniuses, who were frustrated under colonial rule—not only among the slaves but also among workers and peasants of all colors who were deprived of schooling. All this without even counting the many thousands who also lacked schooling under the republic.

How can we talk to these people, who are only beginning to learn of Proust, Kafka, Joyce before we tell them of Marti, Heredia, Varela, Luz and Caballero, without giving them a national consciousness of art, of literature? They first must know who they are, where they come from, where they are going.

But my case is, like those of most Third World intellectuals, truly overdetermined. My experience may be considered a paradigm for what has happened to many Third World writers and artists displaced or alienated in their habitats, or physically exiled and uprooted. It has taken a whole historical process here, in particular the Third World social movements in the United States and my particular identification with the growth of the people's war in the Philippines, thanks to U.S. support of the Marcos dictatorship, to articulate the site of negations and affirmations and reinscribe my otherness not in the hybrid and syncretic *différance* (Derrida) of postcolonial celebrities but in the archive of popular-democratic struggles. It has taken also the mediation of particular thinkers—Fanon, Mao, Gramsci (besides the classics of Marxism-Leninism)—for my own consciousness to realize that it (this subjectivity) is only the arena where historic class forces are constantly colliding and working out daily the tortuous path of their resolution. This work strives to recreate those moments in the staging of trajectories, the scenes of crisis and transformation, in the experience of critical readings. What I am saying is that this volume is the fruit of a historic transactional process in which we, writers and readers, have served both as subjects and objects, players in the discourse of social forces and relations of production, unfolding the concrete, decisive contradictions of this specific stage of the revolutionary development of various social formations.

The "Third World" scene, then, is more ambiguous or complex than *Newsweek*, Lacan, or Derrida might conceive it to be. We witness there a confounding of Imaginary and Symbolic registers, a locus of interpellations that suture and divorce the self and the community, the "I" and "Others," death and desire. Can I really speak about my personal predicament? Or am I simultaneously the bearer of a national allegory which like language articulates my life? Perhaps I can find consolation in the fact that, unlike the ill-fated Jose Arcadio Segundo, eyewitness/participant of the massacre of striking workers in Gabriel Garcia Marquez's *One Hundred Years of Solitude*, I am not a lone survivor of recent upheavals, isolated from the masses, a prophet in the wilderness. Nor do the texts that hide, mystify, or distort reality (like the government textbooks in Marquez's novel) maintain complete monopoly at all times, preempting any resistance and occupying even the fissures, gaps, and lacunae constituting the psyche—or else we would all be solipsists, antinomian pragmatists, or even undeconstructed zombies!

On the contrary, I believe that there is hope in elucidating the truth from concrete events and testifying to this truth with our words and actions, with our bodies and our lives. A reminder from Hegel's Preface to the *Phenomenology of Spirit* might be instructive for anyone who might accuse us of "vulgar" materialism: "Lacking strength, Beauty hates the Understanding for asking of her what it cannot do. But the life of Spirit is not the life that shrinks from death and keeps itself untouched by devastation, but rather the life that endures it and maintains itself in it. It wins its truth only when, in utter dismemberment, it finds itself. This tarrying with the negative is the magical power that converts it into being."

Anyone engaged today in situating the confrontation between Third World cultural practice and the beleaguered hegemony of a reifying and commodifying Eurocentric tradition—as specifically shaped by the idealist or metaphysical world outlook serving capital—must grapple with the total framework of assumptions within which concepts and definitions are played out. Contextualization of ideas and themes is needed for the task of forging the "weapon of criticism." Consequently

I have tried in these essays to provide an explicitly anti-imperialist perspective to the ideological struggle between cultural imperialism and Third World popular-democratic forces. The first and last chapters attempt to sketch a working model for a further microanalysis of diverse themes and tendencies overdetermining specific discursive practices of individual writers. As everyone knows, there is no innocent reader, no *tabula rasa* in interpretation. Each person as a complex and mutable network of relations situates herself or himself in a context of class confrontation, a milieu of practices defined by the dominant reality of the so-called "Free World," namely "alienated labor," racist and sexist oppression, class exploitation, and various forms of domination. In this situation (call it language game, or rhetorical strategy), we know that sides are necessarily chosen, consciously or unconsciously, by us or for us.

Given the different occasions and incommensurable purposes for which the individual chapters were written, I have not tried to superimpose on them a hypothetical and artificial unity that would erase the traces of contingencies and intertextuality in my argument. Worldliness, polemical impulses, and "tarrying with the negative" may be discerned everywhere. A historical materialist orientation, however, provides a frame for the whole collection. In exploring the various manifestations of the cultural changes and mutations in the Third World, I have been guided by the fundamental principle of internationalism enunciated by Marx and Engels: "A people that oppresses other peoples cannot itself be free." Such a principle subsumes the vision of Third World culture as a materialization of popular-democratic needs and aspirations which combines the classic ideals of *utile* and *dulce*; a dialectical synthesis which Lenin described in "The Tasks of the Youth Leagues" as the "logical development of the store of knowledge mankind has accumulated under the yoke of capitalist, landowner and bureaucratic society." This vision serves also as the horizon of expectations for the sensibilities of readers, questioning the limits of the status quo and inspiring the will to move beyond them. It is this vision that radiates from Pablo Neruda's 1972 Nobel Prize lecture, *Toward the Splendid City*, an eloquent inventory and manifesto of the artistic practice not only of Neruda but of a large, heterogeneous group of committed Latin American writers. The following passages propose a strategic agenda for all progressive Third World cultural activists:

> We writers within the tremendously far-flung American region, we listen unceasingly to the call to fill this mighty void with beings of flesh and blood. We are conscious of our duty as

fulfillers—at the same time we are faced with the unavoidable task of critical communication within a world which is empty but which is no less full of injustices, punishments, and sufferings because it is empty—and we feel also the responsibility for reawakening the old dreams which sleep in statues of stone in the ruined ancient monuments, in the wide-stretching silence in planetary plains, in dense primeval forests, in rivers which roar like thunder. . . . I determined that my posture within the community and before life should be that of in a humble way taking sides. . . . In the midst of the arena of America's struggles I saw that my human task was none other than to join the extensive forces of the organized masses of the people, to join with life and soul, with suffering and hope, because it is only from this great popular stream that the necessary changes can arise for writers and for nations. And even if my attitude gave and still gives rise to bitter or friendly objections, the truth is that I can find no other way for a writer in our far-flung and cruel countries, if we want the darkness to blossom, if we are concerned that the millions of people who have learned neither to read us nor to read at all, who still cannot write or write to us, are to feel at home in the dignity without which it is impossible for them to be complete human beings. . . .

For I believe that my duties as a poet involve friendship not only with the rose and with symmetry, with exalted love and endless longing, but also with unrelenting human occupations which I have incorporated into my poetry.

The Chilean poet's eloquent testimony reaffirms the unrelenting solidarity of the creative artist with the "hewers of wood and drawers of water"; the unwashed and unlettered, with that tremendous and powerful agency invoked by Fanon as "the wretched of the earth."

Unlike the alienated "howl" of Ginsberg and the Beat poets, or the decentered screams of French anarchists, Third World writing may be said to resemble that kind of poetry the Scottish-Marxist poet Hugh MacDiarmid compares to "the barrel of a gun/weaving like a snake's head," utterances which abound with "courage, self-assertive unyieldingness, energy, and (above all) a steel-like and combative virility." That engaged, intransigent, partisan practice of writing appears exorbitant in contrast to Establishment apologetics; it exceeds what Hardy calls "the written expression of a revolt against accepted things" and approximates more what the Filipina guerrilla poet Maria Lorena Barros calls an armed fist "to shape reality." From expressing to shaping: this encapsulates, indeed, the tortuous itinerary of Third World writing some of whose memorable projects and adventures I attempt to capture here. These are of course political interventions aimed at mapping the emergence and evolution of Third World aesthetic praxis, a matrix of hope and provocations, a modality of writing committed to incarnating the incandescent and intractable dreams of the masses, giving voice to their grief and joy, inscribing onto the massive palimpsest of their suffering and wrath that hope which has proved as fleeting as fantasy and as solid as earth. Let Lu Hsun's words composed in 1921 be our motto:

> Hope is just like roads across the earth. For actually the earth had no roads to begin with, but when many people pass one way, a road is made.

# Literature and Revolution in the Third World

I come from the Philippines, where, between 1972 and 1986, the martial-law regime headed by the dictator Marcos systematically violated the human rights of forty-four million citizens. These violations were documented by numerous organizations, among them the International Commission of Jurists, the International Red Cross, and committees of the U.S. Congress, and confirmed by the U.S. State Department. Washington's financial support was the main lifeline of the Marcos regime. At the time of this writing [1979], over sixty-five thousand people were being held as political prisoners, including several hundred distinguished intellectuals, writers, teachers, journalists, and artists, whose release was demanded by international bodies like P.E.N. International and Amnesty International.

As one honored by being included in the Marcos dictatorship's "blacklist" of dissident intellectuals, I would like to offer these few remarks on behalf of my colleagues in prison, as well as other progressive writers and artists in the Third World—Kim Chi Ha in South Korea, James Ngugi in Kenya, and many others in Indonesia, Chile, South Africa, and elsewhere.

A U.S. visitor to Manila, John Leonard, wrote in the *New York Times Book Review* of his meeting with a Filipino writer who described himself as a "Brooklyn Dodger." Mr. Leonard explained the context:

> When a writer gets out of jail to find a bunch of magazines and newspapers owned or controlled by the Government, he needs a job to feed himself. He can go to work for a big company in which there are heavy American investments.
>
> United States investment in the Philippines has quadrupled since the declaration of martial law in 1972. . . . When the Government controls the radio and the universities and the taxes affecting big companies, a writer has to Brooklyn Dodge.

What this comment points to is the generally embattled, embroiled, embedded situation of the writer in the Third World, in nations striving to emerge from the economic backwardness and social stagnation of their colonial past. The literary artist in the developing countries, whether he or she is aware of it, is inextricably enmeshed in the manifold contradictions of historical reality. Of course, this is true for any writer anywhere, but more so for Third World artists because of the crisis and crucible of self-interrogation to which their art is subjected by their milieu. In essence, the Third World writer is born already *engagé*, situated in the thick of class struggle.

Observers living in industrialized countries may prefer to think this is just a passing fancy, one ideological interpretation among others. But the interdependent facts of history, ignoring the opportunist impulses of the moment, will always assert their recalcitrant and intractable presence.

About two decades after Mao Tse-tung, Gandhi, Sukarno, and Ho Chi Minh had successfully led national-liberation struggles in their own countries, others in Africa and Latin America began the struggles that would result in the triumphant revolutionary process in Cuba, Guinea-Bissau, Mozambique, and South Yemen. Patrice Lumumba's militant campaign to begin wide-ranging social reconstruction in the former Belgian Congo was aborted, but all these historical developments, consonant with other upheavals, laid the groundwork for a young Caribbean intellectual educated in the colonizer's metropolis, Frantz Fanon, who would articulate the revolutionary principles of the Algerian revolution.

In contrast to Leopold Senghor's procolonial position during the war between France and the Algerians, Fanon expressed in his 1961 essay "On National Culture" what can be seen as the common premise for the programs of Third World cultural workers today:

> A national culture is not a folklore, nor an abstract populism that believes it can discover the people's true nature. . . . A national culture is the whole body of efforts made by a people in the sphere of thought to describe, justify, and praise the action through which that people has created itself and keeps itself in existence. (1968, 233)

In hindsight, given the rise of native entrepreneurs and wealthy property-owners—the native ruling class—only too willing to preserve the status quo inherited from the colonial power, it is necessary to qualify Fanon's concept of the nation as one homogeneous and undifferentiated totality; no such nation has existed since the appearance of private property. Lenin offers the qualification in his dialectical analysis of the phenomenon of "national culture":

> The *elements* of democratic and socialist culture are present, if only in rudimentary form, in *every* national culture, since in

*every* nation there are toiling and exploited masses, whose conditions of life inevitably give rise to the ideology of democracy and socialism. But *every* nation also possesses a bourgeois culture (and most nations a reactionary and clerical culture as well) in the form, not merely of "elements," but of the *dominant* culture. Therefore, the general "national culture" is the culture of the landlords, the clergy, and the bourgeoisie. (1964, 24)

Social classes exist in the heart of Third World countries. Terms like "cultural autonomy," "cultural pluralism," and "acculturation" inevitably acquire class implications. In any case, for Fanon, the primary task for the Third World poet, playwright, or painter is "the liberation of the national territory"—here the examples of Rhodesia, Namibia, and South Africa come to mind, and closer to the United States, the colony of Puerto Rico. In addition, the Third World artist must persist in combating colonialism in a new form, as neocolonialism.

Most Third World countries are, in uneven fashion, undergoing the process of a national-democratic revolution. This revolution is national because it seeks to assert national sovereignty against imperialism and its native clients; democratic because it seeks to fulfill the peasants' struggle for land against domestic feudalism (or its survivals) and to uphold the democratic rights of the broad masses of working people against fascism. For this project to be fully realized, the revolution must be spearheaded by a working class that will unite the peasantry, the petty producers, the intelligentsia, and other sectors in a broad united front. This process, inchoate or advanced, is occurring in various stages in all Third World countries where the masses of people, the workers and peasants, are exploited by U.S. or European transnational corporations—in Chile, Brazil, and Puerto Rico; in Saudi Arabia, Iran, and Morocco; in India, South Korea, Indonesia, and the Philippines.

For Fanon's compatriot from Martinique, Aimé Césaire, the affirmation of an African or Black identity can only be realized simultaneously with the creation of a new system of humane values vis-à-vis the degrading, oppressive colonial society. In *Return to My Native Land*, the surrealist images of violence and destruction derived from the seething, convulsed realm of nature coalesce with ritualistic symbols of organic rebirth and cyclic regeneration:

> And now suddenly strength and life attack me like a bull the wave of life streams over the nipple of the Morne, veins and veinlets throng with new blood, the enormous lung of cyclones breathing, the fire hoarded in volcanoes, and the gigantic

seismic pulse beats the measure of a living body within my
blaze.
I say Hurrah! and more the old negritude
is turning into a corpse. . . .
Between the torn clouds a sign by lightning:
the slave-ship is splitting open. . . . Its belly in spasm ringing
with noises.
The cargo of this bastard suckling of the seas is gnawing at its
bowels like an atrocious tapeworm. . . .
(Césaire 1983, 78)

What was Césaire's urgent motivation in employing a surrealist mode? In an interview in 1967, Césaire confessed:

> We didn't know what Africa was. Europeans despised everything about Africa, and in France people spoke of a civilized world and a barbarian world. The barbarian world was Africa, and the civilized world was Europe. Therefore the best thing one could do with an African was to assimilate him: the ideal was to turn him into a Frenchman with a black skin. (1972, 72–73)

> Even though I wanted to break with French literary traditions, I did not actually free myself from them until the moment I decided to turn my back on poetry. . . . Surrealism was a weapon that exploded the French language. It shook up absolutely everything. This was very important because the traditional forms—burdensome, overused forms—were crushing me. Yes, a process of disalienation, that's how I interpreted surrealism. (66–67)

The South African poet Mazisi Kunene defines Césaire's aesthetic purpose, the "thinking content" of the poem, as identical with Fanon's insight: "the incision of the colonial mentality, the tearing away of the white man's superiority complex and in its place the creation of the ideology of man in his totality as a humane and a civilized being" (cited in Awooner 1976, 197).

Commenting on the poem's epilogue, Kofi Awoonor, a poet from Ghana, stresses the vision of the "unity of man and place" as a signal of renewed hope for humanity. This resurgent consciousness of the "spirit of place" manifests itself in the two dominant themes of Third World novelists. First, the clash between the indigenous sphere of traditional values and the profit-centered goals of European or U.S. imperialism. Its most diligent chronicler in Africa is the Nigerian Chinua Achebe. Second, the intensifying process of decolonization, the conflict of social classes that cuts across both racial and tribal lines and unfolds a dialectical panorama of individual and collective transformation. This may be exemplified in the novels of Ousmane Sembene from Senegal *(God's Bits of Wood)*, Ngugi from Kenya *(Grain of Wheat)*, and Ferdinand Oyono from the Cameroon *(Boy!)*. In Latin America, the tensions underlying the movement of generations and families pervade the novels of Gabriel Garcia Marquez *(One Hundred Years of Solitude)* and Carlos Fuentes *(The Death of Artemio Cruz)*, while a more polemical and topical strategy is adopted by Miguel Asturias in his novels on the plantation system in Guatemala *(Strong Wind)*. And in Asia, the Indian writer Raja Rao's novel *Kanthapura* orchestrates the reverberations of caste, class, and psyche, and demonstrates how a historic sequence of events—the Gandhian movement and the British response—informs individual lives in a single village. The Chinese writer Hao Jan depicts in his novels and short stories the intricate conflicts in thought and action between progressive and reactionary worldviews in scenes of peasant life in the communes.

For most Western scholars and critics, the pivotal issue proposed by Mao Tse-tung in his well-known *Talks at the Yenan Forum on Literature and Art* (1942)—"For whom is the writer writing?"—sounds ominously political and therefore irrelevant to literary inquiry. With some exceptions, the reigning conception of art as divorced from politics or any social extrapersonal criteria—the kernel of what is called the bourgeois liberal dispensation—still forms the basis for critical judgment in the learned journals and universities. This prescribes that culture is neutral, and the values of art are transcendental—timeless and classless. Art has little or no reference to anything outside itself. Form is autonomous and self-sufficient and, as Kant asserts, "judgment about beauty in which the slightest interest interferes is highly partisan and not a pure judgment of taste" (1963, 5).

From Kant to Coleridge, Matthew Arnold, I. A. Richards, the New Criticism, and the now-fashionable school of structuralism, the dominant formalist and idealist worldview of most intellectuals in the metropolitan countries, as well as Third World intellectuals trained in the United States or Europe, automatically condemns writers critical of the view that art conveys classless and nonpolitical universal truths. If writers bother about the immediate problems of life, it is implied, they will forfeit the freedom of the imagination; the delicate sensibility, the complex individual spirit, will be sacrificed for impersonal causes or bureaucratic absolutes.

Fanon, Césaire, and others counter that freedom, if it is not just freedom in the mind, cannot be understood in the abstract, only in the concrete. In a society where people interact mainly through the anarchic laws of the market and through the mediation of commodities (money, wages, etc.), the freedom of one group depends on the servitude of others. For the formalist or structuralist critics, the model and standard of aesthetic integrity and superiority are still too often based on orthodox canonical authors such as Henry James, T. S. Eliot, Ezra Pound, Proust, Yeats, Faulkner, and Flaubert.

Given this ideology of aesthetic formalism and its elitist, reactionary implications—only a few can really appreciate Henry James, etc.—the cardinal sin of the Third World writer is probably his or her passionate commitment to the people's struggle. Themes of classic vintage—the sufferings, anguish, and anger of a whole community; the exploding rebellion of individuals against an unjust system—evoke patronizing criticism. For example, Prof. Charles Larson of the American University, appraising the novel *Petals of Blood* by the Kenyan novelist Ngugi Wa Thiong'o, provides a representative sample of the prevailing critical tendency:

> The weakness of Ngugi's novel as a work of the creative imagination ultimately lies in the author's somewhat dated Marxism: revolt of the masses, elimination of the black bourgeois; capitalism to be replaced with African socialism. The author's didacticism weakens what would otherwise have been his finest work. (*New York Times Book Review,* 19 Feb. 1978, 14)

The reference to the author's "somewhat dated Marxism" is a marker of the critic's ideology. No genuinely revolutionary movement in the Third World has aspired to establish a neocolonial exploitative social system. Practically all of them (one can cite the African National Congress, the Brazilian Workers' Party, the revolutionaries in East Timor opposing the Indonesian generals), sought or seek to establish a socialist society founded on principles first enunciated by Marx and Engels, and subsequently adjusted by Lenin, Mao, Che Guevara, and others to the concrete historical conditions in each country.

The *Declaration on the Establishment of a New International Economic Order,* adopted 1 May 1974 by the United Nations, may be said to formulate in concise language the themes of Ngugi and many other Third World writers. The first point in the document reads:

> The greatest and most significant achievement during the last decades has been the independence from colonial and alien domination of a large number of peoples and nations. . . . However, the remaining vestiges of alien and colonial domination,

foreign occupation, racial discrimination, apartheid, and neocolonialism in all its forms continue to be among the greatest obstacles to the full emancipation and progress of the developing countries and all the peoples involved. (1994, 1–2)

The document further recapitulates the most recent trends in the Third World and affirms the right of each nation to nationalize foreign corporations (which the CIA frustrated in Chile) and the right of self-determination for peoples victimized by foreign occupiers or racist settler regimes.

The choice faced by Third World peoples is not, as often stated in the most banal and chauvinist way, between U.S. democracy (confined only to the wealthy few) and totalitarianism, between *laissez-faire* modernization and feudal conservatism. Rather, it is between a capitalist system, where the major means of social production are owned or controlled by a privileged minority, and a society founded on socialist principles, where those means of production are controlled and managed in the interests of the workers and peasants, for the majority of the people, and where the guiding principle for the whole society is not competition, but cooperation and the spirit of working-class internationalism. Is it possible that our good Professor Larson is himself outdated, left behind by the forward thrust of humanity building a world free from the tyranny of profit-gouging corporations and their political representatives?

It is too easy for many academic critics to dismiss the themes of social justice and militant protest as dated or mere leftist rhetoric, although ironically these same themes evoke cultic devotion when treated by Dostoevsky, Kafka, Conrad, or Malraux. The rhetoric acquires flesh and bones, however, when we confront the reality. For example, in South Africa, where Blacks (seventy percent of the population) have one doctor for every hundred thousand persons, malnutrition and wretched living conditions kill more than half of all Black children before the age of five. The degrading *bantustans*, virtual concentration camps, pose a massive challenge to the craftsmanship of any writer, yet this reality has been powerfully rendered in the fiction of Alex La Guma (*A Walk in the Night, Stone Country*, etc.) and the poetry of the exiled South African militant Dennis Brutus.

In a poem entitled "Sharpeville," Brutus captures not only the fact of seventy people shot in cold blood in Sharpeville on 21 March 1960, but also its significance in the historical perspective of popular resistance.

> What is important
> about Sharpeville
> is not that seventy died:
> nor even that they were shot in the back
> retreating, unarmed, defenceless
>
> and certainly not
> the heavy calibre slug
> that tore through a mother's back
> and ripped into the child in her arms
> killing it
>
> Remember Sharpeville
> bullet-in-the-back day
>
> Because it epitomized oppression
> and the nature of society
> more clearly than anything else;
> it was the classic event
>
> Nowhere is racial dominance
> more clearly defined
> nowhere the will to oppress
> more clearly demonstrated
>
> what the world whispers
> apartheid declares with snarling guns
> the blood the rich lust after
> South Africa spills in the dust
>
> Remember Sharpeville
> Remember bullet-in-the-back day
>
> And remember the unquenchable will for freedom
> Remember the dead
> and be glad
>
> (1975, 38–38)

Propaganda? Didacticism? At any rate, we are light-years removed from the static, mystifying, Confucian-inspired cosmos of Pound's *Cantos*.

Within the dominant European literary tradition, one finds poems where the organizing principle is not an action represented by the plot (as in mimetic forms), but a thematic argument that determines a moral and emotional attitude toward a set of beliefs in such a way as to command action in accordance with it. The final effect of a work with a didactic form is to move the reader's awareness outside the text into an area of common or public concern. Examples range from Lucretius's *De Rerum Natura* to Bunyan's *Pilgrim's Progress* to Orwell's *1984* and Eliot's *Four Quartets*. We need to recognize this category of didactic form (the neo-Aristotelians recognize it) as a separate and distinct aesthetic type, equally valid as its antithesis, mimetic form. (Northrop Frye, an anti-Marxist critic, assigns the term "romance" to designate this fictional mode.)

But I think the reservations of critics like Professor Larson are not really addressed to the presumed "didacticism" of Ngugi's novel, where the ideas are ascribed to fully dramatized characters. Rather, the objection is to the content, an uncompromising critique of imperialism and its ideological consequences in social practice. This is condemned as reductionism, economic determinism, and propaganda.

That response is understandable. In a society where the alienated artist either submits to the subtly concealed commercialization of his art in the "free market," or repudiates "the herd" for the sake of preserving the hermetic sanctity of his vocation, the function of art degenerates into a self-serving form of narcissistic gratification and/or a justification of a status quo based on the fetishism of commodities. Ostensibly both are meant to insure the artist's freedom. In effect both signify a surrender to the deterministic hold of forces the artist has refused to heed, understand, and thus control.

The response of Latin American writers to the demands of their calling offers the sharpest contradiction to aesthetic formalism and structuralism. Nicholas Guillen, the Cuban poet, states the consensus in this manner:

> I cannot comprehend . . . how a truly contemporary writer can, without blushing, give a miner, a cane-cutter, an oil driller, works that are simply not understandable. This is not only a mockery, it is a betrayal. . . . He dare not devote himself to mere plays of the imagination, to useless verbalism, to idle glitter, to amusing crossword-puzzles, to deliberate obscurantism, all of which please those very imperialists who exploit and suffocate us. . . . Poetry is not so much for us as it is for others, and therefore one must be on guard against vulgarity and demagoguery as against the alleged refinements stemming from human decadence. (1974, 12)

The problem of the audience, "For whom is one writing?" cannot be reduced to the stereotyped notion of the conflict between East and West, as popularized by Vera Micheles Dean in *The Nature of the Non-Western World* (1966, 325–40). The decisive issue is whether to conceive art as an abstract entity detached from its concrete historical milieu, its matrix of origin and reception, or to envisage art as part of a total cultural practice, the all-encompassing production and reproduction of social life.

The Chilean poet Pablo Neruda, in his last book, *Incitement to Nixonicide and Praise for the Chilean Revolution*, written on the eve of the coup, rejected the "mystical hermeticism" of his other poems: "I reserve, as an experienced mechanic, my experimental office: I must be, from time to time, a poet of public use, that is to say, I must give the brakeman, steward, foreman, farmer, gasfitter, or the simple regimental fool the capability of cutting loose with a clean punch or shooting flames out of his ears" (5–6).

The Senegalese poet David Diop records a parallel conviction in his essay "A Contribution to the Debate on National Poetry":

> We know that some people wish to see us abandon militant poetry (a term which "purists" jeer at) for benefit of stylistic exercises and formal discussions. Their hopes will be dashed, since for us, poetry cannot be led to "tame the language beast" but to reflect on the world and to keep the memory of Africa "like a splinter in the wound, / like a guardian fetish at the center of the village."
>
> Only thus can we fully carry out our responsibilities and prepare the renewal of our civilizations. (1973, 61)

An analogous sentiment is expressed by René Dépestre, a poet from Haiti, where the Duvalier dictatorship was long supported by U.S. arms and money, oppressing a people with the lowest per capita income in the world, ninety percent illiterate, with a life expectancy of forty-five years. Dépestre rejects "Negritude" and chooses revolution: "Today the Black Orpheus of Africa and Asia only in revolution and by revolution can find again Eurydice that was taken from him by the colonial hell. The revolution is the only power capable of destroying—with the creative energy of the people—all the hells that men have built for men" (1968, 30).

The Guatemalan poet Otto Rene Castillo, killed in 1965 in a guerrilla encounter, voices the idea of the poet's radically democratic responsibility in his satiric poem "Apolitical Intellectuals." One day, he says, the "apolitical intellectuals" will be interrogated by the working people, those who had no place in their books and poems, who will ask: "What did you do when the poor / suffered, when tenderness / and life / burned out in them?" (1974, 267).

In Asia, the experience of the Cultural Revolution in China and the lessons gained from it continue to demonstrate the practical implications of the principle of the "mass line" in culture. This involves two dialectically interrelated tasks: popularization of progressive ideas in works intelligible to the broad masses, and the raising of standards from the level where the masses are. Why these two tasks must be simultaneously wrestled with is indicated by Dr. Nguyen Khac Vien in his book *Tradition and Revolution in Vietnam:*

> An underdeveloped country is essentially a feudal and precapitalist society which totally excludes any ideas about progress. The members of such a society are afraid to change, whether they be peasants, tradesmen or members of the upper classes. Each action and mannerism is above all a rite which cannot be modified for any reason. Society is carefully arranged into a hierarchy according to a supernaturally inspired plan.
> 
> Ideological liberation of the great majority of the people is the sine qua non of development.
> 
> Underdeveloped countries need first and foremost an ideology of progress which is able to mobilize, organize and educate their people.... Underdeveloped countries need more than economic development, the establishment of political institutions, or the presence of the U.N. They need to solve problems concerning the role of women, the national language, and minority and ethnic groups. Attitudes toward religion, folklore and traditional culture must be redefined. The question of human relations in these countries has to be placed in a new context, and new values and practices must be cultivated.... A total restructuring of the foundations and the need for a progressive ideology to overthrow traditional ways of thinking are major priorities. (132, 143–44)

I personally had the opportunity to live in a feudal society for a long time, and later in an industrialized capitalist country. Now I am actively participating in the building of the new Vietnam. I have yet to find a doctrine which sheds as much light on the various problems of rapid development as does Marxism-Leninism.

By juxtaposing this analysis of Third World needs with remarks by Professor David Perkins of Harvard University in a book on British Romantic poetry, we can see the sharp disparity between the two opposing and irreconcilable world outlooks, one historical and materialist, the other metaphysical and idealist. Perkins writes:

Evil may be interpreted as moral or metaphysical, or both, that is, as the selfishness, aggressiveness, and fear embedded in the human heart, or as the limitations, pain, and death to which man is subject in the cosmos. . . . It is no good saying . . . that man is corrupted by society and its institutions, which, if transformed, will transform human nature; for society . . . is the spontaneous creation and outward mirror of human nature. (1967)

In conclusion, I would like to suggest that the culture of the Third World can best be appreciated within the framework of a concrete and dynamic analysis of the sociohistorical formations in which it has emerged and continues to develop. This demands a precise accounting of historical specifications underlying the themes and conventions of literature, the composition of the audience, and the function of the artist. Everything hinges on what Amilcar Cabral, one of the most important theoreticians of the African revolution, calls "the regaining of the historical personality of the people," which has been negated by centuries of imperialist domination.

We are witnessing today among Third World intellectuals a momentous rediscovery of the key insight of the entire tradition of dialectical thought which culminates in Marx, namely, "the human essence is no abstraction inherent in each single individual" but is "in reality the ensemble or totality of social relations" (1978, 175). Marx spelled this out in one axiom: a nation that oppresses another nation cannot really be free. The Third World writer's commitment is inherent in the recovery and elaboration of this fundamental insight.

Lest it be misunderstood, this concept of the "regaining of the historical personality of a people" cannot be equated with a restoration of an outmoded cluster of customs, or a nostalgic search for roots (à la Alex Haley), or a "remembrance of things past" for its own sake. We should remind ourselves that the principal target of the Cultural Revolution in China was Confucius and the value system he represents. What is central to the quest for "historical personality" is not just the sustained effort to demystify the past—which is a priority—but, together with it, the endeavor to make the qualitative leap from the abstract realm of the privatized ego to the concrete arena of social life where all personal acts acquire global import and intersubjective (or objective) meaning. The Palestinian writer Fawaz Turki, born in Haifa and now stateless, author of *The Disinherited,* perceives this principle of materialist dialectics operating in the predicament of a people striving to assert their basic right of self-determination:

The metamorphosis in our national psyche and the controlling images of our active mythology occurred when we had already acquired a past of our own. It occurred when the Palestinian, from the isolation of his world, asked another world that stood with its back to him: who am I and what am I in the scheme of things that seemed to govern other people's lives but not mine? When a Palestinian became aware, along the evolutionary continuum of his consciousness, of that delicate correlation between his political reality and existential concerns, of that pitch in reality that bound his own present to his forefathers' past, the question ceased to bristle with self-pity and acquired historical acumen. For the Palestinian proceeded to ask not who am *I*, but who are *we?* Not what is *my*, but what is *our* place in history? Existence, hitherto governed by private reservoirs of energy and alienation, was now governed by a feeling that history was every man's milieu. (1974, 89)

Whether it is in South Africa, Iran, South Korea, Nicaragua, or elsewhere, revolutionary ideas once grasped by millions of people turn into a material force capable of transforming society. The people then begin to realize that while circumstances inherited from the past, including ideas and habits, to a large degree shape their minds, yet human beings together can also change these circumstances and in the process change their own character. Society shapes humans, but humans also can mold and alter society. The "class-in-itself" becomes the "class-for-itself"; workers and peasants change from historical object to historical subject, the motive force in the making of their destiny. This change, together with the contrast between the perception of the colonizer and the reality of the colonized, is prophetically rendered in a poem by the Turkish poet Nazim Hikmet entitled "Pierre Loti" (excerpts):

Opium!!!
Submission!
Kismet!
Lattice-work, caravanserai
       fountains
a sultan dancing on a silver tray!
Maharajah, rajah
a thousand-year-old shah!
Waving from minarets
clogs made of mother-of-pearl;
women with henna-stained noses
working their looms with their feet.

In the wind, green-turbaned imams
        calling people to prayer;
*This* is the Orient the French poet sees.
This
    is
      the Orient of those books
that come out from the press
at the rate of a million to a minute.
But
    yesterday
        today
            or tomorrow
an Orient like this
    never existed
        and never will.
Orient!
The soil on which
    naked slaves
        die of hunger
The common property of everyone
except those born on it.
The land where hunger itself
        perishes with famine!
But the silos are full to the brim,
full of grain—
        only for Europe. . . .
Orient has had enough!
Orient will swallow
        no more—
we're sick of it, sick! . . .
Those who do not know
        must know now:
you, Pierre Loti, are no better than a charlatan.
A charlatan
who sells in the East
        rotten French fabrics
at a profit of five hundred per cent.
        Pierre Loti,
oh, what a pig of a bourgeois you are!
If I believed in a soul separate from matter,

> on the liberation day of the East
> I would crucify your soul
> at the head of a bridge
> and smoke in front of it.
> I give you my hand
> we give you our hands
> the *sansculottes* of Europe;
> let's ride our horses together,
> look
> the halting-place is near
> the day of freedom nearer still.
> In front of us
> the Year of Liberation of the East,
> waving a blood-red handkerchief!
> Our horses' hoofs
> go deep
> into the belly of imperialism.
>
> (Hikmet 1967)

The original version of this essay was published in *Social Praxis* 6 (1979): 19–34.

## BIBLIOGRAPHY

Awooner, Kofi. *The Breast of the Earth*. New York: Anchor Books, 1976.
Brutus, Denis. *Strains*. Austin, Texas: Troubadour Press, 1975.
Castillo, Otto Rene. "Apolitical Intellectuals." In *American Revolutionary Poetry*, edited by Robert Marquez. New York: Monthly Review Press, 1974.
Césaire, Aimé. *Aimé Césaire: The Collected Poetry, 1939–1976*. Berkeley: Univ. of California Press, 1983.
Dean, Vera Micheles. *The Nature of the Non-Western World*. New York: New American Library, 1966.
Dépestre, René. "Black Nationalism and Imperialism." *Ikon*, no. 6 (Oct.–Nov. 1968): 28–30.
Diop, David Mandessi. *Hammer Blows and Other Writings*. Bloomington, Ind.: Indiana Univ. Press, 1973.
Fanon, Frantz. *The Wretched of the Earth*. New York: Grove Press, 1968.
Guillen, Nicolas. *Tengo*. Detroit: Broadside Press, 1974.
Hikmet, Nazim. *Selected Poems*. Translated by Taner Baybars. London: Jonathan Cape, 1967.
Kant, Immanuel. *Analytic of the Beautiful*. Indianapolis: Bobbs-Merrill, 1963.

Lenin, V. I. "Critical Remarks on the National Question." In vol. 20 of *V. I. Lenin: Collected Works,* by V. I. Lenin, 17–51. Moscow: Progress Publishers, 1964.

Marx, Karl. "Theses on Feuerbach." In *The Marx-Engels Reader,* edited by Robert Tucker. 2d ed. New York: W. W. Norton, 1978.

Neruda, Pablo. *Incitement to Nixonicide and Praise for the Chilean Revolution.* Translated by Steve Kowitt. Austin, Texas: Fly by Night Printing Collective, 1973.

Perkins, David, ed. *English Romantic Writers.* New York: Harcourt, Brace & World, 1967.

Turki, Fawaz. "To be a Palestinian." *Journal of Palestine Studies* 3 (Spring 1974).

United Nations General Assembly. *Declaration on the Establishment of a New International Economic Order.* Cambridge: American Friends Service Committee, 1974.

Vien Nguyen Khac. *Tradition and Revolution in Vietnam.* Berkeley: Indochina Resource Center, 1974.

# Transgression and Deliverance

Apart from the Spanish-American War in 1898 and the fall of Bataan and Corregidor to the Japanese military invaders in 1942, the Philippines dominated the world's attention, and only for a few days, in February 1986. In the face of tanks and soldiers armed to the teeth, an urban mass insurrection of over a million people overthrew the long-entrenched Marcos dictatorship without firing a single shot. Scenes of this uprising were televised throughout the world, images exuding an aura of the miraculous. Distanced from the original context, those images and representations that mediated this singular event became an inspiration to the popular rebellions that soon exploded around the world, particularly in Eastern Europe, China, Pakistan, Haiti, and other countries in the Third World.

But like most Third World societies plagued by colonial underdevelopment (from the time of its conquest and annexation by the United States in 1898 up to the present), the Philippines today, although nominally independent, still suffers the classic problems of neocolonial dependency: its economy is controlled by the draconian "conditionalities" of the IMF-World Bank, its politics by semifeudal warlords, bureaucrats, and military officials beholden to Washington, its culture by U.S. mass media and Western information and knowledge-production monopoly (also known as the culture or consciousness industry). With over seventy-five percent of sixty million Filipinos extremely impoverished, the Philippines also has (despite some attenuation) the only active socialist-led guerrilla insurgency in all of Asia. The fate of U.S. military bases as well as U.S. business, cultural, and political interests will soon be decided by the unfolding of these contradictions, primarily by the action of the Filipino masses, in the first decades of the twenty-first century.

What happened to this much-touted U.S. experiment in colonial entrepreneurship that claimed to produce the "showcase of U.S. democracy" in Asia after World War II? Why did it fail? From the beginning, the entire discursive apparatus of U.S. academic scholarship has been committed to providing an explanation for this historical vicissitude.

Challenged by mounting popular resistance from the late sixties on, the rationale for U.S. support of the Marcos dictatorship—from Nixon to Ford, Carter and Reagan—for almost two decades has drawn its logic and rhetoric from the scholarship of American historians, political scientists, sociologists, and functionaries in other disciplines. Complicit with state policies since the advent of Empire, their intellectual authority in the field of actual implementation remains to be scrutinized and evaluated. The gravity of the crisis of U.S.-Philippines relations can be gauged by the "axe grinding" of Stanley Karnow's five-hundred-page production entitled *In Our Image: America's Empire in the Philippines* published in 1989. Karnow's journalistic and popularizing summary of over eighty years of massive American archival and theoretical labor to understand the dynamics of U.S. involvement in the Philippines has yielded only the most banal but not invidious conclusion: the effort to Americanize the Filipinos partly succeeded in terms of introducing the *forms* of institutions like electoral democracy, mass public education, civil service system, and so forth; but it completely failed in altering traditional "Filipino" values, in particular those sanctioning the patron-client relationship.

Now this theme of "imperial collaboration" between the Filipino elite and the U.S. colonial administration has been a recurrent leitmotif in the canonical apologetics of U.S. diplomacy since W. Cameron Forbes's two-volume inventory of U.S. accomplishment in the Philippines, *The Philippine Islands* (1928). It was extended to the Commonwealth years by Joseph Hayden's *The Philippines: A Study in National Development* (1942) and elaborated against the background of Cold War geopolitics by George Taylor's *The Philippines and the United States: Problems of Partnership* (1964). Notwithstanding their authors' claims to objectivity, these texts have now been compromised by the realities of poverty, social injustice, racism, and exploitation exposed by Filipino intellectuals, among them Filipino writers and artists who have courageously dared to speak up and in the process duly suffered the consequences of opposing U.S. imperial oppression from the forcible annexation of the islands in 1898 up to the Marcos dictatorship (1972–1986), its latest postcolonial reincarnation.

Logos yields to the immediacy of praxis, transcendence to historical contingency. Given the intensifying threat of Filipino nationalism to expunge once and for all the myth of U.S.-Philippines "special relations," the compulsive desideratum of contemporary U.S. scholarship on the Philippines (as demonstrated by the works of David Steinberg, Theodore Friend, and particularly Peter Stanley) is to reconceptualize the experience of U.S. imperial domination as a transaction of equal partnership between Filipinos and Americans. It is essentially an interpretive strategy to revise the canonical, orthodox narrative of imperial success. This project of revaluation, what I would call a *post hoc ergo* construal to underscore its status quo instrumentalism, would center on a refurbishing of the patron-client paradigm; the notion of reciprocal obligations entailed by it would arguably serve as the theoretical framework within which one can then exorcise the burden of U.S. political and ethical responsibility for what happened in the Philippines from 1898 to 1946 by shifting the cause of the failure of U.S. tutelage to the putative shrewdness of Filipinos in "manipulating" their masters.

We tried to do our best, but— This is the basic thesis of Peter Stanley's *A Nation in the Making: The Philippines and the United States, 1899–1921* (1974), an updated sequel to the family of metanarratives cited earlier. It is an argument replicated by Karnow and numerous exfoliating commentaries before and after the February "people power" insurrection. A dialectical twist of historical sensibility seems to have occurred. The sharp contrast between these revisionary texts and previous works critical of U.S. imperialism—to cite only the most accessible, James Blount's *The American Occupation of the Philippines* (1913), Leon Wolff's *Little Brown Brother* (1961), and Stuart Creighton Miller's *"Benevolent Assimilation"* (1982)—may be read as symptomatic of a cleavage in elite consensus, a change in tactics attuned to the reactionary climate of opinion now ascendant since the midseventies. It can also be conceived as a defensive mechanism set into play to counter a resurgent, nomadic movement of anti-U.S. imperialism around the world in the wake of the Vietnam debacle and the renewed revolutionary struggles in Central America, South Africa, the Middle East, and elsewhere.

The issue needs to be clarified further because of its impact on contemporary cultural politics and the function of intellectuals in the Philippines. In reviewing a volume edited by Peter Stanley entitled *Reappraising an Empire: New Perspectives on Philippine-American History* (1984), Robert B. Stauffer (1987) acutely points to the dogmatic ideological framework of the new apologetic historians cited earlier. The revisionary thrust of scholars employing the paradigm of patron-client linkage instead of a concept like dependency or even (in the pedantic jargon) "asymmetrical relation" within the capitalist world system with its uneven and overdetermined geography is meant to recast the exploitative relationship of dependency into a reciprocal one where responsibility is equalized if not dispersed. By downplaying any serious U.S. influence on Philippine social structures and inflating the ingenious duplicity of the subaltern, Stauffer contends, Stanley and his colleagues make "empire" into a romantic ideology: "it is as if to give a Victorian legitimacy to past conquests and in so doing to justify ... future imperial ventures" (103). Since a seemingly immutable patron-client pattern of relationship determined political life during U.S. colonial ascendancy, Filipino nationalism is relegated to the "manipulative underside of the collaborative empire," a phrase that euphemistically reformulates McKinley's "benevolent assimilation proclamation" of 21 December 1898, the foundation of U.S. rule over the island colony. Stauffer's reservation is amplified and sharpened by Peter Tarr in another context. Reviewing Karnow's book in *The Nation* (5 June 1989), Tarr cogently attributes the fallacy of the new apologetics to the "Immaculate Conception" view of U.S. imperial policy as a glorious and selfless "civilizing mission," this last phrase evoking the period of a socioeconomic transition from European mercantilism to a new international division of labor. In retrospect, one can describe this "civilizing mission" as the ideological impetus behind the march of Anglo-Saxon progress over the conquered territories and subjugated bodies of African slaves, American Indians, Mexicans, Chinese workers, and so on from the founding of the pilgrim colonies to the closing of the western frontier at the end of the nineteenth century.

Of all the varied instruments mobilized by the United States to subjugate the Philippines after the violent suppression of the native revolutionary forces in the Filipino-American War of 1898–1902, culture had the most powerful and enduring effect. In general, culture here can be defined as that ideological sphere of representations in which hegemony (in Gramsci's terms, the moral-intellectual leadership of a social bloc avowed by consent of the ruled) is defined, organized, destroyed, reconstructed. Culture subsumes all social practices and *habitus* that generate identities and reproduce a hierarchy of differences in the modalities of class, gender, race, nationality, etc. In its quest for hegemony, U.S. colonialism harnessed the educational system as the chief vehicle of "benevolent assimilation," of acculturation. Within the educational sector of what Althusser calls "the ideological state apparatus" and other disciplinary regimes of the colonial formation, it was the English language that forged the chains of acquiescence to the "superior" racialized nation-state power.

Writers and intellectuals then constituted the most effective mediation or relay between the colonizing power and the subjugated populace. The first Filipino writers in English (e.g., Paz Marquez-Benitez, Jose Garcia Villa) were educated in the University of the Philippines founded in 1908; their writings were first published by the college journals. The idiom of American English displaced both Spanish and the vernaculars as the primary symbolic system through which Filipinos represented themselves, that is, constituted themselves as colonial subjects with specific positions or functions (rights, duties) in the given social order. It was through this hegemonic language that the colonized subjects, especially the organic intellectuals of the emerging middle strata (merchants, professionals, rich peasants), represented their subordination and validated their serviceability to the norms and projects of the U.S. imperial dispensation. The Filipino historian Renato Constantino emphasizes this use of the ruler's language as the root-cause of the Filipino's inveterate self-alienation: "The first and perhaps the master stroke in the plan to use education as an instrument of colonial policy was the decision to use English as the medium of instruction. English became the wedge that separated the Filipinos from their past and later was to separate educated Filipinos from the masses of their countrymen" (1987, 47). In short, the implantation of U.S. imperial ideology in the Filipino psyche and the routine of everyday life cannot be dissociated from the use of English in business, government, education, and media; this instrumentality of language acted as the synthesizing force that unified a repertoire of social practices through which the public and private identity of the Filipino as "bearer" of a commodity (labor power) was constituted and subsequently valorized.

But what I think transformed the Filipino into the ideal accommodating subject was not just his Americanization through language and with it his internalizing of a decorum of submission—an imaginary relation to the real conditions of existence—that at the minimum guaranteed survival. That decisive conversion occurred with William Howard Taft's policy of "Philippines for the Filipinos," a slogan more revealing for its disingenuous opportunism than for its diplomatic substance. It was really a strategy of co-optation articulated in terms of equal exchange, as manifested for example in Taft's words: "and when the Filipino, in seeking a position in executive offices where English is the only language spoken, fits himself, as he will with his aptness for learning languages, in English, he will have nothing to complain of, either in the justice of the examination and its marking or in the equality of salaries between him and Americans doing the same work" (Veneracion 1987, 61). What this hegemonic strategy performed with finesse is its formal conversion of a relation of domination into a relation of exchange, an exchange of services, a contractual relation. Maurice Godelier observes that "no domination, even when born of violence, can last if it does not assume the form of an exchange of services" (1986, 161). With this mode of representing colonial oppression as a service rendered by the powerful, a form of exchange carried out in the colonizer's language that establishes a reciprocal commitment (analogous to a voluntary compact) between the parties involved, the consent to be subordinated is won and the sublimating bondage of the Filipino sealed. In short, subjugation is transcoded into freedom, albeit freedom to dispose of one's body in the reifying marketplace.

In the symbolic exchange of the liberal polity, the counters of bondage can circulate as freely as tokens of autonomy. Nothing could be more emblematic of this paradox than what a leading *ilustrado* of that time, T. H. Pardo de Tavera, advocated in his campaign for rapid assimilation. De Tavera expressed an opinion that, though initially disclaimed by the "nationalist" bloc, deserves to be honored as the implicit principle of the colonial elite's platform of achieving independence via the route of incremental reforms: "After peace is established, all our efforts will be directed to Americanizing ourselves; to cause a knowledge of the English language to be extended and generalized in the Philippines, in order that through its agency, the American spirit may take possession of us, and that we may so adopt its principles, its political customs, and its peculiar civilization that our redemption may be complete and radical" (Veneracion 1987, 60). Viewed from this perspective, the question of language—of replacing English with a "national" language—appears today as the most crucial site of cultural-political struggle in the Philippines, and this has been the case ever since the converted cattle ship *Thomas* brought the first five hundred American teachers of English into the country. Despite the interventions of sociolinguistic experts and congressional compromises, this problem of a "national" language will remain unresolved for the neocolonial government; meanwhile, the clandestine and outlawed New People's Army seems unimpeded in popularizing "Pilipino" in its liberated zones throughout the islands.

In many Third World countries where massacres have occurred over language boundaries and loyalties, this foundational question cannot be detached from its complicity with major ideological and political issues. Writers like Ngugi Wa Thiong'o and Chinua Achebe (in Africa), Edward Brathwaite and Wilson Harris (representing the Caribbean and South America), and Raja Rao (representing Asia) have rehearsed the sociocultural context and ideological resonance of the debate over language as medium of imaginative expression and intellectual reflection in their respective societies (see Ashcroft et al. 1989, 38–115). In the Philippines, the dispute over one "national language" has been sublimated into the politics of affirming—more precisely during U.S. colonial rule, gesturing toward—popular self-determination.

Because of its history of separatist resistance, the aesthetic mode of syncretism conceived as a process of abrogation and appropriation of the alien tongue, together with the alternative choice of inventing hybrid interlanguages, have never been considered viable options in the Philippine setting for the reasons already outlined. Over the years of anti-imperialist struggle, the sign has invariably become the site of what Deleuze and Guattari call "deterritorializations"—the index of "minor" or dissident discourse (1988). By 1986, the "language problem" can no longer be dissociated from the quest for popular self-management and democratic sovereignty. After heated exchanges in public forums and special hearings, threats of boycott and sabotage from non-Tagalog speakers, the Constitutional Convention of 1986 agreed to reaffirm "Filipino" (based on a modified Tagalog base) as the evolving national language of the land. This was the sequel to a political-cultural battle that had been waged by antagonistic classes and regions since the early decades of this century. Although English continues to be used predominantly in business and in government, Filipino-in-the-making as propagated by the mass media—television, films, radio—has practically become the *lingua franca* throughout the islands. A systematic program of replacing English with Filipino in all universities is now under way so that within the next two or three decades, the use of English as the traditionally sanctioned medium of intellectual communication will be gradually phased out. Eventually, writing in English will be relegated to the museum and antiquarian archives. In the meantime, it may be instructive for those engaged in Third World cultural studies to inquire: What are the deeper implications in the larger society of this struggle over English as the language of aspiration, of social practice and artistic expression?

In essence, the conflict over language is a struggle over renegotiating hegemony. Who will articulate the sovereignty of the nation, the identity of the Filipino people? In their monograph *Neo-Colonial Politics and Language Struggle in the Philippines* (1984), Virgilio G. Enriquez and Elizabeth Protacio-Marcelino have forcefully presented the nationalist perspective in the context of a broadly based mass movement for genuine political, economic, and cultural liberation. They advance the view that the possession of a national language is an essential precondition for autonomy. They assert that the continued use of English in a U.S.–oriented educational system (textbooks, curriculum, methodology, etc.) not only suppresses the democratic aspirations of the Filipino masses but also "undermines Filipino values and orientation and perpetuates the miseducation and captivity of the minds of the Filipino people to the colonial outlook" (3). For them, the English language symbolizes the belief in the superiority of U.S. culture, values, society, as we have noted earlier; thus it can only serve the exploitative, profit-seeking ends of U.S. power. To eradicate the persisting effects of an inherited dependency syndrome manifest in the neocolonial structures of the economy, government, schools, and in the institutions of civil society, linguistic nationalism must be promoted to insure the cultural survival and preserve the unique identity of the Filipino people. Pursuing the logic of this pedagogical and heuristic endeavor, Enriquez and Protacio-Marcelino demonstrate their case by showing how U.S. psychologists have insidiously diagnosed the Filipino character as an embodiment of certain behavioral patterns (like *utang na loob* or *hiya*) based on a perverted, basically Eurocentric, construal of their meanings and contexts of reference. In the process of arguing that research in psychology should proceed by searching for the "right words" in the vernacular languages that "will truly reflect the sentiments, values and aspirations of the Filipino people," and not through superimposing Western concepts, Enriquez illustrates how the repertoire of significations condensed in the word *"kapwa,"* for example, captures a truly indigenous mode of social interaction. Vernacular usage in effect registers the mutations of what is both national and popular. The genius of the native languages is thus shown to be the most accurate reflection of the Filipino psyche contextualized in its interface with local and global environments. Here in this micropolitics of psychosocial linguistics, it seems that the Whorf-Sapir hypothesis of language as shaper of one's worldview is resurrected with a vengeance.

Now it is precisely this hypothesis that Filipino writers in English seem to have implicitly rejected when they chose English as their privileged medium of artistic expression. Of course, as everyone knows, the choice is not a genuine free choice given the constraints of dysfunctional literacy, limited access to resources like channels of publication, audience, rewards, and so forth; on the other hand, it conveys more than a mere aesthetic/personal decision. A politics/ethics of signification is implied. No one has really explored this terrain of personal responsibility and complicity of vocation; this essay is only scratching the surface.

In assessing the fate of English as a literary medium in the Philippines for the last half century, the noted linguist Andrew Gonzalez has come up with an ambiguous but ultimately ironic conclusion (1987). Gonzalez has documented the process whereby the code or signalling system of the English language "was transferred without its cultural matrix" and this resulted in a variety of Filipino English with distinctive speech patterns in accord with "Pilipino styles of thought." This is a phenomenon underlying the development of diverse kinds of "english" (as sociolinguists put it)—conceived now as an international idiom no longer fixated on a British or U.S. model—spoken and used in Jamaica, India, South Africa, Australia, New Zealand, Canada, and elsewhere. A genre called "world literature written in English" is even proposed by humanitarian fellow travellers to abolish the invidious distinction between margin and center in the geopolitical reckoning of nation-states, between the canonical and the optional/elective, between what is major and what is minor.

In the Philippine scene, this encounter between the alien and the indigenous triggered a curious mutagenesis. When it comes to discourse patterns evinced in Filipino prose, Gonzalez notes the phenomenon of a new contextualization of English, the "transplantation of English structures and poetic discourse applied to a new environment, a new cultural matrix" (148). Pointing out that since the indigenous discourse conventions and techniques of a native tradition have all been practically destroyed by Spanish and American colonization, the indigenous creativity of Filipino writers has been released in their appropriation of a new language and the need to innovate within this new system. In the process, however, their imagination has been circumscribed by its strict adherence to Western canonical standards. Discourse structure and grammatical code are all foreign; only the reference hierarchy, themes or *topoi*, and their cultural matrix are Filipino. Hence Gonzalez's judgment that Filipinos write poetry in the English language concerning Philippine topics and realities and themes, "but there is no Filipino art form to speak of as transferred from the indigenous culture to the new tongue. There are no traces in this literary language born of academic and English schooling and modelled on the poetic experiments of America, of the local traditions of versification and poesy" (149). What results then is a "monstrous" production, an enigmatic sport defying the wisdom of taxonomists. Is this proof of "indigenous creativity"? Or is it unwarranted to call it self-induced alienation and schizoid experimentation?

Obviously Gonzalez's mode of divorcing form from content, diverse signifying practices from changing historical circumstances, essentially fails in its attempt to grasp that peculiarly Filipino "creativity" he is positing. The alloy seems inferior compared to the pure ingredients. While I acknowledge Gonzalez's linguistic expertise in canvassing conformities and deviations to the code, his account ignores the whole contextual field of writing practices that critics like Voloshinov [Bakhtin], and linguists like Jakobson, Halliday, Rossi-Landi, and other social semioticians have brought to our attention particularly in the last two decades. In my books, especially in *Toward a People's Literature, Only By Struggle,* and *Writing and National Liberation* among others, where I analyzed classic texts like Juan C. Laya's *His Native Soil,* Stevan Javellana's *Without Seeing the Dawn,* and other deviant or nonconformist texts; and especially in *Subversions of Desire,* where I provide substantive metacommentaries on the major writings of Nick Joaquin, by consensus the leading Filipino writer in English, I concretize the parameters of the "sign," a privileged locus of ideological contestation, within the "uneven and combined development" of the Philippine social formation. My main project is to recapitulate this complex interweaving of history, ideology, and form implicating a metropolitan power, the United States, in the fate of its former colony in Asia, the Philippines, and of at least two million Filipinos scattered over the North American continent.

Indeed Filipino writers read the West—the tradition-sanctioned discourses of Shakespeare, Wordsworth, T. S. Eliot, Faulkner, Hemingway according to canonical standards—but they write their hermeneutic responses with an "Eastern" signature. As I have indicated earlier and will elaborate later, this dialogic conjuncture derives from the historical specificity of the Philippines as the only U.S. colony in Asia at the turn of the century, a focal point of condensation and displacement for numerous conflicting political, ideological, economic, and social trends. The Philippines conceived as the site of contradictory forces and heterogeneous actors with their own transitional genealogies is what underlies the antinomic modernizing imagination of Nick Joaquin (which I have already examined in a dialectical critique of his major texts in *Subversions of Desire*). Likewise, the prodigious artifacts made by Carlos Bulosan cannot be properly understood without appreciating how the rhythm of oral storytelling and the calculated inversions of folklore pervade the stories in *The Laughter of My Father.* Nor can one comprehend his syncretic alchemy of mapping events in *America Is in the Heart,* which combines picaresque motifs and autobiographical notations without contextualizing it in the experience of peasant unrest in Pangasinan and the hardships of migrant labor and racial violence on the West Coast—the existential "lived experience" of Filipinos in the master's territory. (Both those aspects I have thoroughly explored in my *Carlos Bulosan and the Imagination of the Class Struggle* [1972] and countless essays). The same applies to the prison writings of Father Edicio de la Torre, Jose Maria Sison, and others incarcerated by the national-security state; with recent oppositional texts and emergent cultural practices particularly in the spheres of musical and theatrical performances and in what has now become in our postmodern milieu the hegemonic cultural signifiers of universal commoditization: film and television. One example of recent work whose form is conditioned by historic impulses and circumstantial pressures is the 1980 underground novel *Hulagpos* [Break Free], a realistic but also polemical critique of the Marcos martial-law regime. While the plot is ostensibly patterned after Jose Rizal's *Noli Me Tangere*, its technique of montage—abrupt cuts and syncopated juxtaposition of incidents—and collage of characters clearly derives from *inter alia* the method of the serialized novels in the weekly comic books and underground pictorials popular among the masses today and from the techniques of the avant-garde cinema.

It might be instructive to briefly sketch the dialectical crossbreeding between the autochtonous tradition and modern Filipino writing in English with three examples. I would like to suggest that, contrary to Gonzalez's positing of a dichotomy between native sensibility and alien tongue, a subtle intertextual symbiosis actually obtains in their transactions. In this sense Jose Garcia Villa's poetic art, long held to be an exercise in imitation of modernist styles to the point of mannerism and parody, cannot be reduced to a matter of eccentric prosody such as "reversed consonance" or "sprung rhythm." Again, here, form and substance cannot be so easily disjoined. Villa is the exemplary case of the offspring of *ilustrado* gentry who rejects his class origin but paradoxically valorizes the caste privilege of the artist. This cannot be understood except as a revolt principally against the commercial, materialistic, philistine milieu of colonial society. Despite his ultravanguardist exhibitionism, Villa's art cannot deny the influence of over three hundred years of Spanish-Malayan cultural interaction (more on Villa's career in the chapter "Art against Imperialism"). If we compare the design and texture of Villa's representative texts in *Selected Poems and New* (1958), with their characteristic surface of aphoristic verbal play and quasi-parody (even pastiche) of metaphysical conceits, with the native tradition of didactic and allegorical indirection—from the pre-Christian riddles, oratory, song, and *dagli* (vignette) to Balagtas's epic *Florante at Laura* to the satires of Rizal and M. H. Del Pilar—we can begin to understand how and why his individualist revolt in the colonial milieu of the twenties and thirties assumed the form it took: exile, adoption of masks, aristocratic ventriloquism, and other eccentric poses. Whatever the merits of Villa's response to his dilemma, the persistence of generic conventions in his poetry seems to override changing social contexts. As a provisional orientation, it may be helpful to illustrate a still undefined genealogy of modernist Filipino writing by comparing the tropological scheme of the first stanza of Villa's poem No. 123:

> What,is,defeat?
> Broken,victory.
> Darkest,sanctuary,
> But,solider,far,
> Than,the,triumphal,star.
> (Villa 1958, 101)

with a poem (transcribed by a Spanish priest/lexicographer) dating back to precolonial times when Indian, Arabic, and Chinese cultural currents blended in the Malayan aesthetic intelligence:

> Ang sugat ay kung tinanggap
> di daramdamin ang antak
> ang aayaw at di mayag
> galos lamang magnanaknak.
> (Lumbera 1982, 9)

(Freely translated: When one submits himself/to wounding,/the intensest pain is bearable;/when one is unwilling,/even the merest scratch/can fester.)

As for the invention of an authentic Filipino discourse in the short story anchored in the peasant *habitus* (Bourdieu's term) and the ethical milieu of an organic community, it might be sufficient to present a synecdochic example: consider the nuanced tonality and figurative resonance of this passage from Manuel Arguilla's "A Son is Born," whose peculiar mix would be difficult to find in Chekhov, Maupassant, Hemingway, or any other Western practitioner of this art:

> My mother's face was small in the growing dusk of the evening, small and lined, wisps of straight, dry hair falling across it from her head. I could see the brown specks on my mother's cheekbones, the result of working long under the sun. She looked down upon Berting and me and her eyes held a light that I dimly felt sprung from the love she bore us, her children. I could not bear her gaze any longer. It filled me with a longing to be good and kind to her. I looked down at my arms and I was full of shame and of regret. (Lumbera 1982, 177)

My third example of the hybrid but recuperative nature of neocolonial discourse production is different from the first two instances. Here the linguistic code of English is seized and subdued, refunctioned to serve emancipatory ends, when it is incorporated into a modernized form of the *sarsuwela*, a theatrical spectacle mixing songs and dances, with a melodramatic plot of threatened romantic love suturing the unravelled "thickness" of contemporary social and political issues. Introduced by the Spaniards in the nineteenth century as a popular form of entertainment, it has been Filipinized by major artists like Severino Reyes, Vicente Soto, Mena Pecson Crisologo, and others. Here is a passage from Nicanor Tiongson's *Pilipinas Circa 1907*, a rewriting or adaptation of Reyes's 1907 play of the same title that has been cross-fertilized by the "seditious" drama and novels of the first decade, the paramount cultural signifiers of anticolonial resistance to U.S. aggression. In Tiongson's script, the anticipated overcoming of American economic-political power is symbolically enacted by the ironic chorus of modernizing "girls"—part of which I quote below. The second stanza may be read as an emblematic specimen of counter-hegemonic renegotiation of the dominant linguistic code:

*Ba't nga ba may Pilipino*
[Why are there Filipinos]
*Na masyadong atrasado*
[Who are still so backward]
*Dumaong na'ng Amerikano*
[The Americans have already landed]
*Ay! pusakal pa ring Indio!*
[But my, they're still wild Indios!]
*I do not know to them*
*I do not know to them*
*We do not know to them!*
*Kundi kay William Mckinley*
[If not for William McKinley]
*We are still swinging from a tree*
*Walang statue of liberty*
[We wouldn't have a statue of . . . ]
                    (Tiongson 1985, 46–47)

Given this complex historical background absent in most literary histories, writing in English in the Philippines is no doubt an ideological practice firmly imbricated in the conflicts and problems of subaltern existence. Writing finds itself historicized, so to speak, without knowing it. Unless the production of such discourse is historically situated, one cannot grasp its power of producing meaning, of communicating what Foucault calls knowledge/power and its dual effects of inhibiting and in the same breath mobilizing people into action. This imperative of contextualizing literary form becomes more compelling if we accept Earl Miner's theory that Asian poetics is fundamentally affective-expressive rather than mimetic or dramatic like European poetics in general, a distinction originating from incommensurable cultural-social disparities (1990, 82–87). Conversely Third World mimesis, unlike the Western kind, can be deciphered as ultimately allegorical and collective in meaning and motivation, as Fredric Jameson (1986) has so persuasively argued (see also Gugelberger 1991). This is why I suggest that it is important to situate Filipino literary expression in the specific historical conjuncture of political, economic, and ideological forces—the transition from colonial dependency to the initial stages of national-popular autonomy—I have outlined above. While everyone recognizes the axiom that the linguistic system (Saussure's *langue*) is self-contained, a differential system of signifiers structured in binary oppositions, it is also the case that (as Voloshinov [Bakhtin] has shown) *parole* or speech is what sets the system in motion and generates meaning among interlocutors in the speech community (1986, 65–106). Speech acts or performances of enunciation are social, not individual phenomena. In other words, discourse is always intertextual; the world, the concrete historical life-situation of speakers and horizon of listeners, is a necessary constitutive element of the semantic structure of any utterance (Todorov 1984, 41–45). Consequently, it follows that the character of any discourse cannot be fully understood without reference to its intertextuality, its axiological embeddedness in social process, in the thickness of circumstances. To separate code from the context of enunciation is thus to annul discourse, to negate utterance in its modalities of communication and artistic expression. In the social text foregrounded here, the conjuncture of colonial occupation, U.S. hegemony and Filipino resistance are two moments or phases of the same event.

This is the reason why I would strongly endorse the deployment of what Mary Louise Pratt calls a linguistics of contact instead of the conventional linguistics of community (or its late-capitalist variant, Habermas's "communicative action") in order to displace the "normative vision of a unified and homogeneous social world" and accentuate instead "the relationality of social differentiation" (1989, 59). Dialectics then instead of functional empiricism. This mode of linguistic comprehension would decenter a self-identical community, highlighting instead "the operation of language *across* lines of social differentiation." It would focus on modes and zones of contact between dominant and dominated groups and on "how such speakers [with multiple identities] constitute each other relationally and in difference, how they enact differences in language" (60). Tiongson's *sarsuwela*, Villa's poems, and Bulosan's fiction may thus be conceived as attempts to explore the operation of an aesthetics of contact and disjunction between U.S. hegemonic culture and the Filipino artistic response to it.

There is, I might suggest at this point, a felicitous correspondence between the subject-position of the writer in the Philippines and her counterpart in Latin American societies, given the historical parallels in their colonial domination by Spain and by their subordination to U.S. economic-military supremacy. Investigating the literary institution as an ideological practice in Central American revolutions, John Beverley and Marc Zimmerman remark that "the ideological centrality of literature in Latin America has to do with the effects of colonialism and capitalism combined and with uneven development in the region, which have left intact and/or specially marked elements of earlier cultural formations that have become extinct or marginal in the metropolis" (1989, 15). I concur with this stress on the uneven, nonsychronized field of forces—textual practice or symbolic inscription being one force—where precisely a hegemonic politics relative to local circumstances becomes the only feasible long-range strategy for confronting a militarily and economically superior enemy. (To forestall misunderstanding, I should like to stress here that I take "hegemony" to imply varying proportions or ratio of the war of maneuver and war of position, privileging neither, the mix dependent on the social field of forces at any given time.)

Unlike Ruben Dario's *modernismo* or Ernesto Cardenal's Christian-Marxist repertoire of prophetic jeremiads and exempla, no contemporary cultural text—except perhaps the writings of former political prisoners like Sison, Angel Baking, and Karl Gaspar; interviews of quasi-charismatic personalities like Bernabe Buscayno or Father Edicio de la Torre; or certain poems of Amado V. Hernandez—has so far exercised the role of a central ideological signifier that could generate a national-popular culture with overwhelming mass appeal, one strong enough to mobilize an intraclass bloc that could successfully challenge the U.S.-supported oligarchic machine and the military-ideological agencies at its command. A likely candidate for this status would be the cinema-texts of Lino Brocka and of Kidlat Tahimik (if the latter's films are thoroughly popularized), or the lore of myth and filmic aura surrounding certain personalities like ex-movie star Senator Joseph Estrada. But the future cannot be totally mortgaged to past or present achievement. In this interregnum, I consider the primary and urgent task of criticism to be the revitalization of texts and the invention of a wide range of disruptive, oppositional practices that would fulfill the function of such a charismatic signifier in a highly disintegrated society that is nevertheless structured in dominance by the reactionary apparatus of terror and the state's dependence on foreign financing and investment. Without this emancipatory practice of critical reading/writing and its mediation of meaning, literary texts can be used to advance the ends of reproducing exploitative social relations and reinforcing the victims' *ressentiment*. This expropriative praxis entails the risk of historicism, of invoking a teleology based on superimposed values and convictions. However, since everyone is implicated in historical becoming and one is (sometimes without knowing it) forced to take sides in a struggle whose stakes are life or slow death for millions of Filipinos, I take this risk. It is a small price one must pay for unfolding the power of literature—the submerged Orphic voices prophesying the revenge of the oppressed generations in limbo, victims of injustice and ruthless calculation of profit; prophesying the fulfillment of dreams, hopes, desires: justice for the living and the dead—not only in interpreting our personal and communal experiences but also in changing the direction of our lives together with others.

A convergence of my position as a Filipino intellectual based in the metropolis and an unprecedented nationalist resurgence in the Philippines situates my critical commentaries and researches as necessary interventions in the realm of cultural politics. In the process of comparative cultural investigation, margin and center, like inside and outside, ultimately coalesce. It is now generally acknowledged that any person engaged in a critical commentary on Philippine culture and society is always a participant in the arena of ongoing political and ideological antagonisms encompassing two polities, the United States and the Philippines. My larger ongoing project (in which the essays gathered here function as a heuristic reconnaissance of the terrain) of assessing English writing in its historical inscription is modest, however; it is basically revisionist in a sense antithetical to that of Karnow's *In Our Image* and mainstream scholarship mentioned at the outset. It is heretical and dissident in conceiving of literature in the Philippines as an ideological practice of national liberation, the paradigm of an alternative "emergency" politics with a national-popular agenda. It is fundamentally counterhegemonic because it strives to articulate the Filipino subversion of the "received," legitimizing identity imposed on it by the metropolitan power and reproduced daily by local and transnational institutions. Finally it is oppositional in its effort to construct a sovereign Filipino identity, multiple and protean, in the process of rereading and rewriting the U.S. inscription of the Filipino subject-position in the text of Western metaphysics and its fetishizing instrumentalities. Revision then is a form of what Nietzsche calls "creative destruction." In this otherwise reconstructive task, I share the burden of responsibility with my Filipino brothers and sisters in numerous organizations in the homeland, in Europe and elsewhere, committed to egalitarian social justice, participatory democracy, and true national independence.

Despite the unavoidably particularizing impulse of constructing indigenous signifiers, the context-specific vernaculars, of each national or regional literature, a partisan of anti-imperialist theory from the "boondocks" shares a general orientation with all those who have non-elective affinities in being victims of colonial power, in facing common obstacles in the present (there is nothing postcolonial about the Northern hegemony of capitalist-industrial powers over the poor nations of the South), and who entertain visions of a cooperative future. This does not signify a levelling or homogenizing orientation where differences that really matter are erased—indeed, all determination is negation (Spinoza), so a negative hermeneutics that questions everyone's referentiality and logic except itself is indeed a sorry affair, if not downright fraudulent. What is needed is a dialogic, more precisely a dialectical, horizon of communication sustained by mutually supportive reciprocal goals. Can a Filipino writer, given the confluence of Asian, Spanish, and Anglo-Saxon imprints on his or her collective psyche, really choose to be singular and idiosyncratic? How could that be demonstrated in living practice? These essays in fact explore the conjunction and disjunction between a Eurocentric discourse of autonomy (initiated by bourgeois Enlightenment thought) and an embattled Asian sensibility trying to define itself in opposition, trying to assert what in retrospect could be original or indigenous, relationally speaking. Reckoning globally, I take comfort in the thought that this is not a solitary enterprise. In the community of Third World intellectuals and partisan activists, I have found inspiration in the models of solidarity personified by Frantz Fanon, Amilcar Cabral, Lu Hsun, Che Guevara, C. L. R. James, Adolfo Sanchez Vasquez, George Jackson (to cite only the most publicized names), and numerous Asian, Latin American, and African combatants for popular democracy and socialist internationalism. But without being necessarily sectarian about it, some tactical demarcations with those claiming a theoretical edge sometimes need to be drawn.

Within the framework of dependency/world systems analysis, Australian critics Bill Ashcroft, Gareth Griffiths and Helen Tiffin have espoused an anti-Empire position with commendable erudition and rhetorical force. They have emphasized the hybrid and syncretic nature of postcolonial writing, mainly Commonwealth writers from former British possessions, in their theoretical synthesis *The Empire Writes Back* (1989). While I agree with their basic thesis of a dialectical relationship between metropolitan and peripheral cultures and the impossibility of recuperating "an absolute pre-colonial cultural purity," I disagree with the corollary belief that it is impossible to create a national formation geared to realizing autonomy within the given hegemonic global system—even after the collapse of a so-called socialist Soviet Union in the post-Persian Gulf War era, in the grisly hard times of the "New World Order" of capital. Needless to say, Ashcroft and his colleagues ignore the Third World outside the Commonwealth; for example, they have nothing to say about the rich, diverse cultures of the American Indians in the north and south, nor do they manifest any awareness that something is going on in their neighbors' space (Indonesia, New Caledonia, the Philippines), or in Cuba, Palestine, and other sites of fierce anti-imperialist struggles. "The Empire" is clearly delimited by the authors' national experience.

This is where the centrality of the category "nation" (and its corollaries, national democracy and national liberation) for literary theory intrudes. Whether through mimetic or allegorical modes, in either imaginary or symbolic registers or both, the quest for national autonomy (even though the postmodern configuration of "nation" appears problematic) seems inescapable (see Bhabha). Will subaltern, minority, postcolonial discourse always be reactive, a vertiginous psychodrama of resistance? Is there no possibility for the *novum* (after Bloch) to materialize in symbolic exchange? If there are no closures and no beginnings either, the power of capital in the New World Order *in medias res* will always win.

Whatever the answers to those questions, I hold that it is not enough simply to multiply ingenious deconstructive rereadings and rewritings of the European or U.S. historical and fictional records. Ashcroft et al. claim to legislate what Third World/postcolonial artists should do: "These subversive manoeuvres [mentioned before], rather than the construction of *essentially* national or regional alternatives, are the characteristic features of the postcolonial text. Postcolonial literatures/cultures are constituted in counterdiscursive rather than homologous practices" (196). The guerrilla-writer in the jungles of Peru or Timor queries: why "rather than"? Is there no room for the homology of *testimonio*—those of Rigoberta Menchu or of Domitila Barrios de Chungara? A foreclosing judgment seems to punctuate the aporia of postcolonial normative speculation and immediately suspends dialogue. Is it possible that we are confronting here once again, resurrected in the guise of unsolicited "friendly" advice, the imperial hubris of Western logocentrism and power? But can we, "the hewers of wood and drawers of water," not decide for ourselves? Is a clean break foreclosed? Are all the boundaries fixed? Can we not stake new ground? What indeed are the real stakes in this antifoundational discourse? Whose lives are on the line confronting imperial power? We—if I may presume to use this editorial pronoun—in the decolonizing societies of the Third World of course understand the historical predicament and susceptibilities of a settler state like Australia and its "White Australia" heritage (Miles 1989, 90–98) so that, despite our own scholarly interest in "advanced" theory, we have no illusions about the heterogeneity and radical Otherness of postcolonial theory arising from even the pulpits of the submetropolitan centers. But reversals and disruptions that clear the ground are bound to happen, as Gramsci observes: "A historical moment . . . is rich in contradictions. It acquires a personality, it is a moment of development in that some basic activity of life dominates others and represents a historical 'advance'" (Thibaudeau 1976, 19). What historical experience has shown is that interventions from new social agencies are bound to erupt in places least expected, not necessarily weak links, so we remain vigilant and hopeful that the changes going on will not repeat the narratives of the past.

In the ongoing *perestroika* of the whole planet, the coordinates of periphery and core are constantly being scrambled. Icons are recurrently destroyed, cries of convulsive birth pangs resound. Subterranean rumblings charged with "auguries of innocence and of experience" can be heard even from seemingly pacified frontiers like New Caledonia, "zones of occult instability" (Fanon's phrase) like Timor, the former Spanish Sahara, and large parts of the Amerindian regions. I am hopeful that from the struggles of peoples in Haiti and El Salvador, South Africa, Palestine, Northern Ireland, Guatemala, and other outposts of the Empire, new theories and practices of popular resistance art will spring—not just one or two but many—and only then will a real dialogue or colloquy with the West begin. As Ernst Bloch and Walter Benjamin have discovered in the darkest days of European fascism, the *new* is permanently possible and in the fullness of time will blast the continuum of history.

In the meantime I would urge partisans of the emancipatory imagination in the "postcolonial" zones of "occult instability"—whether inner cities in Chicago, free-trade zones in South Korea, or the desert of

Saudi Arabia—to engage in inventing new modes of renegotiating the terms of the hegemonic transnational discourse embracing "justice," "democracy," and "freedom" and articulating them toward a collective project of national-popular liberation. This oppositional task is unavoidable if we want to challenge the disciplinary regimes of imperial power and their liberal or even "libertarian" surrogates. It can be synchronized or merged with that of producing alternative, oppositional, and utopian discourses and practices. One task in this project is propaedeutic or heuristic in nature: the effort to draw up a provisional cognitive mapping of one terrain in which the fates of two cultures, two peoples, have been joined—a radical, deconstructive rewriting of how U.S. hegemonic culture has read and "produced" the Filipino, more precisely the "truth/knowledge" concerning the Filipino; how the subaltern engendered by interlocking if polarized and originally discordant cultures (Malayan, Chinese, Arabic, Spanish, North American) has finally begun to speak and act (perhaps to curse, like Caliban) in a new language inscribed in oral or written texts, gestures, body movements, songs, cinematic and video images, weapons native and imported—all signs of a new beginning.

## BIBLIOGRAPHY

Ashcroft, Bill, Gareth Griffiths, and Helen Tiffin. *The Empire Writes Back.* New York: Routledge, 1989.
Beverley, John, and Marc Zimmerman. *Literature and Politics in the Central American Revolutions.* Austin: Univ. of Texas Press, 1990.
Bhabha, Homi, ed. *Nation and Narration.* New York: Routledge, 1990.
Blount, James H. *The American Occupation of the Philippines, 1898-1912.* New York: G. P. Putnam's Sons, 1913.
Constantino, Renato. "The Miseducation of the Filipino." In *The Philippines Reader,* edited by Daniel B. Schirmer and Stephen Shalom. Boston: South End Press, 1987.
Deleuze, Gilles, and Felix Guattari. "What is Minor Literature?" *Mississippi Review* 11, no. 3 (1988): 13–33.
Enriquez, Virgilio, and Elizabeth Protacio-Marcelino. *Neo-Colonial Politics and Language Struggle in the Philippines.* Quezon City: Akademya ng Sikolohiyang Pilipino, 1984, 1989.
Forbes, W. Cameron. *The Philippine Islands.* 2 vols. Boston: Houghton Mifflin, 1928.
Godelier, Maurice. *The Mental and the Material.* London: Verso, 1986.
Gonzalez, Andrew. "Poetic Imperialism or Indigenous Creativity? Philippine Literature in English." In *Discourse Across Cultures,* edited by Larry Smith. New York: Prentice-Hall, 1987.

Gugelberger, Georg. "Decolonizing the Canon: Considerations of Third World Literature." *New Literary History* 22 (Summer 1991): 505–24.
Hayden, Joseph R. *The Philippines: A Study in National Development*. New York: Macmillan, 1942.
Jameson, Frederic. "Third World Literature in the Era of Multinational Capitalism." *Social Text*, no. 15 (Fall 1986): 65–88.
Karnow, Stanley. *In Our Image: America's Empire in the Philippines*. New York: Random House, 1989.
Lumbera, Bienvenido, and Cynthia N. Lumbera. *Philippine Literature: A History and Anthology*. Manila: National Book Store, 1982.
Miles, Robert. *Racism*. London: Routledge, 1989.
Miller, Stuart Creighton. *"Benevolent Assimilation": The American Conquest of the Philippines, 1899–1903*. New Haven: Yale Univ. Press, 1982.
Miner, Earl. *Comparative Poetics*. Princeton: Princeton Univ. Press, 1990.
Pratt, Mary Louise. "Linguistic Utopias." *The Linguistics of Writing*. New York: Methuen, 1989.
San Juan, E., Jr. *Carlos Bulosan and the Imagination of the Class Struggle*. Quezon City: Univ. of the Philippines Press, 1972.
———. *Toward a People's Literature: Essays in the Dialectics of Praxis and Contradiction in Philippine Writing*. Quezon City: Univ. of the Philippines Press, 1984.
———. *Only by Struggle: Reflections on Philippine Culture, Politics and Society in a Time of Civil War*. Manila: Kalikasan Press, 1988a.
———. *Subversions of Desire: Prolegomena to Nick Joaquin*. Honolulu: Univ. of Hawaii Press, 1988b.
Stanley, Peter W. *A Nation in the Making: The Philippines and the United States, 1899–1921*. Cambridge: Harvard Univ. Press, 1974
Stanley, Peter W., ed. *Reappraising an Empire: New Perspectives on Philippine-American History*. Cambridge: Harvard Univ. Press, 1984.
Stauffer, Robert B. "Review of *Reappraising an Empire*, by Peter Stanley." *Journal of Asian and African Studies* 12, nos. 1–2 (1987): 103–4.
Taylor, George E. *The Philippines and the United States: Problems of Partnership*. New York: Praeger, 1964.
Thibaudeau, Jean. "Preliminary Notes on the Prison Writings of Gramsci: The Place of Literature in Marxian Theory." *Praxis* 3 (1976): 3–29.
Tiongson, Nicanor. *Pilipinas Circa 1907*. Quezon City: Philippine Educational Theater Association, 1985.
Todorov, Tzvetan. *Mikhail Bakhtin*. Minneapolis: Univ. of Minnesota Press, 1984.
Veneracion, Jaime. *Agos ng Dugong Kayumanggi*. Quezon City: Educational Forum, 1987.
Villa, Jose Garcia. *Selected Poems and New*. New York: McDowell Obolensky, 1958.
Voloshinov, V. N. [Mikhail Bakhtin]. *Marxism and the Philosophy of Language*. Cambridge: Harvard Univ. Press, 1986.
Wolff, Leon. *Little Brown Brother: America's Forgotten Bid for Empire Which Cost 250,000 Lives*. London: Longman's, 1961.

# Ngugi's *Petals of Blood*: The African Novel as a Weapon of Decolonization

Despite an international furor over his arrest in 1978, Kenyan writer Ngugi Wa Thiong'o is definitely not a household word in the United States. Given the hegemony of the banal and the sensational on the drugstore shelves and bestseller lists, the dominant culture of the marketplace excludes not only Third World progressive writing but also any mixture of art and politics—other than the politics of the IMF-World Bank and the transnational corporations. The daily consciousness of the public must be made safe from critical, not to say radical, thinking.

But it is precisely this privatization of daily life under capitalism, its ethnocentric confinement to Anglo-Saxon superficialities, its compartmentalized puritanism, that Ngugi's fourth and most powerful novel, *Petals of Blood*, places on exhibit. The novel is a sustained interrogation of the modern dilemma of alienation: Why do individuals feel lost, their lives meaningless, their souls devalued, in the great liberal "marketplace of ideas"?

The novel begins with the four major characters—Munira, Abdulla, Wanja, Karega—arrested for the alleged murder of three African directors of the Theng-eta Breweries in Ilmorog, Kenya. The first part focuses on Munira, a withdrawn and introspective schoolteacher, who is later revealed as the arsonist of the brothel where the directors died. He provides the most extreme example of the isolation of the psyche which all the others, in varying degrees, share. His moralizing recollection of the past, his obsessive probing into his family history and the painful traumas of his youth in Siriana, sets the framework for a series of recollections by the three other characters also uprooted from their origins and drifting. Haunted and driven by unresolved personal crises and the upheavals of history, all of them have settled in the village of Ilmorog, temporarily immobilized until their past returns and compels them to act.

We next meet Abdulla, an aging veteran of the Mau-Mau rebellion against British colonialism in the fifties. Cheated of any honor after independence, the lame Abdulla manages a store to which Munira and Wanja, the central woman figure and granddaughter of Nyakinyua, a village elder, are drawn. Wanja is Ngugi's paragon of the protean self. She epitomizes the problematic consciousness of Kenyan activists. Rejected by her family and ruined by Kimeria (one of the slain directors), Wanja's plight typifies the ordeals of city women in the Third World who are victimized by feudal authoritarianism, sexism, and competitive "free enterprise."

In such a world, where labor power is bought and sold as a commodity, where the quality of life is reduced to an abstract measure, a quantity scaled by money or private property, the reality of Wanja is an inexorable fact. Her role as prostitute, and later as manager or proprietor profiting from the sale of other women's bodies, symbolizes the acquisitive and predatory system that is the main target of Ngugi's uncompromising critique.

All three characters are suspects in the "crime," an assault on the sanctity of the status quo. But only one, Karega, is relentlessly pursued by the law because he is "a trade-union agitator" whose militant organizing of the brewery workers threatens the hitherto unchallenged logic of exploitation. Karega is the youthful hero whose education or apprenticeship informs one underlying pattern of the novel.

Karega shares a common background with Munira: both went through the disillusioning experience in Siriana where Chui (another of the slain directors) demonstrated the deformation of the anti-British intellectual into the native elitist tyrant. But Karega, unlike Munira, does not succumb to cynicism or stoic indifference. On the contrary, he immerses himself in the working masses, in the project of uniting theory and practice, ideas and action. Karega falls in love with Mukami, Munira's sister. Her suicide, precipitated by her father's objection to Karega (whose brother, a Mau-Mau rebel, cut off the father's ear for his complicity with British oppression), inflicts a psychic wound on Munira, but spurs Karega to action, while indicting the whole patriarchal morality of religion and exploitation.

One of the novel's principal contradictions is represented by Munira's metaphysical egotism and Karega's proletarian commitment to anti-imperialist revolutionary change. Their passion for Wanja joins them in a unity of opposites analogous to Wanja's "cohabitation" with the native bourgeoisie personified by the slain directors of the brewery.

When the novel begins in the manner of a whodunit, we are confronted with the end, the climax of our characters' dramas. Confined in jail, Munira thinks back twelve years to the time when all four gravitated to Ilmorog, a remote rural village which, for Karega, still preserved the pristine virtues of a communal Africa long gone. Everything seemed harmonious until drought overtook the village. Led by Nyakinyua, the villagers make a journey or pilgrimage to the city to appeal to the member of parliament. Salvation comes after a few years, in the form of capital investment: Ilmorog becomes the entrepreneur's happy hunting ground. This is vividly illustrated when theng-eta, once a vision-inducing herb for poets and soothsayers, is commodified or transformed into the main ingredient for beer.

Ilmorog is "saved" by business and profit making. With a cash-economy come robberies, lockouts, "prowling prostitutes in cheap night clubs," police raids, police cells, etc. Wanja sets up her establishment, which becomes the trap for the three African bourgeois. Munira, in trying to save Karega from the diabolic temptress Wanja, sets fire to the house—an act evoking an adolescent exorcism of guilt that has never quite vanished from his memory. Abdulla, deliberately planning to kill Kimeria ("the time, the day, and the place was not of his making, but to act was his freedom"), comes to rescue Wanja from the fire, an ironic fulfillment of his quest.

The novel, as suggested above, concludes with Munira confessing to his responsibility for burning Wanja's house. In the trial he condemns his father's hypocrisy and infidel ways. Our attention then is shifted to Wanja, who, pregnant with Abdulla's child (which compensates for her killing her child by Kimeria in the past), emerges as the catalyst who, in Karega's judgment, reveals the diverse possibilities in everyone. Read allegorically, Wanja thus personifies an Africa (or Kenya) going through the ordeals of rectifying its mistakes and seizing the opportunity for self-renewal.

The ending of the novel thematically foregrounds Karega's consciousness agitated by Wanja's voice:

> Imperialism: capitalism: landlords: earthworms. A system that bred hordes of round-bellied jiggers and bedbugs with parasitism and cannibalism as the highest goal in society. . . . The system and its god and its angels had to be fought consciously, consistently and resolutely by all the working people! . . . Tomorrow it would be the workers and the peasants leading the struggle and seizing power to overrun the system of all its preying bloodthirsty gods and gnomic angels, bringing to an end the reign of the few over the many and the era of drinking blood and feasting on human flesh. Then, only then, would the kingdom of man and woman really begin, they joying and loving in creative

labour. . . . For a minute he was so carried on the waves of this vision and of the possibilities it opened up for all the Kenyan working and peasant masses that he forgot the woman beside him.

The last sentence of that tremendously prophetic passage is symptomatic of the novel's major theme: the recovery of individuality through collective, liberating action.

The passage also conveys what I think is the most significant argument or principle of the novel's action: Ngugi's demonstration that the quest for identity, and with it one's personal destiny, cannot be successfully conducted in the usual solipsistic, privatized mode exemplified by the dominant culture (its models, let me remind the readers, are the "innocent" narrator of Fitzgerald's *The Great Gatsby* and Camus' alienated outsider in *The Stranger*) of which Munira's fanatical casuistry and impotence are the practical realizations.

Through his novel, Ngugi is telling us that this search for personal validation can only proceed in the context of the tortuous and constrained milieu we find ourselves in today, a realm of necessity, where ultimately the level and mode of material production (and reproduction) determine the parameters of choice and action. Within this realm occurs class struggle, the combat between ideologies, the tension of wills and nerves and bodies.

This content of Ngugi's vision may be glimpsed in the formal construction of the narrative. Ngugi establishes in part one a sequence of involved exercises of memory (chiefly engaged in by Munira in his prison cell, an appropriate metaphor). This is disrupted by a social fact, the drought, also a spiritual analogue for the impasse suffered by the protagonists. Ngugi then stages a recovery of the popular, collective tradition of protest in describing the journey. It is the pivotal conduct of the journey which crystallizes the dispersed sentiments of the villagers, unifies the disintegrating sensibilities of Munira, Wanja, and Abdulla, and finally reveals the heroic potential of Abdulla (the Mau-Mau past) and Nyakinyua (the village ethos nourished by the land).

In effect, the journey shatters the paralyzing hold of the past on the present and unleashes energies that converge in the destruction of Wanja's brothel (the shameful humiliations and defeats of the struggle) and the directors (the present oppressors).

After the journey, Karega realizes that the duty of the revolutionary is not to reinstate an antiquarian, idealized past but rather to question it, learn from it, and use it to build a more humane future. His vision is thoroughly and genuinely dialectical—like the novel's action.

Although part three's title, "To be Born," continues the biblical motif announced in part two, "Toward Bethlehem," the rubric for part four, "Again ... La Luta Continua!" with epigraphs from Whitman and Cabral, the leader of the revolution in Guinea-Bissau, underlines Ngugi's affirmation of a visionary utopian orientation. For it is in the last part, the description of how profit and commodity production envelope Ilmorog, dispossess the inhabitants of the ancestral lands, and reduce passion into cash, that we perceive how ideology—the world-outlook shaped by class position—interpellates the characters, prodding them to action along determinate paths.

Thus, in contrast to Wanja's and Munira's fragmented and atomized view of experience, which pinpoints or accuses individuals as sole, independent agents and causes of events, Karega's relational or structural perception is seen to derive from his practice, in particular his grasp of contradictions while working with people. He replies to the Inspector, the bureaucratic specimen of a predatory society: "I don't believe in the elimination of individuals. There are many Kimerias and Chuis in the country. They are the products of a system, just as workers are products of a system. It's the system that needs to be changed ... and only the workers of Kenya and the peasants can do that." Here the religious allegory vanishes, to be replaced by the insistent language and imagery of revolutionary praxis.

Ngugi's novel is a dynamic, intensely searching exploration of the problems of contemporary Kenya, an East African nation independent since 1963, but still dominated by British and U.S. transnational corporations. Monopoly capitalism services, and is served by, local agents, the formerly anticolonial group of the late Jomo Kenyatta, now the only legal party, the African National Union. Today Kenya is a classic neocolony, saddled with multileveled contradictions.

Given its dependency status, the monopoly of land and other resources by a few settlers and a privileged native minority, the control of the state apparatus by a reactionary ensemble of bureaucrats, capitalists, landlords, and compradors, Kenya—except for the complicated tensions among its forty ethnic groups—typifies the situation of most Third World countries today. For this reason, Ngugi's novel can be viewed as a revealing microcosm of the "Free World," including the United States, to whose racist and decadent tendencies Ngugi repeatedly alludes.

*Petals of Blood* not only dramatizes the agonies of isolated and tormented individuals (the imagery suggesting that their blood must be shed before their spirits can blossom) striving in vain for escape or for ambiguous contact with others. It also registers the impact of large historical forces on individual consciousness. It delineates how actions result from the clash of subjective motives and objective situations. It projects the recognition of the Other in the process. Finally, it provokes the reader to participate and choose sides in the ongoing life-and-death struggle presented. It incites you to produce the meaning of the text by a profound involvement with those very same implacable forces that Ngugi invokes, forces that you wrestle with, blindly or purposefully, in solitude or with others, in every moment of your life.

Originally published in *Theoretical Review* (Sept.–Oct. 1981): 31–33.

# Palestine, Incarnation of Our Desire: Texts from Fawaz Turki

The last time I talked to Fawaz Turki, one of the most charismatic Third World intellectuals living in the United States today, was in December 1978, months before Yasir Arafat, with symbolic gusto, would occupy the abandoned Zionist embassy in Teheran.

After talking to participants of a United Nations Honors Program Seminar, where the specter of the *fedayeen* as a hairy terrorist shrouded the "sweetness-and-light" atmosphere of petty-bourgeois liberalism, Turki declared that although Israel is armed to the teeth with missiles, it is powerless and destined to be conquered by his people with their inexhaustible spiritual resources.

Was that mere bravado, or left-wing rhetoric?

One answer: witness the example of Palestinian courage and determination at Tel Zaatar in 1975 resisting the genocidal assault of the Lebanese fascists and their Syrian and Israeli accomplices. Provoked by this testimony of his people's capacity to "suffer, endure, survive, struggle and etch their reality and ethos" (to quote Turki) on the world, the poet composes an elegiac homage to the martyrs and survivors, a surrealist meditation which provides the title to the collection, *Tel Zaatar Was the Hill of Thyme* (1978). In that poem, Turki celebrates the heroic resistance of the ghetto, thus exploding the static and mechanical stereotypes of the passive, pathetic refugees or victims begging for U.N. handouts.

Beginning with his intensely searing memoir, *The Disinherited: Journal of a Palestinian Exile* (1972), Turki has sought in his writings to capture what he calls the "psychodynamics" of the Palestinian diaspora and the "collective mythologies" surrounding it. His task has been to affirm the Palestinian revolution, whose goal is not just "a place in the sun" but "human dignity and national identity." In his journal, Turki's obsession with "the Return" expressed itself in a seething anguish defined by communal rituals and shared familial memories. The exile of the Palestinians embodies global contradictions that propel them forward, together with the entire Third World. Their hopes and desires thus sprout from, and are rooted in, the concrete sociohistorical base of the Palestinian homeland.

In the first group of poems, we find the experience of the *ghourba* (exile) poignantly imaged: "In alien cities / I am clothed / in thick raincoats of otherness / long before it rains" ("When I Shake Hands with a Stranger in Every Other Season"). Abandoned cities and homes saturate the poet's sensibility. An organic attachment to definite locales and habitats dominates the psyche: "I lie in my bed / tangled in the hair / of her deserted streets / under curfew" ("Nablus Under Occupation"). In "Beirut," the poet speaks of "disinherited selfhood / walks in rags / looking for a Western wedding to attend" (1978).

Palestine was and is, before 1948 (when the Zionists expropriated and transmogrified it into Israel) and after. But the homeland before captivity has been preserved in Palestinian poetry. There, geography is transformed into an existential unfolding, the time of lived experience. Turki articulates this urgent, militant drive to materialize time in an apocalyptic fulfillment: "I am just a violent blow / vanishing into a vanishing point / preceding the beginning" ("Doing Time Inside the American Dream"; see also "The Future of a Past" and "Waiting for the Return").

The process of planting or impregnating and the rhythm of the seasons are sometimes used to vitalize the quest to establish Palestinian identity. This is associated with the phenomenon of exuberant, spontaneous generation in nature; see "One Day" and "The Seed Keepers."

What Turki envisions is not a fated, mechanical victory, but rather a consciously planned, calculated, or engineered product. A sister-comrade visits; the exiles expect the banal litany of grievances, but instead "She only says / our people are still in the tunnel / in the dark, / digging, / digging" ("News from Salwa"). In "Questions," the Palestinian resolves no longer to speak but to act after he has analyzed the dynamic, multidimensional contradictions in class-divided society.

In the title poem, Turki voices this fierce determination to act—within the ideological sphere of art—in sympathy with partisans and combatants. Only in Tel Zaatar, he sings, "can I define our Palestinian solitude in a fraternity of screams of sunrise. . . . Between the Tower of Towers (a refugee site in Beirut where Turki grew up) and the Hill of Thyme (Tel Zaatar), between my original leap to a maturing consciousness and my helpless rage, lies my Palestinian sensibility. Thus when I roamed foreign cities, all these years, I never window-shopped for ideologies. I already had one. I just looked for stores that sold guillotines."

Turki expresses in his writings this fundamental need to integrate the developing consciousness of the committed intellectual with the organized mobilization of the masses. Underlying the style of his poetry is a scientific knowledge of the physical and social universe which he encapsulates, for example, in the epilogue of "Yousef": "Only the energy of the universe / is contained in its endlessness. . . . / The finite system of our oppressor / will be dust." Turki also evokes this personalized cosmic energy in "The Village Where the Living and the Dead Join Hands in the Promised Land."

In an essay entitled "The Palestinian Estranged," Turki outlines the evolution of Palestinian poetry from its pivotal fixation on Palestine as woman/mother; "the total, phantasmagoric fusion of *ard* (home) and *aard* (women)." Absent are the machismo complex and the competitive impulse. Instead, the political objective of a secular democratic state (as formulated, say, in the PLO program) "represents the vision of sharing the *ard*—a dialectic of liberation that is the organic outgrowth of the changes that Palestinian society has undergone."

Turki notes how Palestinian writers have identified the homeland with the beloved: Palestine "is always the womb to return to, the breasts to suckle, the lap to sit on, the power to appeal to in a moment of crisis." Such images may be embarrassing or platitudinous, smacking of Freudian psychology. But let us treat them as provisional or dispensable figures of speech, symbolism that functions as dramatic vehicle or medium to render with flesh-and-bone immediacy the Palestinian predicament of uprootedness, fragmentation, and dispersal.

To overcome this paralyzing alienation, a general condition in capitalist society where everything (without exception) is reduced to a commodity, Turki shapes the premises for a dialogue with, and an embrace of, the Other. In "A Discussion," he lays down the parameters of cooperation: "for until we light a fire / And I see the first spark leap through, / I cannot give you a rose, / and you can not profit from my tragedy." Because he envisages the United States as a prison (Camp David a slave camp), the more insistently cathartic is Turki's need for communication in the hope that the chance colloquy of strangers may yield shocks of recognition.

It is in solidarity with Third World struggles that Turki projects the inevitable recovery of authentic selfhood. His metaphors fuse the prophetic and the prosaic, concrete and abstract, present and future tenses, in the moving poem "In the Night Sky of Zimbabwe": "And in the backyard of African homes / settler colonialism / will lie in winter puddles / like cigarette butts in the rain. / Every day the blood of memory / and the passion of dreams / are delivered by the midwife of revolution."

With ironic distance, Turki can probe into the problematic realm of subjectivity and objectify its tensions. In "Palestinians in Exile," my favorite poem here, the agony of desire for the Return metamorphoses into a craving for the beloved—a powerful erotic cry for a tryst long overdue, the unquenchable anguish "between dream and nothingness" when chains and barbed wires will snap: "Like lovers from Palestine, / agonizing over who is really in exile: / they or their homeland." Somehow, to use philosophical jargon, the Self and the Other are wedded inextricably in Turki's verse, mediated through the ritualized critique and reflection of everyday gestures and mannerisms.

Turki's preface to his book, his cultural manifesto, invokes the classic role of the poet as the folk shaman, healer and visionary combined. It coincides with that of other Third World poets—one thinks of the Guatemalan Otto Rene Castillo, the Turkish Nazim Hikmet, or the Filipina Maria Lorena Barros—who, plunged in the crisis-charged arena of their vocation, are profoundly embedded in "the geography of his people's soul," in the "syntax of its mass sentiments" (to quote Turki).

In our meeting that December, Turki told me that he belonged to the "Rejection front" which, unlike the PLO, refuses any concession of a ministate, or anything short of recovering the whole of Palestine. I cited Lenin on tactical compromises, but Turki was adamant. Subsequently, however, his principled flexibility affirmed itself. Asked by a student from North Dakota why Palestinian culture is pervaded with military nuances, Turki alluded to the ongoing synthesis of the imagination and the actual practice of the masses.

Appealing to a middle-class audience, Turki sometimes lapses into metaphysical obscurantism when he extols the humanism that binds both Palestinian and Zionist Jew, ignoring ideology or class allegiance. But his poetry corrects the lapse with its inherently demystifying function. Turki's art inserts the spirit back into the recalcitrant materiality of life. Consider, for example, the feudal or bourgeois milieu of the poems in part 3, which effectively satirize the obscene Arab compradors and sellout puppets of foreign interests.

Turki's poems serve as valuable propaganda and agitational instruments for all revolutionaries. In them, the aesthetic moment and the instant of political decision crystallize in a unity of opposites. The poet explores the immense reservoir of moral and emotional possibilities inspiring the will and the reasoning power of the Palestinian people. They prove once more the dialectical materialist proposition that it is the inexhaustible richness of social life, its scientifically comprehensible vicissitudes and contingencies, that energizes art and imbues it with enduring purpose and concrete use value. However, without the aesthetic dimension provided by Palestinian poetry in general, our understanding of the Palestinian struggle for self-determination—the key to unlocking the Middle East tangle—would be seriously impoverished.

## POSTSCRIPT 1993

In September 1993, Israel's Prime Minister Yitzhak Rabin and PLO Chairman Yasir Arafat signed a historic document in Washington, D.C., whose preamble or "Declaration of Principles" includes the PLO's recognition of the right of the state of Israel to exist in exchange for Israel's recognition of the PLO as the sole legitimate representative of the Palestinian people. It provides for the grant of Palestinian "limited autonomy" in the interim five-year period to the Gaza Strip and the West Bank city of Jericho following the withdrawal of the Israeli Defense Forces. The Occupied Territories are inhabited by roughly one million seven hundred fifty thousand Palestinians, with about 137,000 Jewish settlers. Not spelled out in the agreement are such crucial issues as: the question of the powers of the Palestinian self-governing authority, the future of Israeli settlements, the prospect for a healthy and independent Palestinian economy, the final disposition of Jerusalem (with 152,000 Palestinians and 133,000 Jews; *Newsweek*, 13 September 1993, 23), the right of return for millions of refugees (about three million expatriates around the world) and compensation for those forced off their land (in places like Jaffa, Haifa, Lod, etc.) in 1948 and 1967. This agreement obviously lends itself to multiple and often incommensurable interpretations. While many observers explain Israel's virtual abandonment of the Zionist idea of the Judaization of the Galilee and further territorial expansion as an effect of its loss of status as the most important strategic ally of Western imperialism in the Middle East, others view it as a result of the "stability-oriented" policy mandate of the United States premised on the politics of resources (oil), not on justice (Bloice 1993, 19).

The public consensus is that this "historic breakthrough" or "honorable compromise," to quote media epithets, promises to end twenty-six years of Israeli domination of the Occupied Territories. It will not restore seventy-seven percent of Palestine—all the lands conquered in 1948—nor honor the basic provisions of United Nations Security Council Resolutions 194, 242, and 338, and General Assembly Resolution 3236 which, among others, "reaffirms the inalienable rights of the Palestinian people . . . to self-determination," national independence and sovereignty. By conceding Israel's sovereignty and renouncing the use of violence, has the PLO (to echo its critics) bargained away forty-five years of militant resistance, ninety percent of Palestinian land (only about twenty-three percent of the land is the object of negotiation), and its own singular future for a small West Bank town and a string of refugee camps in the Gaza Strip? So far three generations of Palestinians have endured intense poverty and misery, repression, total dislocation, futility, and insecurity—for what? Only to have the world finally acknowledge the "terrorists" as freedom fighters? What else awaits them?

One dissenting voice is that of Edward Said, a member of the Palestine National Council and distinguished intellectual whose books, among them *The Question of Palestine*, *After the Last Sky*, and *Culture and Imperialism*, have helped project a seminal Palestinian presence in world culture. Said notes that this new phase of reconciliation leaves Israel still in charge of East Jerusalem, the settlements (land, water, security, foreign affairs), and the economy, while the PLO becomes a subordinate small-town government assigned to suppress the Islamic fundamentalists in Hamas (Islamic Resistance Movement), Islamic Jihad, and other recalcitrant trends among its constituency. It will also mean the final dispossession of fifty percent of Palestinians not resident in the occupied territories—350,000 stateless refugees in Lebanon, twice that number in Syria, and many more elsewhere. The fate of 13,000 political prisoners is left for future negotiations. Can life be normalized for six million Palestinians whose struggle is for full freedom, equality and democracy, and who have not fully participated in the negotiations? Joining his colleagues Mahmoud Darwish and Shafiq al-Hout, Said criticizes the PLO leadership for secrecy, "lack of care, precision and seriousness," and above all for having irresponsibly mortgaged the people's future without disclosing "the full and bitter truth" (1993, 270). In short, the settlement does not answer Palestinian needs expressed for years by UN resolutions and PLO pronouncements, nor solve the leadership crisis.

For his part, Shafik al-Hout, who resigned from the PLO Executive Committee, asks: "If this is the maximum Arafat could get after all the years of the *intifada*, what will he get now that he's in the hands of the Israelis, on the really important things like sovereignty, Jerusalem, the return of Palestinians who have been driven out since 1948?" (Cockburn 1993). It is more reprehensible that the agreement in effect even legitimizes the occupation by referring to captured land as "disputed territories" in much the same way as the U.S. formula "land for peace" reflects a racial/racist view in which Palestinians give up their violent resistance (not their right to their historic homeland) in exchange for sacred Israeli property (see Massad 1993). The Israeli state's colonial aggression and violent oppression of the Palestinians are totally erased in the ascendant discursive axioms of U.S./Western diplomacy.

Such a critique reflects what may be called a mainstream perspective between Zionist absolutism (the primacy of the Jewish state) and pan-Arab nationalism, the two polar opposites that have so far governed inquiries into the Middle East crisis since 1948 or even before. One example of this mediatory position is that of the American Friends Service Committee. Their 1981 paper entitled *A Compassionate Peace* proposed a two-state solution peacefully arrived at to resolve Israel's dilemma of either securing long-term peace or promoting dangerous broad-scale settlements in the West Bank and Gaza:

> For Israel's commitment to peace to be fully appreciated, Israel must drop its claim to extended sovereignty over the West Bank and Gaza and deal openly and positively with Palestinian desires for self-determination and statehood. Israel should be generous in its interpretation of U.N. Security Council Resolution 242 and, in return for withdrawal to the approximate pre-1967 borders and recognition of Palestinian nationalism, require Palestinian and Arab recognition of Israel's legitimate right to live peacefully within secure borders. . . .
>
> We hope for more than an end to conflict and seek more than a mere coexistence of two states sharing a nervously guarded border. Important as these are, their very achievement should be used to propel Israelis and Palestinians toward a new relationship with each other. These two peoples who have common histories of persecution and dispersion will, we hope, come to respect—and support—each other's quests for self-determination and self-identity. (186–87)

In contrast, Noam Chomsky in 1969 sketched a left-oriented diagnosis that claims to transcend the ontology of orthodox nationalisms: "The alternative to the framework of national states, national conflict, and national interest, is cooperation between people who have common interests that are not expressible in national terms, that in general assume class lines. Such alternatives are open to those who believe that the common interest of the great masses of people in Palestine—and everywhere—is the construction of a world of democratic communities in which political institutions, as well as the commercial and industrial system as a whole, are under direct popular control and the resources of modern civilization are directed to the satisfaction of human needs and libertarian values" (8). It is plausible to argue that this stance finds general resonance with the radical premises of the programs of Nayef Hawatmeh's Popular Democratic Front for the Liberation of Palestine (see Chaliand 84–129) and Dr. George Habash's Popular Front for the Liberation of Palestine. In October 1976, the PLO itself voiced the idea that if the regime in Israel becomes non-Zionist, "Israel's Jews and Palestine Arabs will discover that partition will be nothing more than a transitional step toward the establishment of a unitary democratic state. A truly democratic state is the only effective guarantee for political and economic independence" (Al Hout 1983, 65).

What has really produced the decisive break with the inertia of the past three decades in which the Palestinian struggle served as a testing-ground for Cold War diplomatic maneuvers and as the principal obstacle for U.S. hegemony in the oil-rich Gulf region, is the *intifada*, the popular uprising of more than two million Palestinians in the occupied territories, which erupted on 9 December 1987, exactly nine years after my exchange with Fawaz Turki. I think this is the major catalyst for the sudden accommodationist posture of both parties, the challenge of a genuinely grassroots, popular-democratic initiative unthinkable and anathema to the hierarchical dogmatism of propertied elites.

Offhand one can say that the *intifada*, an explosion of organized and spontaneous mass resistance, is a political-military expression of the Palestinian revolution as a national-popular process of mobilization of all the oppressed and exploited classes. It accords with Lenin's theory of insurrection as a convergence of vanguard organization and popular spontaneous actions, where "armed actions are carried out within the framework of civil disobedience, rallies and constant strikes against the occupation and by putting the new institutions of people's power into motion" (El Masri 1990, 13).

The *intifada* is a completely original creation of the Palestinian national-popular forces. One must point out here the distinct difference between the goal of "the liberation of Palestine" found in the Palestine National Charter of the PLO and the *intifada*'s stated general slogan of March 1988: "Freedom and Independence." The specific demands raised at the outset were premised on the right of return, self-determination, and an independent Palestinian state. Among the specific slogans issued by the Unified National Leadership were: An end to the Iron Fist policy and the repeal of past Emergency Regulations and the immediate repeal of all deportation decisions; prohibition of the desecration and defilement of the holy sites; withdrawal of the army from the towns, camps, and villages; and a halt to the confiscation of lands (Proclamation No. 2). According to Yusuf Mustafa, the general slogan of the *intifada* cannot be fixed "since it is the balance of forces that defines the form of the slogan and the struggle's goal" (51). With the breaking of administrative and legal relations between Jordan and the West Bank on 15 November 1988, the insurrection announced the establishment of the Palestinian state.

What is striking here is the key role of the organized leadership constructed from within the besieged community. One can trace from the unfolding of events how the communiques of the leadership of the uprising delineated its strategy as a response to emergent practical and theoretical demands in the struggle—that is, they articulated the dynamic process of interaction between people and leaders, between "inside" and "outside." Indeed, it is this dialectic of "inside" and "outside" that effectively disrupted Israel's strategic game of relocating the problem of occupation of the Palestinian people from the inside to the outside—to the Arab exterior (Jordan and Lebanon)—and transforming it into an internal Arab problem. In short, Israel tried to displace its burden of occupation into an Arab problem at the expense of its victims, of course. For Elias Khoury, the *intifada* overhauled the structural dichotomy of inside and outside, of occupation and exile, of Palestinian history since the founding of the state of Israel in 1948. Israel was faced with the dilemma of choosing between the South African or the Algerian solution. In the first, Israel would be a settler state with the Jewish minority practicing racist oppression on the original inhabitants, thus forfeiting its "western democratic" appearance; in the second, by recognizing the right of the Palestinian people to self-determination and to an independent state, it would call into question the legitimacy of the state of Israel. Khoury's acute analysis of the historical vicissitudes of the Israel-Palestinian antagonism can also elucidate for us the precise symbolic value of Tel Zaatar, celebrated by Turki in the realignment of global forces in the entire region:

> The Palestinian relocation to inside and the re-posing of the question from the West Bank and Gaza is not only an expression of the political failure of the outside but of the old and conflicted trajectory of the Palestinian struggle as well, one that emerged amidst innumerable difficulties from the rubble of the two disasters of 1948 and 1967.
>
> The withdrawal to the outside following 1967 was not born of a Palestinian choice but was the result of an Israeli military and strategic superiority as well as of the vicious repression in Gaza and the West Bank that led to the creation of the resistance

in the Arab "outside" and a long series of wars. But, and here lies the distinction-dilemma for Israel, the outside is not outside for the Palestinians and was transformed instead into an "inside" factor. The Israeli attack on the "outside," intended to turn it into a tool for the elimination of the Palestinian people, an attack which reached its peak in the 1982 invasion of Lebanon, the Palestinian departure from Beirut, and the massacres in the two refugee camps [of Sabra and Shatila], was made an inside factor that expressed itself in two moments.

While the moment of the Lebanese national resistance did not succeed in unifying Lebanon, it did succeed in undermining the Israeli idea of a serviceable "outside" by making this outside into a form of resistance compelling Israeli withdrawal. The moment of the *intifada* and its overthrow of all Israeli balances restructured the struggle as a struggle between the Palestinian people and the occupation, nothing more and nothing less. (40–41)

The trajectory of the Palestinian revolution has thus reached a mature stage in which the internal conditions (the resistance of the popular masses in the occupied lands) has made the outside (the refugee camps and the diaspora) as a reserve for the inside, "a bridge which the Palestinian struggle, its very heart and central point, crosses to enter into the Arab nationalist question." Accompanying this imperative to reconceptualize Palestinian political and social structures is the transformation of Palestinian rights on the inside into a weapon of struggle. Fundamentally, the *intifada* translates into a demand for the basic right to political action which lays the groundwork for independence. It is possible to grasp the deconstruction of the outside/inside dichotomy in the uprising as a form of ideological struggle: popular practices of resistance, while not yet synonymous with theoretical axioms, can theorize resistance by "their materially-grounded disarticulations of conventional structures and inherited organizational paradigms and by their clearing the site for new possibilities of 'meaning-generation,' for the making of a new historical narrative" (Harlow 1990, 36–37). This narrative is now directed to a telos of liberation, sublating the stage of nationalist independence, a new alternative which (to quote Said) "involves, in Fanon's words, a transformation of social consciousness beyond national consciousness" (1990, 83), an exorcism of the logic of imperial identity which has dehumanized all the peoples that suffered the proverbial "civilizing mission" of Western capitalist powers.

We now begin to comprehend why both Israel and the PLO

bureaucracies with their statist orientation are sensitive, if not wholly alarmed, at the emancipatory radical potential of the *intifada*. Hence the precipitous and secret nature of diplomatic negotiations. Of immense and lasting significance is the mobilization of women in the whole region. Nahla Abdo sums up the gains in this area: "Women's mass participation in the *intifada* had given them a sense of empowerment and conviction of their ability to effect change in the social, gender, and economic structures of their society. . . . A major achievement for the women of the *intifada*, one which is not likely to fade out, is the role they have played in politicizing the Israeli women's movement as well as in generating not only sympathy but also solidarity and support among various feminist groups internationally" (122–23). Not only has this popular insurrection revealed the genuine character of Israel's apartheid and racist system, but also its ultimate dependence on violence; in short, it testified to Israel's loss of hegemony and total political bankruptcy. One can also sense the profound impact of six years of insurgency by an Israeli general's comment that the occupation "has corrupted a whole generation of Israelis" (*Newsweek*, 27 September 1993, 29).

The return (*auda*) to the homeland is a central theme in Palestinian culture, a utopian or anticipatory drive aiming to redeem the disaster (*nakbah*) of 1948 and the defeat or setback (*naksah*) of 1967. In allegorizing this journey or quest, writers like Turki, Mahmoud Darwish, Jabra Ibrahim Jabra, and others are compelled to map the trajectory of borders and boundaries and discriminate the coordinates of what's outside and inside. Long before the *intifada*, Ghassan Kanafani has defined the Palestinian literary renaissance as an integral part of the armed struggle for a democratic secular state; Palestinian writing expresses a desire for liberation coeval with "resistance in its broadest sense" as refusal and as a firm grasp of the roots and the situations." Barbara Harlow has brilliantly described the emergence of this unique concept of resistance literature in Kanafani's pathbreaking novel *Return to Haifa* and his critical essays. This theory of resistance writing fundamentally derives from Kanafani's perception that in 1967, when Palestinians living in the West Bank and the Gaza Strip were transformed from exiles into dispossessed subjects of an occupying state and its military administration, their literary imagination moved from exile to another site: "the language and speech of the Arabs of occupied Palestine." Consequently the reseacher or critic who intends to articulate the narrative of the Palestinian people must be "located within the resistance movement itself inside the occupied land, taking his testimony from the place in which it is born, lives and is propagated: the lips of the people" (Harlow 1987, 3). But where are the voices now coming from? What the *intifada* has achieved is precisely the problematization of the fixed loci of inside and outside, the decentering of any strategic Archimedean point from which the totality can be apprehended, so that the historic agency of the people began to acquire nomadic, shifting, protean shapes that pay homage to their inexhaustible potential. Especially after the Israeli invasion of Lebanon in 1982, borders opened up—in more senses than the physical. It is clear that the complexity of the Palestinian fate is not just one of exile or occupation. In his eloquent testimony, *After the Last Sky*, Said repudiates Palestinian alterity and incompleteness as simply identical with victimage. He writes: "Whatever the claim may be that we make on the world—and certainly on ourselves as people who have become restless in the fixed place to which we have been assigned—in fact our truest reality is expressed in the way we cross over from one place to another. We are migrants and perhaps hybrids in, but not of, any situation in which we find ourselves. This is the deepest continuity of our lives as a nation in exile and constantly on the move" (1985, 164). While Said deplores this life as anxiously subsumed in a "protracted not-yet," a process of suspension or postponement, yet for the Marxist thinker Ernst Bloch this moment of transition and movement, this process of becoming, is exactly the privileged scene in which what is new, what releases the deepest energies and fulfills the most urgent needs of the collective body, approximates the joy of the return that Palestinians persevere in realizing. Darwish, the Palestinian poet in exile, offers sibylline images for that emancipatory vision: "I carry the key to legends and ruined monuments of slaves./ I see history an old man/ Tossing dice and gathering the stars . . . /In the rubble I rummage for light and new poetry."

Original version published in *Alive Magazine* no. 129 (31 March 1979): 14–15.

## BIBLIOGRAPHY

Abdo, Nahla. "New World Order: Old Arab World Problems." In *Global Visions*, edited by Jeremy Brecher, John Brown Childs, and Jill Cutler. Boston: South End Press, 1993.

Al Hout, Bayan Nuwaihed. "The Palestinian Identity." *Tricontinental*, no. 85 (1983): 49–65.

American Friends Service Committee. *A Compassionate Peace*. New York: Hill and Wang, 1982.

Bloice, Carl. "'A Historic Turning Point of Tremendous Importance.'" *Corresponder* 2, no. 6, (Oct.–Dec. 1993): 19.
Chomsky, Noam. "Nationalism and Conflict in Palestine." *Liberation*, Nov. 1969, 1–12.
Cockburn, Alexander. "Beat the Devil." *The Nation*, 4 Oct. 1993, 342–43.
El Masri, Rafik. "Intifada–Present and Future," *Tricontinental*, no. 129 (1990): 4–20.
Harlow, Barbara. "Constructions of the *Intifada*: Introduction." *Polygraph* 4 (1990): 35–38.
———. *Resistance Literature*. New York: Methuen, 1987.
Khoury, Elias. "The Names, All of Them." *Polygraph* 4 (1990): 39–42.
Massad, Joseph. "Palestinians and the Limits of Racialized Discourse." *Social Text*, no. 34 (1993): 94–114.
Mustafa, Yusuf. "A Reading of the Specific and General Goals and Slogans of the *Intifada*." *Polygraph* 4 (1990): 43–53.
Said, Edward. *After the Last Sky*. New York: Pantheon Books, 1985.
———. "Yeats and Decolonization." In *Nationalism, Colonialism, and Literature*, by Terry Eagleton, Fredric Jameson, and Edward W. Said. Minneapolis: Univ. of Minnesota Press, 1990.
———. "Arafat's Deal," *The Nation*, 20 Sept. 1993, 269–70.
Turki, Fawaz. *The Disinherited: Journal of a Palestinian Exile*. New York: Monthly Review Press, 1972.
———. *Tel Zaatar Was the Hill of Thyme*. Washington, D.C.: Free Palestine Press, 1978.
Watson, Russell. "Peace at last?" *Newsweek*, 13 Sept. 1993, 21–26.

# Art against Imperialism: For the National Liberation Struggle of Third World Peoples

For the majority of Third World peoples brutalized by the nightmare reality of a colonial past and a neocolonial present, art is literally a matter of life and death. It reflects in varied forms the ongoing class struggle. It reflects the sharpening contradictions between the oppressed masses in revolt and disintegrating monopoly capitalism with its feudal or comprador lackeys. Art thus cannot deny its social origin nor its historical destiny.

In the *Economic and Philosophic Manuscripts of 1844*, Marx pointed out how integrally commensurate, even identical, is the development of the aesthetic and creative faculty with social practice, i.e., work, productive transaction between humanity and nature in history:

> Only through the objectively unfolded richness of man's essential being is the richness of subjective *human* sensibility (a musical ear, an eye for beauty of form—in short, *senses* capable of human gratification, senses affirming themselves as essential power of *man*) either cultivated or brought into being... *human* sense, the human nature of the senses, comes to be by virtue of *its* object, by virtue of *humanised* nature. The *forming* of the five senses is a labour of the entire history of the world down to the present. (1975, 301-2)

Whether they like it or not, artists in the "undeveloped" countries of Asia, Africa, and Latin America serve as witnesses and participants in a complex but law-governed process in which a new configuration of human relations, both the antithesis and fulfillment of the present, is assuming integrity and substance in the womb of the old dying system. Depending on the artist's choice, aesthetics in the context of the class struggle may serve either as midwife or executioner. Like humanity itself, its ministry submits to Engels's maxim of freedom as "the recognition of necessity."

This conception of art's role, its import and efficacy in mediating consciousness and reality, is implicitly committed to the goal of radical social change. Either one decides to take a stand in full awareness or one yields to "blind necessity"—on the surface, a dualism that art as a kind of human engagement seeks to resolve. But surely many aestheticians in the metropolis, scrupulously calculating the decorous mixture of pleasure (*dulce*) and usefulness (*utile*), would dissent. Those who believe that art contains a self-sufficient or autonomous terminal value transcending contingent interests and needs may be scandalized by what they call "vulgar instrumentalism." For them, the genuine artist takes the side of all humanity and universal truth in the creation of immortal beauty. The artist's only responsibility is to the *métier*, the vocation.

Perhaps it is wiser to subsume this hackneyed theme of the bankruptcy of "art for art's sake," whether it disguises itself in Kantian categories, New Critical scholasticism, or structuralist metaphysics, in the far more challenging responses of the ultraleft, anarchist orthodoxy and the "right" opportunists who try to revise Marxism-Leninism to suit compromised subjective ends.[1]

The Third World countries, from the time when the emerging bourgeoisie of Europe proceeded to accumulate capital by plundering the colonies, have been systematically "underdeveloped." They have been reduced to the classic status of supplier of cheap raw materials and labor, and dumping ground for expensive industrial products and other manufactured commodities.[2] With the consolidation of bourgeois hegemony in the nineteenth century, finance capitalism intensified its exploitation through the export of capital, territorial division, war, and other insidious schemes first described by Lenin in *Imperialism, the Highest Stage of Capitalism.*

Imperialism, in effect, wrested from the Africans, Asians, and Latin Americans the right to control their productive resources and to determine their lives, manipulating the ideological superstructure—cultural forms embodying value-systems, modes of self-interpretation, etc.—to maintain the natives in the bonds of self-hatred, impotence, and awe at the slavemaster. In the pit of colonial domination, the native's sense, no longer effective powers of worldly intervention, is finally deprived of any awareness of identity as producer, as a motive force of history.

Amilcar Cabral formulates the problematics of this experience succinctly:

> Both in colonialism and in neo-colonialism the essential characteristic of imperialist domination remains the same: the negation

of the historical process of the dominated people by means of violent usurpation of the freedom of development of the national productive forces. On the basis of this, we can state that national liberation is the phenomenon in which a given socio-economic whole rejects the negation of its historical process. In other words, the national liberation of a people is the regaining of the historical personality of that people, its return to history through the destruction of the imperialist domination to which it was subjected. (1970, 102)

To effect the maximization of profit, imperialism disrupted the historic process of internal class struggle within the different societies it violated and subsequently instituted racial, chauvinistic discrimination. Co-opting a privileged stratum of the indigenous ruling class, it enforced alienation. This alienation, transmitted through the various media of communications, schools, etc., may be conceived of as the over-all mystification of the forms of consciousness (values, habits, fashions, tastes, ideals) arising from, and affirmed by, the loss of vital decision-making powers. From this comes the African's Europeanized sensibility; the myth of French, British, or American cultural and technological supremacy; the fetish of capitalist investment as the miraculous key to modernization; philosophy, art, literature, etc., as neutral, privately disposable property and attribute of individuals freed from mundane concerns, receiving from the anarchy of the capitalist market the dividends of catharsis, self-actualization, and so forth.

Because art crystallizes one's way of perceiving reality in accordance with one's generic, historically unfolding needs and potencies, we cannot ignore the concrete material situation, the uneven development of the socioeconomic formation, in which the artist functions.

In other words, art cannot be divorced from praxis. People make themselves, reproduce their own nature, in association with other people. To deny this is to fall into idealist mystification. If art is conceived not as an inert product for contemplation but as a mode of interpreting and changing reality, then the real motive force of the imagination exists not in the sphere of noumenal freedom, but in the actual tension of the class struggle. The much-vaunted freedom of the imagination acquires meaning only within the limitations of the artist's sensory world, a world located within the historical domain. The artist's sensibility registers the pressures of material forces and acts on them to the degree that the artist's reason succeeds in grasping the dialectical movement of the historical experience inhabited. This is why a class analysis of the intellectual's role and the cultural differentiation in Third World societies should precede any attempt to understand the significance of art there for the masses, the agents of production and progress.

The historical experience of Third World societies in general shows that the petty-bourgeois intelligentsia, the university-trained elite which includes writers, painters, teachers, scientists, etc., constitutes a privileged segment (perhaps the "weak link" in the state apparatus) removed from the peasants and workers by their role in the production process.[3] On the whole, they tend to rationalize and justify what exists, the status quo of imperialist domination. They are the "whores" of appearance. Tutored in France, England, the United States, etc., the native intellectuals, while enjoying their marginal share of the surplus value stolen from the laboring masses, are nevertheless still exposed to the humiliating paternalism of their Western employers and the cunning suspicion of their countrymen.

Two alternatives are open to them. They can deny the objective inequality in their minds and exalt the supraclass, supraracial status of the artist. Disembodied spirits, they ironically enact a naturalistic and empirical transcription of everyday reality, surrendering to the illusion of the statistical average. They are happy, their consciences are at rest. Their benevolent impartiality is rewarded with cash and sinecure. This is what we may call "right" opportunism.

Or they can get rid of their petty-bourgeois hang-ups, the egotistic lifestyle encrusted on them by the decadent and parasitic milieu of Paris, London, or New York, and "go native" again, this time extolling a mystical essence like "Negritude" or an authentic Oriental (Gandhian?) spirit. This we may call "left" opportunism. Kim Il Sung repudiated this trend of "restorationism." He stressed self-critical discrimination, endorsing the immediate priority of Lenin's thesis on the dialectical growth of the cultural tradition:

> Restorationism is an anti-Marxist ideological trend which restores and glorifies the things of the past uncritically, in disregard of the demands of the times and the class principle. If restorationism is allowed in the field of cultural development, all the unsound aspects of the culture of the past will be revived, and reactionary bourgeois and feudalistic Confucian ideas, as well as other outmoded ideas, will grow in the minds of the people.
> 
> A relentless struggle should be waged against the tendency to copy blindly the antiquated, reactionary things of the past,

idealizing and embellishing them on the pretext of taking over the heritage of national culture. We must discard backward and reactionary elements in the cultural heritage, and critically inherit and develop progressive and popular elements in conformity with the realities of socialism today. (1971, 199)

One example of the first alternative is the Filipino poet Jose Garcia Villa. Born of the landed gentry class and reared in the dominant capitalist ethos of competitive individualism, conspicuous consumption, and bohemian elitism, Villa damned his countrymen, migrated to Greenwich Village, and aped the techniques of Gertrude Stein until he was finally glorified by the Edith Sitwell clique of modern-day aesthetes. Asked why his poetry was abstract, Villa revealed the kernel of his reactionary apriorist and ahistorical outlook in his reply:

> The reason for it must be that I am not at all interested in description of outward appearance, nor in the contemporary scene, but in *essence*. A single motive underlies all my work and defines my intention as a serious artist: The search for the metaphysical meaning of man's life in the Universe—the finding of man's selfhood and identity in the mystery of Creation. I use the term *metaphysical* to denote the ethico-philosophic force behind all essential living. The development and unification of the human personality I consider the highest achievement a man can do. (1955)

This is a paradigmatic statement, instances of which one can see in Jorge Luis Borges's metaphysical puzzles, Lewis Nkosi's or John Nogenda's image of the artist as the Elect, and Kamala Markandaya's self-indulgence in grotesque pathos and sentimental voyeurism. One can cite a dozen Third World artists whose expertise in the banality of the Absurd wins them kudos in the cocktail circuits of the "free world."

Of the second alternative, the most instructive case is Leopold Senghor.[4] To achieve decolonization in a mechanical fashion, Senghor proposes a mystical affirmation of "Negritude" as a distinctly African essence which cuts across class boundaries. Contrast this with Aimé Césaire's idea of "Negritude" as a weapon of resistance to the assimilation/acculturation strategy of neocolonialism. Senghor's "Negritude" is a kind of escapist narcissism which obscures the class contradictions between the African comprador bourgeoisie and African workers, peasants, and other exploited sectors. As an ahistorical idea, "Negritude" negates art as social praxis. It is ultimately counterrevolutionary. Such a sectarian reaction to the imperialist technique of monopolizing all history, relegating the past of the colonized and their memories to the inert realm of prehistoric barbarism, may justify such misleading phenomena as a unique "African socialism" more realizable by legislative fiat than by class struggle.

Given the national dimension of the class struggle in the Third World countries, with the masses, except for the comprador minority, being oppressed by alien rulers, there exists a tremendous revolutionary potential in the emergence of a consciousness of national culture, the birth of national self-esteem. This is a necessary first stage in the liberation struggle against imperialist aggression. It has been voiced by Che Guevara, by the recent discovery and revitalization of Afro-Cuban culture, by the collective endeavors of Nicolas Guillen, Pablo Neruda, Carlos Fuentes, Luis Valdez's Chicano guerrilla theater, the Ramona Parra Brigade in Chile, etc. It characterizes the cultural nostalgia of Tagore and other Asian intellectuals.

In *The Wretched of the Earth*, Frantz Fanon eloquently articulated the need to destroy the colonial system, its base and superstructure, which broke the historical continuum of the colonized, deluding the native into thinking that he can only be the passive consumer, while the alien intruder is the sole creator of commodities and spiritual goods. But it is also Fanon who emphasized the primacy of the national struggle: "To fight for national culture means in the first place to fight for the liberation of the nation, that material keystone which makes the building of a culture possible. . . . The nation is not only the condition of culture, its fruitfulness, its continuous renewal, and its deepening. It is also a necessity" (1968, 233, 244).

But what Fanon failed to point out, and what others who reject a Marxist-Leninist framework ignore, is that the concept "nation," in this moment of world history cannot be a homogeneous, reified totality. In fact the national struggle today can only be a triumphant anti-imperialist transformation of a colonized or neocolonized country if the working class, in broad alliance with the peasantry and other democratic forces, leads the struggle. Proletarian politics, implemented by the vanguard party comprised of the most advanced elements of the toiling masses, must command any cultural revolution aimed not only at recovering national pride but also at changing permanently the alienating social relations of individuals by abolishing the exploitative material conditions: private ownership or control of the means of production, tyranny of exchange value (profit) over use value, devaluation of work, etc. Hence the spirit of proletarian internationalism orients the culture of "new democracy." In the Third World liberation struggles, only the leadership of the working class can release the productive forces and thereby adjust the form and quality of human association with the content of productive life. In their obsession with form and the "independent" subjectivity of the artist, theoreticians of the New Left have sometimes forgotten the cardinal premise of radical thought: ideas spring from social praxis, ideas become a material force when consciously grasped by the masses in revolutionary action. Art then begins to function as a sensory manifold of values and qualities that heightens our cognition of the world, its limitations and possibilities for collective action. It ceases to be simply an autonomous mode of self-realization. Compelled by his attack against "repressive de-sublimation" and his passion for utopian extrapolations, Marcuse defines the aesthetic sense as "the capacity of receiving the impression of Form: beautiful and pleasurable form as the possible mode of existence of men and things" (cited in Baxandall 1972, 58). This may be fine Hegelian philosophizing, but it is not a historical-materialist or class-oriented elucidation of art's humane service. The medium is not the only message. Even for the "engineer of the soul," technique is not everything. What is required is an intelligent concern with the meaning being formed which is needed to raise political consciousness, awaken the spectator of fate to become an actor, and intensify the people's commitment to revolution.

Could we salvage from the fictitious ethical objectivity of corporate liberalism any poetics to promote the all-round development of all people? In what sense can Third World cultural workers be mentally equipped and mobilized for destroying feudal/bourgeois culture by contemplating the constellation of symbols and archetypes in Nabokov or Samuel Beckett, in the artifacts of the much advertised exponents of Angst-ridden, modernist sophistication?

To enable us to appreciate the differences in aesthetic criteria due to underlying ideological premises and milieux, it may be worthwhile to juxtapose the convictions of Third World artists with a remark made by the well-known novelist Jerzy Kosinski, a president of American P.E.N. (Poets, Essayists, Novelists), apropos of the topic "Literature and Revolution—Can a Writer be Uncommitted?" Kosinski observes:

> While a writer's primary commitment does not seem to have changed, his audience's receptivity has diminished. The majority of contemporary society, trained by the mass media to expect the simplest situations and emotions, can no longer digest the novel, whose intent is the expansion of individual consciousness. The "normal" readership is continually bombarded by visual images, and has been trained by television to observe

without becoming engaged, to experience "art" as passive reception. Ironically, the only truly unaffected audience now is the blind, whose access to literature is wholly through imagination. Thus at a time when so much of the mass media—both visual and verbal—tends to retard individual and social awareness, the writer's ability to counteract fragmentation and isolation is particularly valuable. In the absence of any religious sustenance, the creation of an internal imaginative world is the only remaining means to emotional integration. (1973)

In the "atomized society" Kosinski refers to, the artist grapples with "the unknown, his own existence." Skeptical despair, cynicism, withdrawal into an abstract subjectivism open to irrational (fascist) machinations, the metaphysical dilettantism of artistic experiments divorced from the mass struggles of working people—these characterize the self-appraisals of bourgeois writers published in *Partisan Review, New York Review of Books, Encounter,* etc.

On the other hand, we have the intransigent principles of Third World writers:

> The poet does not have a different personality when he writes than when he talks or fights. A poet is not a degenerate dreaming that he is flying in the clouds, he is a citizen engaged in life, organizing life.
> 
> Nazim Hikmet (1954, 7), (Turkey)

> Today, for the first time, the writer's valid words prove that the words of Power are invalid. . . . The fact is that the head of the most powerful nation in the world was run out of his post by the students, intellectuals, journalists, writers, by men with no other weapon than words. . . . Nobody can remember the Alamo, the *Maine,* the *Lusitania* or Pearl Harbor to justify daily murder and destruction in Vietnam. No "manifest destiny" convinces us that in order to insure the doubtful democracy of South Vietnam's oligarchs a country must be erased from the map with napalm and phosphorus. Similarly, nobody can be content with simply asking for proper legislation to resolve the black problem, which is not a legal problem but one of alienation and which is not a conflict of feelings but of being. In those conditions, words become rhetoric on the side of power and heresy on the side of dissent: words deny the orthodox position assigned to them by the Founding Fathers.
> 
> Carlos Fuentes (1972, 114), (Mexico)

The days are over when the artist was a new Narcissus who, before the mirror of the stream, marvelled and adored the shadow of his own self. The artist is now a witness and part of the immediate present. ... The artist is directly involved, as participant and member of society, in the lot of men with whom he has been destined to live. He knows that he is part of society, a part that contributes to the whole but also receives from the whole. Like Antaeus in mythology who fought with Hercules, the artist must needs stand always on solid earth, his feet on the soil, because from the heat and power of the soil spring the life and strength of his body.

Amado V. Hernandez (1984, 182), (Philippines)

I would be quite satisfied if my novels (especially the ones I set in the past) did no more than teach my readers that their past—with all its imperfections—was not one long night of savagery from which the first Europeans acting on God's behalf delivered them. Perhaps what I write is applied art as distinct from pure. But who cares? Art is important but so is education of the kind I have in mind. And I don't see that the two need be mutually exclusive.

Chinua Achebe (1988, 45), (Nigeria)

In the uneven development of social forces in the Third World, the central task of the artist is to demystify the class-distorted picture of the world established by imperialist domination. The artist's vocation is to undermine, not reinforce, the predominant interest of the ruling class. In order to dismantle the sacrosanct engines of repression, one must reform public opinion and restore to the masses their self-confidence, their long-suppressed tradition of resourcefulness and creativity. The principal task, namely, to transform the people from an object to a subject, also presupposes and entails converting the deracinated native intellectuals into revolutionary cadres serving the people. That is what the May 4th Movement in China essentially accomplished. It is the task the National Democratic Cultural Revolution in the Philippines pursued when the petty-bourgeois writers and artists committed "class suicide" (to use Cabral's phrase) and integrated with the masses in militant practice. Art followed the principle of the mass line: "from the masses, to the masses" (Mao Tse-tung).

Literary critics and aestheticians in monopoly capitalist society react violently and often ignorantly to the radical conception of art as an ideological weapon in the class struggle. Rejecting art as a coherent mode of apprehending the contradictions of society, they define art as an autotelic structure of qualities expressing nonclass attitudes and values. They reject art's function of mediating between class consciousness and the historical situation, not simply mirroring but revealing in typical synthesis the interconnected trends and tendencies of the whole historical process: what is coming into being, what is passing away. They deny the mimetic process and its educational impact because they accept exclusively, perhaps with some nuanced qualifications, the organic-expressive-formalistic notion of art. In striving to refute the bourgeois concept of "economic determinism," they denounce the tendentious, didactic theory of art. In doing so, they betray utter contempt for art as a social performance, a powerful instrument for shaping minds and therefore the collective vision of the good life.

Meanwhile, for the Third World peoples confronted daily with degrading poverty, hunger, disease, racist bigotry, and genocidal weapons, art spells life or death.

Unquestionably there are moral and material incentives to combat art propagating imperialist domination. Should not the partisans of "socialist realism," the followers of Plekhanov, Lukács, Gramsci, Sartre, Althusser, Brecht try to link up the proletarian cultural revolution in the metropolis with the Third World's anti-imperialist struggle in the ideological realm—as Lenin exhorted time and again? Should we welcome the transitional third way of "critical realism" to afford liberal reformist writers room to exercise their subtle wit, their moralizing paradoxes, their ironic satire which often leads to cosmic nihilism if not to self-pitying ego trips? Should artists in Asia, Africa, and Latin America overthrow the stranglehold of U.S. corporations and the Hollywood-Madison Avenue apparatus by expropriating the techniques of John Cage, Le Corbusier, Norman Mailer, Robbe-Grillet, Pop Art, and Happenings?

To repeat a commonplace: Marxism is a method of analysis, a critique, a guide to action, not a set of metaphysical dogmas. Consequently, one cannot legislate on what artistic method or style revolutionary artists participating in the national liberation struggle should adopt. Moreover, there is a combined unity and struggle of opposites in every conjuncture of events, at every stage of the total revolutionary process.

At the same time, however, one cannot be so eclectic that, in trying to avoid the fixation on a doctrinaire mystique of the "proletariat" regardless of prevailing class alignments, especially in the Third World societies, one succumbs to the futile notion that since the bourgeoisie (according to the *Communist Manifesto*) was once historically progressive, Third World artists should assiduously cultivate their knowledge of Shakespeare, Milton, Dante, Goethe, Cervantes, etc. Recall that these names, representing the great Western dispensation, have been used by the colonial administrators to justify bludgeoning to death millions of Africans, Asians, Arabs, and Latin Americans.

We are surely not accusing Shakespeare and company, but this only proves that we cannot measure the humane worth of art and literature apart from the unified structure of values or world outlook, the ideological motivations and judgments, the resolutions and programs for action incorporated in them. This is not to say that art is equivalent to agitprop. In his "Talks at the Yenan Forum on Literature and Art," Mao Tse-tung suggests that, for the revolutionary artist, the question "For whom?" is a fundamental question of principle. Mao asserts:

> In the world today all culture, all literature and art belong to definite classes and are geared to definite political lines. . . .
>
> Although man's social life is the only source of literature and art and is incomparably livelier and richer in content, the people are not satisfied with life alone and demand literature and art as well. Why? Because, while both are beautiful, life as reflected in works of literature and art can and ought to be on a higher plane, more intense, more concentrated, more typical, nearer the ideal, and therefore more universal than actual everyday life. Revolutionary literature and art should create a variety of characters out of real life and help the masses to propel history forward. For example, there is suffering from hunger, cold and oppression on the one hand, and exploitation and oppression of man by man on the other. These facts exist everywhere and people look upon them as commonplace. Writers and artists concentrate such everyday phenomena, typify the contradictions and struggles within them and produce works which awaken the masses, fire them with enthusiasm and impel them to unite and struggle to transform their environment. (1971, 266)

Of course, Mao's thought should not be regarded as absolute dogma. His talk does not deal, and is not meant to deal, with the intricate criteria for judging the efficacy of certain modes, techniques, idioms, in achieving a socialist goal. But Mao's summing up—"the raising of standards is based on popularization, while popularization [N.B. not to be confused with 'vulgarization'] is guided by the raising of standards"—precisely states in dialectical form the Party policy for doing artistic work among the masses. (Note that Mao is not at all preoccupied with the "liberated psyche" of the artist, self-confrontation, etc.)

We can illustrate how Mao's principle is applied by the Palestinian poets of the Resistance (e.g., Mahmoud Darwish) in their unrelenting project of demystifying their exile, exposing its historical alterability, and thus energizing their audience into directed political action. But that will require another essay in its own right.

Suffice it here to demonstrate in brief how false consciousness evolves to class consciousness, how social practice vindicates the viably humane function of art, by quoting at length the words of two Vietnamese authors recorded in Peter Weiss's inspiring testimony and tribute to the genuine avant-garde, the people's artists:

> We wrote out of hate and out of sympathy. We wrote about the lives of oppressed people. At the beginning our class point of view was not clear. For the most part we writers came from the *petite bourgeoisie*. We had little education. Yet the *petite bourgeoisie* in colonial conditions is close to the have-nots. To their misery and also to their stubbornness. Still, we had not as yet become aware of the root causes of want and impoverishment. Not until the revolution did we grasp the full extent of the crime that had been perpetrated on our country.
>
> We lived in the midst of the masses, who were demanding their rights. This much is common to all of us: we took our themes from the daily existence of the peasants, the industrial workers, the fishermen, and the soldiers in combat.
>
> At first we simply transcribed events. In their raw, unorganized form. We kept to the surface of things. We still did not know enough about the thoughts of the people with whom we were living. That was our childhood sickness. We were blinded by the light of the revolution. But one night I saw the true face of my fellow man:
>
> We were in a heavily contested area. The enemy was sending up flares. The road and the shell-cratered fields were bathed in white light. Then I saw the faces. Faces of soldiers, of women, girls, children. They all stood there heavily laden, weighted down, carrying weapons, ammunition, and heavy loads of food carried on yokes. They held their heads high. These faces burned themselves into my gaze. They are imperishable.
>
> Formerly we reproduced our impressions in brief sketches. Today we go beyond the immediate event. We describe the

struggle in its basic outlines. Behind the uplifted radiant faces we see the goal, the objective of the war.

Bui Hien (Weiss, 1970, 62–63)

These peasants and soldiers, these self-taught people, are not trying to change literature by experimenting with the use of language. What they want to do is change the reader, their own world. For us a book is a weapon....

With us everything has to do with realistic action. At the present time we need, above all, descriptions of the situation as it exists. We try to analyze events. Insofar as we make clear what is happening within people, show how they are holding firm, what they are accomplishing, we contribute to a strengthening of the power to resist. It is natural that from time to time the toil, the pain of losing some member of the family, the never-ending pressure of destruction, should overshadow hope. It would be inhuman to suppose that deprivations continuing year after year would leave no mark. Our consciousness for the time being is satisfied with a clear presentation of the perspectives of the people's war. We remind people of the indignities of colonialism, of the gigantic efforts which led to revolution, of the successes achieved during the years of construction. Our literature holds fast, it affirms. It assimilates the difficult experiences since the bombing attacks. Literature absorbs what the people have accumulated by way of thinking power and self-control.... We use a mode of expression understood by all.... Aesthetics interests us only as a means of advancing elucidation. Our literature is intended to be political, to have a practical application.

Nguyen Dinh Thi (Weiss, 1970, 70–71)

Original version published in *Weapons of Criticism*, edited by Norman Rudich, 147–60, © 1976 by Ramparts Press.

## NOTES

1. Vestiges of this abstract mode of thinking inhere in Fidel Castro's formula of "Within the Revolution, everything; against the Revolution, nothing" as guideline for Cuban artists; see his "Words to the Intellectuals" (cited in Baxandall 1972, 267–300). For recent developments, see Roberta Salper (1970)

2. The literature on imperialism is enormous. The most useful are:

Magdoff 1969, Baran 1957, Woddis 1967, Fann and Hodges 1971, and Gunder Frank 1967.

3. The lessons of China's Cultural Revolution should highlight the crucial role of the intelligentsia in revolutionizing the superstructure as well as the total social relations. In his article "Marxism and Mao," sociology professor Alvin W. Gouldner comments on the unique Chinese policy undergirding the educational reforms brought about by the Cultural Revolution, especially the changing of the traditional nature and function of the intelligentsia: "In the self-understanding of Maoism, the aim is to debourgeoisify the intellectual, to eliminate the rift between intellectuals and masses, to change the class character of intellectuals predominantly from workers or peasants, and themselves have an extensive personal experience of laboring as peasants or workers. This, to repeat, is Maoism's self-understanding of its policy toward the intelligentsia" (1973).

4. I am deeply indebted to Professor Omafume F. Onoge's unpublished essay, "The Crisis of Consciousness in Modern African Literature: A Survey," for many valuable insights into the African cultural scene.

## BIBLIOGRAPHY

Achebe, Chinua. *Hopes and Impediments: Selected Essays 1965–87*. London: Heineman, 1988.
Baran, Paul A. *The Political Economy of Growth*. New York: Monthly Review Press, 1957.
Baxandall, Lee, ed. *Radical Perspectives in the Arts*. Harmondsworth, U.K.: Penguin, 1972.
Cabral, Amilcar. *Revolution in Guinea*. New York: Monthly Review Press, 1970.
Fann, K. T., and Donald C. Hodges. *Readings in U.S. Imperialism*. Boston: P. Sargent, 1971.
Fanon, Frantz. *The Wretched of the Earth*. New York: Grove Press, 1968.
Fuentes, Carlos. "The Enemy: Words." In *Literature in Revolution*, edited by George Abbot White and Charles Newman, 111–22. New York: Holt, Rinehart and Winston, 1972.
Gouldner, Alvin W. "Marxism and Mao." *Partisan Review* 40 (1973): 243–60.
Gunder Frank, Andre. *Capitalism and Underdevelopment in Latin America*. New York: Monthly Review Press, 1967.
Hernandez, Amado V. "Beyond Narcissus, Toward Antaeus." In *Toward A People's Literature*, edited by E. San Juan, Jr., 181–83. Quezon City: Univ. of Philippines Press, 1984.
Hikmet, Nazim. *Poems*. New York: Masses and Mainstream, 1954.
Kim Il Sung. *Revolution and Socialist Construction in Korea*. New York: International Publishers, 1971.
Kosinski, Jerzy. "Literature and Revolution—Can a Writer be Uncommitted?" *American PEN Newsletter*, Summer 1973.

Magdoff, Harry. *The Age of Imperialism.* New York: Monthly Review Press, 1969.
Mao Tse-tung. *Selected Readings from the Works of Mao Tse-tung.* Peking: Foreign Languages Press, 1971.
Marx, Karl. *Economic and Philosophic Manuscripts of 1844.* In vol. 3 of *Karl Marx, Frederick Engels: Collected Works,* 229–346. New York: International Publishers, 1975.
Salper, Roberta. "Literature and Revolution in Cuba." *Monthly Review* (Oct. 1970): 15–30.
Villa, Jose Garcia. "Autobiography." In *Twentieth Century Authors,* edited by Stanley Kunitz, 1035–36. New York: H. W. Wilson, 1955.
Weiss, Peter. *Notes on the Cultural Life of the Democratic Republic of Vietnam.* London: Calder & Boyars, 1970.
Woddis, Jack. *Introduction to Neo-Colonialism.* New York: International Publishers, 1967.

# Ho Chi Minh: Writing as Praxis

In August 1924 Ho Chi Minh, then known as the Vietnamese patriot Nguyen Ai Quoc, was arrested by the Kuomintang police on his way to Chungking to represent the Vietminh Front and win support for it from the Chiang Kai-shek government.

In retrospect, the incident was a fine ironic lesson for the poet. Ho was subsequently confined in numerous filthy jails, starved, and humiliated. By some uncanny dialectical twist, his predicament begot enduring works of art: Ho's prison poems. His places of confinement —Tsingsi, Nanning, Kweilin, Liuchow, etc.—mark the stations of the heroic spirit of Ho Chi Minh. They incarnate in their sordid and outrageous existence the triumphant revolutionary will of the Communist leader who led the courageous people of Vietnam—the masses of workers and peasants—to victory.

## Practical application of materialist dialectics

Ho's prison poems, entitled *Prison Diary* (published in English translation by Real Dragon Press, Berkeley, 1971, with a preface by Phan Nhuan), reveal the essential humanity of this great fighter for socialist democracy and human liberation. His poetic interpretation of experience embodies in dramatic and lyrical form the fundamental truths enunciated by Mao Tse-tung, such as: "The people, and the people alone, are the motive force in the making of world history"; "Revolutionary culture is a powerful revolutionary weapon for the broad masses of the people"; and "Revolution is the main trend in the world today."

Ho Chi Minh's *Prison Diary* exemplifies in structure and substance the main objective of the lucid and seminal guidelines established by Mao Tse-tung concerning art and literature in his widely read "Talks at the Yenan Forum on Literature and Art" (May 1942). Intensely subjective and moodily introspective, *Prison Diary* subsumes the private consciousness of the poet in the fictive persona of Ho the prisoner. Ho's poetic method validates the ego's insights by focusing on the typical figure of the poet, who then speaks for all the mute victims of colonial injustice and imperialist oppression. Consequently the subjective appeal is qualified and included in the larger design of the representative and typical consciousness of the revolutionary agent. In effect, Ho's poetry exhibits the practical application of materialist dialectics in transforming personal experience into moving and persuasive universal works of art.

## The poem as revolutionary weapon

Ho's poems are charged with the authentic vibrations of moral revolt against colonial exploitation. They are singularly animated by the complex sensibility of a man with an abundant love for his suffering fellow humans and an enormous gusto for life. In "Autumn Night," the poet subdues his distress poignantly:

> ... My dream intertwines with sadness like a skein of a thousand threads.
> Innocent, I have now endured a whole year in prison.
> Using my tears for ink, I turn my thoughts into verses.

These verses are not merely self-indulgent exercises; rather, they serve the prime function of collective protest because they are conceived in the full awareness of the historical demands of the class struggle:

> ON READING *ANTHOLOGY OF A THOUSAND POETS*
> The ancients used to like to sing about natural beauty:
> Snow and flowers, moon and wind, mists, mountains, and rivers.
> Today we should make poems including iron and steel,
> And the poet also should know how to lead an attack.

Ho kept the immediacy of the class struggle and the national democratic revolution spearheaded by the proletariat in the forefront of his mind. He elaborated frequently on the theme of revolutionary dedication:

> AT THE POLITICAL BUREAU OF THE FOURTH ZONE OF RESISTANCE
> I have travelled the thirteen districts of Kwangsi Province,
> And tasted the pleasures of eighteen different prisons.
> What crime have I committed, I keep on asking?
> The crime of being devoted to my people.

The poet's ordeals in jail, a subject liable to sentimental exaggeration by self-centered petty-bourgeois writers, receive a homely but powerful metaphoric representation. Ho's technique of analogy recalls the Oriental tradition of the Japanese *haiku*, the Malay *pantun*, and the Filipino *tanaga:*

> LISTENING TO THE RICE-POUNDING
> How much the rice must suffer under the pestle!
> But, after the pounding, it comes out white like cotton.
> The same thing often happens to men in this world:
> Misfortune's workshop turns them into polished jade.

That is why, as the poet claims in "Seriously Ill," amid his intolerable afflictions, "instead of weeping, I prefer to keep singing."

## Toward a Marxist poetics

Social being or social practice determines human consciousness. This principle Ho embodies in his reflections on the educational value of suffering. In the time-honored fashion of freedom fighters everywhere, Ho believes that experience forges the character and tempers the iron in the soul. But the sufferings, privations, anguish, and pain are not tolerated or accepted merely for their own aesthetic merit. On the contrary, they are reshaped and assimilated in the poet's ideological outlook. Ho regards his prison-stay not as a necessary ritual for ascetic sainthood—a goal alien to Marxist humanism. On the contrary, his agonizing ordeals serve in the final analysis to heighten humanity's spontaneous and creative appreciation of the world.

A mature, realistic perspective emerges from the poet's totalizing assessment of his sojourn in prison, as conveyed in "At the End of Four Months":

> "One day in jail is equal to a thousand years outside it . . . ."
> How right were the ancients, expressing it in those words!
> Four months leading a life in which there is nothing human
> Have aged me more than ten years.
> Yes: in a whole four months I have never eaten my fill,
> In four months I have never had a comfortable night's sleep,
> In four months I have never changed my clothes, and in four
>     months
> I have never taken a bath.
> So: I have lost a tooth, my hair has grown grey,
> And, lean and black as a demon gnawed by hunger,
> I am covered with scabies. Fortunately
> Being stubborn and patient, never yielding an inch,
> Though physically I suffer, my spirit is unshaken.

He confronts the truth of his particular condition with a mixture of stoic fortitude, anxious detachment, and constantly renewed militant daring. Thus he refuses to be resigned, and instead he vows to strengthen his determination in combating wayward thoughts, ultimately hoping to vanquish the enemy that incarcerates his body. One memorable testimony of Ho's dialectical vision of the revolutionary experience is found in "Advice to Oneself":

> Without the cold and desolation of winter
> There could not be the warmth and splendor of spring.
> Calamity has tempered and hardened me,
> And turned my mind into steel.

The poet's conviction of the positive value of suffering informs a majority of the poems in *Prison Diary*. It underlies his conception of a person's worth as unfolded and guaranteed in class war, especially in the revolutionary strivings of the oppressed peoples against imperialism and for national liberation.

The philosophy of Marxism-Leninism—historical and dialectical materialism—provides Ho's art with a correct, dynamic, and progressive orientation. For example, Ho recognizes that labor creates everything of value in this world ("Road Menders," "Prison Life," etc.). People's natures are shaped by changing historical circumstances while they endeavor to alter or modify these circumstances. Ho affirms this thesis in "Midnight":

> Faces all have an honest look in sleep.
> Only when they wake does good or evil show in them.
> Good and evil are not qualities born in man:
> More often than not, they arise from our education.

History is presented as a purposeful record of the colonized people's struggle against the decadent forces of imperialism and its local "running dogs." The traditional image of the dragon invests the didactic thrust of these lines with sensuous immediacy and classic dignity:

> ... People who come out of prison can build up the country.
> Misfortune is a test of people's fidelity.
> Those who protest at injustice are people of true merit.
> When the prison-doors are opened the real dragon will fly out.
> (from "Word-Play")

In "The Eleventh of November," Ho captures graphically the evolving panorama of the war against Japanese fascism in epigrammatic strokes, summing up thus:

> . . . All over Asia flutter the anti-Japanese flags:
> Big flags or little flags—they are not all the same.
> Of course, big flags we must have, but we need the little flags, too.

Compare this with the poem "Alert in Vietnam," notable for its austere simplicity of utterance, a style which functions as the vehicle of a recurrent emotional tension:

> Better death than slavery! Everywhere in my country
> The red flags are fluttering again.
> Oh, what it is to be a prisoner at such a time!
> When shall I be set free, to take my part in the battle?

In "A Milestone," Ho chooses a common object to symbolize the progressive motivation that propels history. Using the same dominant image of the road, the poem "On the Road" allegorizes the truth of social practice as the test of ideas, theory, hopes, plans, and aspirations:

> Only when out on the road can we take stock of our dangers.
> After we climb one mountain, another looms into view:
> But, once we have struggled up to the top of the mountain range,
> More than ten thousand li can be surveyed at a glance.

The metaphor of the way or path of struggle recurs in "Hard Is the Road of Life" as a counterpointing motif to the static condition of imprisonment. But here the personal vicissitudes of the poet-prisoner are sublimated, dwindle in importance as a special category, and become simply an instance of a general but historically defined occurrence. The tone and framework of parable used by the poet evoke a peculiar response in us, a response akin to what Brecht calls "alienation effect"—an illusion of distance resulting from the gestural and reportorial cast of the whole poem. Hence, the quantity of facts undergoes a qualitative change—a transmutation mediated by Ho's sensibility:

> I
>
> Having climbed over steep mountains and high peaks,
> How should I expect on the plains to meet greater danger?
> In the mountains, I met the tiger and come out unscathed:
> On the plains, I encountered men, and was thrown into prison.
>
> II
>
> I was a representative of Vietnam
> On my way to China to meet an important personage.

> On the quiet road a sudden storm broke loose,
> And I was thrust into jail as an honored guest.
>
> III
> I am straightforward man with no crime on my conscience,
> But I was accused of being a spy for China.
> So life, you see, is never a very smooth business,
> And now the present bristles with difficulties.

## A commitment to the human world

Throughout his incarceration, Ho never yielded to despair, for the simple reason that he never abandoned the concrete sensuous reality around him. That is, he never surrendered himself to the temptations of futile idealism and utopian romanticism—a common malady of intellectuals in crisis, as attested to by the lugubrious confessions in *The God That Failed* and other shameless apologetics. "Twilight" confirms this loving commitment to the world in motion:

> Now the wind's edge is sharpened on mountain rocks.
> The spear of cold pierces the branches of trees.
> The gong from a far-off pagoda hastens
> The traveler's steps, and boys are playing flutes
> As they drive the buffaloes home across the twilight.

Opposing forces in the world unite and struggle together, just as contradictory forces in society unite and impel social development on to a higher historical stage. "Arrival at Tienpao" witnesses the morning's splendor framed by the edge of a cesspool. Changes in the material environment register the meaning of time and space in the response of living persons:

> MORNING SUNSHINE
>
> The morning sunshine penetrates into the prison,
> Sweeping way the smoke and burning away the mist.
> The breath of life fills the whole universe,
> And smiles light up the faces of all the prisoners.

In life, appearances deceive but the person who grasps the truth of objective reality based on the mode of production, a reality that transcends private notions and impulses, is sustained by a knowledge on which the efficacy of revolutionary practice is based. Two poems indicate Ho's radical and impassioned faith in the existence of a law-governed reality containing the limits and possibilities of action:

MORNING

I

Every morning the sun, emerging over the wall,
Darts its rays against the gate, but the gate remains locked.
Inside the prison, the ward is shrouded in darkness,
But we know outside the rising sun has shone.

II

Once awake, everyone starts on the hunt for lice.
At eight o'clock the gong sounds for the morning meal.
Come on! Let's go and eat to our heart's content.
For all we have suffered, there must be good times coming.

NIGHTFALL

Wearily to the wood the birds fly seeking rest.
Across the empty sky a lonely cloud is drifting.
Far away in a mountain village, a young girl grinds out maize.
When the maize is all ground, the fire burns red in the oven.

This latter poem exhibits in an oblique manner Ho's commitment to the Marxist principle that their productive activity ultimately conditions the relations among people and the cultural or ideological milieu of a given society at a certain historical period.

*Dialectic of the imagination*

Throughout his reveries and meditations on his plight, Ho repudiated escapism to an ivory tower of metaphysical idealism. He repudiated the tendency of petty-bourgeois individualists to succumb to desperate fantasies. The whole of *Prison Diary* implicitly attacks petty-bourgeois alienation and opportunism. Consider Ho's strong attachment to the inescapable demands of objective reality:

NOON

In the cell, how lovely it is to have a siesta!
For hours we are carried away in a sound sleep.
I dream of riding a dragon up into heaven . . . .
Waking, I'm brought abruptly back into prison.

A wry and sometimes sardonic humor characterizes many poems consisting of notations of prison life: "No Smoking," "Leaping," "The Charges," "The Inn," "The Dog-Meat at Paosiang," and others. Ho records the restrictions of prison life as absurd and antihuman disruptions of the human moral order actualized in revolutionary action.

While sharply critical of the degrading conditions of prison and the brutal treatment of prisoners by the vicious Kuomintang soldiers, Ho refrains from abstract generalizations.

Ho's virtue principally inheres in his consistent application of Lenin's dictum concerning dialectics as "the concrete analysis of concrete conditions." This may be illustrated of the poem "Mr. Mo, the Head-Warder":

> The head-warder at Pinyang has a golden heart.
> He buys rice for the prisoners with his own money.
> At night he takes off the fetters to let us sleep.
> He never resorts to force, but only to kindness.

Here Ho perceives the exceptional case—the negation of the negation, so to speak. In actuality, Ho simply pursued his vocation as a sincere revolutionary artist, exercising a strenuous but discriminating sympathy within the limits of the virile discipline imposed by the partisan stand of Marxism-Leninism.

## From knowledge to pleasure

Accompanying the poet's warm generosity of spirit, compassion, and solidarity with the oppressed is a knowing detachment required of the artist who seeks to transcribe the complex process of objective reality. Ho can thus afford the luxury of ironic witticism in poems like "Something to Smile At" or "Wife of a Conscript Deserter":

> One day you went away, not to come back again,
> Leaving me alone in our rooms, with sadness for companion.
> The authorities, having pity on my loneliness,
> Invited me to live temporarily in the prison.

In "Writing a Petition for a Jail-Mate," where Ho helps a fellow prisoner draw up a petition, aping officialese jargon, the poet is astonished by the exuberant gratitude of his friend. People can remain human in prison, Ho asserts, so long as they adhere firmly to their identities as revolutionary protagonists. Even prison is dominated by the corrupt business practices of the bourgeoisie, as Ho critically points out in "Entrance Fee" and other pieces. In "The Leg-Irons," Ho describes how people readily sacrifice freedom for the comfort and security of unthinking servitude. Even in prison, the rich and the poor are treated differently, as Ho observes in "Imprisoned for Gambling."

## Beyond the charity of absolutes

It would be a mistake, however, to assume that Ho, in trying to comprehend the exigencies of the prison system, forgave his enemies and (like Tolstoy, for example) failed to resist what are generally held to be remediable historical evils. On the contrary, Ho vigorously denounced the antipeople tyranny of the Kuomintang and, by implication, the monstrous abuses of the colonial exploiters. Ho raged intensely against the deprivation of freedom as an insufferable violation of the natural process, of life's primordial rhythm:

### RESTRICTIONS

To live without freedom is a truly wretched state.
Even the calls of nature are governed by restrictions!
When the door is opened, the belly is not ready to ease itself.
When the call of nature is pressing, the door remains shut.

Amid and beneath the contradictions of the social process, the struggle of the poet's mind proceeds with the inevitability of the season's maturation:

### AUTUMN IMPRESSIONS

#### I

At about ten o'clock the great Bear tops the mountain.
The cricket's song, rising and fading, announces autumn.
What does the prisoner care for the changing seasons?
Only one change he dreams of: his liberation.

#### II

Last year at the beginning of autumn I was free.
This year autumn finds me in the depths of a prison.
As for services rendered my country, I surely may claim
This autumn has been just as productive as the last.

## *Style and ideology*

What is probably the most distinguished quality of Ho's poems, which may be identified with the tradition of classical Japanese and Chinese poetry, is sensitive attention to the flux of natural phenomena. This is deepened and complicated by his visionary but paradoxically realistic rendering of psychological responses and impressions. This style is attributable to Ho's revolutionary faith, his vision of socialist equality and prosperity arising from the concrete grasp of objective material reality. A profound belief in the truth of material reality, mirrored for instance in the modulation of the seasons, manifests itself in the calm and assured statements of "Fine Weather":

Everything evolves, it is the cycle of nature:
After the rainy days, the fine weather comes.
In an instant, the whole world shakes off its damp clothes,

> Thousands of li of mountains unfurl their brocade carpet.
> Under the warm sun and the clean wind, the flowers smile.
> In the big trees with branches washed clean, the birds make chorus.
> Warmth fills the heart of man, and life reawakens.
> Bitterness now makes way for happiness,
> This is how nature wills it.

Characteristically, Ho achieves a quiet and subtle expression of his emotions by a constant fidelity to what is happening around him, as in "On a Boat for Nanning." Describing the swift gliding of the fishermen's boats around him while his legs are manacled, Ho suggests the antinatural injustice of his plight. His materialist poetics succeed in fusing the impulse to freedom and the obedience to the order of a humanized nature. It succeeds also in harmonizing the will of the revolutionary and the objective demands of sociohistorical existence, as many poems confirm.

But, as in all revolutionary poets, nature is there not to be worshipped but to be understood and transformed in revolutionary practice. Nature acquires significance only because people interact with it in the social process of making a living.

In "Morning Scene," Ho notes how the prison-cell bars the sunlight from penetrating into his quarters. This fact is, however, only a temporary accident, not a permanent condition. Indeed the force of nature and life—the life of the working class, in particular—cannot be suppressed.

## Ho's example today

On 19 May 1969 Ho Chi Minh drew up his testament, affirming his faith that "Our rivers, our mountains, our people will always be; the American aggressors defeated, we will build a country ten times more beautiful." His prison poems anticipate Ho's declaration of unshakable faith in the Vietnamese people's indomitable will, in the victorious destiny of the mass line.

Ho's materialist poetics brilliantly fulfill what Mao Tse-tung in his Yenan lecture asserted as the purpose of culture: "All our literature and art are for the masses of the people, and in the first place for the workers, peasants and soldiers." Ho Chi Minh's revolutionary practice in art and in life serves today as a mighty weapon, an inexhaustible inspiration to all artists and intellectuals in Asia, Africa, and Latin America who are today waging the ideological and armed struggle against U.S. imperialism, for the cause of national democracy, freedom, equality, and socialist liberation.

Original version published in *Eastern Horizon* 11 (1972): 20–26.

# Toward an Aesthetics of National Liberation: On Sergio Ramirez and Roque Dalton

## I. *The example of Roque Dalton*

*Poetry*
*pardon me for having helped you to understand*
*that you are not made of words alone.*
—"Ars Poetica 1974" by Roque Dalton

Whenever the term *aesthetics* (the study of the beautiful) is used, it almost automatically evokes the experience of pleasure for its own sake, as an end in itself and not a means or instrument for some ulterior motive. Counterposed to an extrinsic purpose or use, aesthetic pleasure is often ascribed to the perception of formal qualities of an object, qualities devoid of any utilitarian, moral, or pragmatic import. What the art object is, its *quidditas*, becomes the chief source of aesthetic pleasure. Thus one experiences the aesthetic pleasure of reading Wallace Steven's "Sunday Morning" or of beholding Andy Warhol's canvas entitled "Green Coca Cola Bottles" by attending to the formal arrangement of its parts. Unity, organic harmony, synesthesia, autotelic ontology—all these terms denote the essence of beauty, in the lexicon of Western aesthetics.

Whether experienced in museums or libraries or in private solitude, aesthetics becomes synonymous with anesthesia: disinterestedness, psychic distance, Kant's "purposiveness without purpose"—ultimately, art self-destructs. Indeed, postmodernist art (after Ezra Pound and James Joyce) may already have incorporated this self-destructive impulse in its fetish of self-conscious parody, in ironic pastiche or ambiguous mimicry. How do the Third World artists, aware of their position in its historic specificity, confront this challenge of Western aesthetics—Indian *rasa* theory and Zen Buddhist aesthetics should be strictly differentiated from the European kind—and its hegemonic imperative?

One instructive response is the anti-aesthetic, partisan poetics of Roque Dalton of El Salvador, whose writings were translated and widely circulated here amid unceasing U.S. imperialist repression in Central America as part of the strategy to destabilize and overthrow the Sandinista government in Nicaragua. Born in El Salvador in 1933, Dalton was a student of law and anthropology in El Salvador, Chile, and Mexico. In 1955, when he won the Central American Poetry Prize together with the Guatemalan poet Otto Rene Castillo, Dalton joined the Communist Party of El Salvador. Before he went to exile in Czechoslovakia, Cuba, and elsewhere, he suffered imprisonment several times. A story is told that when he was once in jail awaiting execution, an earthquake disintegrated the walls of his prison cell, permitting him to escape. In 1975 he returned to El Salvador as a member of the People's Revolutionary Army; but, soon after, he was killed by a rival faction. Dalton's achievement consists of six books of poems, critical and political treatises, a biography, and a novel. Aside from an essay "Culture in North Korea" (published in *Tricontinental*), Dalton's single most important essay is *Poetry and Militancy in Latin America* (originally published in the journal *Casa de las Americas*, Sept.-Dec. 1963), published in English translation by Curbstone Press in 1981. Instead of explicating his poems, I focus on this essay as an example of a Third World artist articulating his vocation in a country undergoing rapid structural mutations.

Unlike analogous pronouncements such as Brecht's "Little Organon for the Theater," or Mayakovsky's *How to Make Verses*, Dalton's theorizing inflects the aesthetic-political demand with a personal problematic: he questions the interface between the "ideological content and social consequence of poetic work" (16).

Dalton notes retrospectively the "painful scars" left by his Jesuit education and his irresponsible lifestyle nurtured in the "womb of the mean-spirited Salvadoran bourgeoisie"; his career exemplifies the predicament of the Third World artist bifurcated by a "long and deep bourgeois formative period" and "communist militancy." His text registers the hesitancies, reservations, misgivings, and scruples of this hybrid genealogy. The writer engages in self-criticism not by jettisoning the past but by sublating it in a dialectical mode of absorption and negation. Dalton believes that, far from exhausting its potential, the bourgeois outlook offers "creative possibilities" and that by discarding its essentially negative aspects, the artist can "use it as an instrument to create ideal conditions for the new people's art that will spring up" in the process of Salvadorans fashioning a new autonomous life for themselves. Dalton does not offer proofs of these concrete possibilities, however, except to emphasize the uneven, combined development in any Third World formation:

> and so it's well that we revolutionary writers open the way to future art, to the future revolutionary Salvadoran literature, from within the very bowels of bourgeois culture, hastening at the same time its collapse and disintegration by confronting it with its insurmountable internal contradictions, making it face itself and what it springs from—taking it, finally, consciously, with the people's blessed cunning, to the dead end it would come to anyway if we let it develop untroubled in the hands of its logical creators, the bourgeois artists, the artists/ideologues of the bourgeoisie. (12)

Here an enigmatic paradox surfaces: the constructive use of bourgeois culture appears as a site for the subversive operations of "the people's blessed cunning." Unlike Hegel's "cunning of Reason" manifest in the historical dialectic, Dalton's popular cunning exhibits a worldly, ubiquitous practicality—sensuous and productive consciousness—that serves as the opposite of the humanistic idealism of Dalton's inheritance, which renders this text a starkly revealing testimony of the this-worldly nomadic sensibility Dalton has acquired.

Dalton is caught on the horns of this perennial dilemma. Fundamental to his thesis of inventing a committed Marxist-Leninist but also Salvadoran *praxis* is the conceptualization of class stratification in El Salvador *vis-à-vis* North American imperialism. He correctly diagnoses the failure of various social classes in El Salvador to attain "consciousness of themselves as classes" so that it becomes "necessary to propose that all problems of the artistic superstructure correspond to a single, basic, general contradiction, that is, between the people and the nation on one side, and imperialism and its middleman on the other" (13–14). Hence the priority of constituting the nation, of constructing a subject-position for the "people" denied by the hegemonic power.

Dalton formulates two categories of art, one promoting the interests of the "two-headed monster" (the Creole oligarchy and U.S. imperialism) and the other expressing "the people's life, their problems and struggles and hopes." The fusion of national liberation and popular democracy characterizes this judgment. But Dalton expresses a caveat: he refers to his country's "truly impoverished cultural tradition" as a symptom of El Salvador's "semifeudal wasteland" status. He thus ignores the oral traditions, nonverbal cultural practices, noncanonical indigenous forms. He contends that the extant corpus of writings fails to express the nation, to provide "a vision of the whole of our social development." Because of the fragmented and inchoate condition of the classes, the Salvadoran nation has failed to materialize. Dalton's nationalistic project is to create this polity "in a revolutionary way" by universalizing "the principal constant features" of the tradition "so as to confer on the fragmented Salvadoran culture the essential characteristics of any culture whatever: organic unity, interconnectedness, the grounds of existence at once particularized and whole." This synthesizing function of the Third World artist, the task of the organic intellectuals (in Gramsci's historicist framework) identified not with a single class but with a national-popular bloc, finds confirmation in the works of all the writers treated in this book, but more urgently in such a people's allegory as Sergio Ramirez's *To Bury Our Fathers* (which I discuss next).

What finally occupies the foreground of Dalton's concern is the writer's drive toward wholeness, toward a particular but also totalizing subjectivity rooted in the "fundamental community interests," the evolving "free sovereign nation." He refers to this as "the human medium that grants me roots," a reality to hold onto in time and space, and, at the same time, serves as the basis for progress. The signifier embodying national progress is the Communist Party where the artist can practice the integration of a "scientific understanding of our reality (Marxist-Leninist method) and creative work"–this integration being for Dalton the "grand objective of all modern literature or art dedicated to the elevation of humankind." Specifically, party work offers the means where the poet can fulfill his "sense of responsibility regarding the human struggle." But the poet's practice, while "safeguarding this responsibility with its own particular resources" (that is, art cannot be reduced to class), transcends its status as "mere ethical instrument." Dalton strives to uphold the classic Horatian fusion of *prodesse* and *delectare*, learning and pleasure, betraying in the process the powerful seduction of his bourgeois past as he valorizes the Platonic or prophetic effect of the imagination: by heightening the real and affording us "a primary understanding of the real–which would be enough for the fight for liberty"–imagination puts people "in touch with the truly transcendent ... eternal aspects of that reality." It seems that here Dalton has renounced historical materialism and has succumbed to the lure of bourgeois aesthetics, although he qualifies that art's political end (to make people conscious of themselves and their needs) generates in the process the artistic choice of "the reality that needs to be expressed."

To clarify this somewhat dense crux of the quotation, Dalton then tries to mediate the totalizing or homogenizing drive of the Communist activist with the sensuous, practical energies of the imagination (recall Marx's *Theses on Feuerbach*). The artist has to "live intensely," in the thick of what is "nature and what is human." Immersed in the "glorious dramas of the people," the artist will acquire a "profound understanding of life" and at the same time exercise "creative freedom." Under the rubric "beauty," Dalton subsumes the poet's internationalist vocation—the adaptation of myth and symbol appropriate to each epoch—even though he warns against privileging art above other kinds of craft or calling. For Dalton, however, one cannot conflate the responsibility of "co-existence" (read: empathy with the people) and the strictly individual consciousness of the artist. In the passage numbered eight, Dalton anticipates the objection that his notion of beauty has become idealist or metaphysical: if the "great obligation of the poet, communist or not, . . . is to the very essence of poetry, to beauty," his or her "degree of revolutionary consciousness" compels the poet to respond to the "concrete demands of time."

I have pointed out earlier that Dalton's thinking is necessarily decentered, antinomic, or paradoxical precisely because in countering bourgeois reification (to borrow Lukács's useful concept) it takes account of the spectrum of residual and emergent tendencies, objective givens and speculative possibilities. Class struggle becomes internalized, with dialectics becoming the rhetorical and figural mechanism to generate discontinuities and ruptures amid humankind's march toward a classless future. Dalton, of course, is fully aware of the danger of essentialist thinking when he devalues Plato and modernist aestheticism even as he insists on "the grounds of form." While he stresses that the concept of the beautiful should be conceived "as cultural realities, endowed with historic scope and social roots," he imposes an obligation on the communist poet above all "to articulate all of life: the proletarian struggle, the beauty of the cathedrals left us by the Spanish colony, the wonder of the sexual act, the prophecies of the fruitful future that the great signs of the day proclaim to us." Lest this surprising allusion to the prophetic mislead us, Dalton is careful to advise the administrative secretary of the party's Central Committee to love "St. John of the Cross, Henry Michaud, or St. John Perse."

Dalton arrives at an impasse, a classic aporia, stemming from the joining of two terms: communist and poet. On the one hand, Dalton's view tends to valorize universality as such, "life in all its intensity"; on the other hand, communist militants must immerse themselves in people's everyday life. They must attend to heightening "the contradictions, disasters, defects, customs and struggles of our present society." But the gap between the militant's commitment to help forge the nation and liberate the people from oligarchic and imperialist domination, and the poet's fidelity to timeless beauty—the aesthetic injunction—widens when Dalton invokes the French professor Roger Garaudy's apotheosis of Marxism-Leninism as "the most thoroughgoing *humanism* . . . the most dependable *scientific method*," etc. The nationalist agenda of defeating imperialism seems marginalized by Dalton's final affirmation of "love of humanity" as the guarantee of hope and truth, allowing the bourgeois past to return with a vengeance.

One finds at the end a dualistic opposition between the future and the present, between the prophetic impulse and the social-realistic notation of the immediate, forcing Dalton to conclude with a moralizing prescription. Before the "prospectus of the future" can be shaped, the poet's labor is mainly destructive during the "insurrectional" and "triumphal" stage of the Latin American revolution. Dalton argues that the revolutionary poetic task par excellence is to convince one's generation of the necessity of revolutionary action—the only epic theme possible today—before the fact of death. Poetry reaffirms its dignity by valorizing the historical process. Lyric solitude dissolves, supplanted by the primacy of an epic vision.

In an illuminating commentary on Central American poetics, the U.S. critic John Beverley underscores the ironic duplicity of Dalton's poetic system—his ideas and their embodiment in his signifying practice—as reflective of the specific response of the postsixties generation to the debates on the strategy of guerrilla warfare *vis-à-vis* reformist and parliamentary roads to national liberation (1984/85, 56–57). The polarity of "immediate perspective/destructive activity" epitomized in the last section of Dalton's essay can be traced back to the poet's situation as an active cadre in the Salvadoran Communist Party up to 1969 and as leader of the underground People's Revolutionary Army until his death in 1974. Dalton's self-mocking and amphibious persona is manipulated to produce a conversational poetry which oscillates from bitter sarcasm and tough anger to tender solicitude and generous candor. On the whole, Dalton's poetry gives us a new model of the revolutionary subject complicit with the nationalpopular sentiments predominant in El Salvador in the sixties. In contrast, Beverley explains the ascendancy of the Catholic-populist modernism of Ernesto Cardenal in Nicaragua, which possesses a historical specificity different from El Salvador. Obviously Cardenal's discourse on *exteriorismo*, born from a historically defined Nicaraguan conjuncture, attempts to resolve the suspended or hypostatized dialectic one senses in Dalton's grappling with what orthodox metaphysicians conceive of as the antithetical demands of political commitment and aesthetic integrity. It might be appropriate to conclude here with Cardenal's eloquent declaration of his aesthetic project prior to overt advocacy of the Sandinista ideal since, as a prophetic gesture to the approaching birth of the Salvadoran nation redeemed from imperialist domination, it felicitously enacts the submerged visionary exuberance of Dalton's thought:

> Exteriorism is a poetry created with images of the exterior world, the world we see and sense, and that is, in general, the specific world of poetry. Exteriorism is objective poetry: narrative and anecdote, made with elements of real life, and with concrete things, with proper names, precise details and exact data, statistics, facts and quotations.... In contrast, interiorist poetry is a subjectivist poetry made with abstract or symbolic words: rose, skin, ash, lips, absence, dream, touch, foam, desire, shade, time, blood, stone, tears, night. ... I think that the only poetry which can express Latin American reality, reach the people and be revolutionary, is exteriorist.... Poetry can serve a function: to construct a country, and create a new humanity, change society, make the future Nicaragua, as part of the future great country that is Latin America (cited in Aldaraca 1985, 17)

## II. Approaching the Nicaraguan Revolution

> I believe that the contemporary Latin American novel is profoundly committed to its time—this vital moment in the history of our age. Just as Breton said "beauty must be disturbing or it isn't beauty," so we could say that the Latin American novel must be committed or it can't exist.
>
> Alejo Carpentier

Elected vice-president of Nicaragua in November 1985, Sergio Ramirez is internationally recognized as one of the most intelligent revolutionary intellectuals of Latin America. His apprenticeship began with the rebellious "Autonomy Generation" of university students in the late fifties; he was founding editor of the avant-garde literary journal *Ventana*. In the late seventies, he became one of the "Group of Twelve," intellectual supporters of the Sandinista movement; with the victory of the Sandinista Front for National Liberation (FSLN) in July 1979, Ramirez, joined by poet-priest Ernesto Cardenal and other artists, has emerged as one of the leading forces in the socialist reconstruction of Nicaragua and in its defense against continuing U.S.-supported Contra attacks. It was during his exile in West Berlin in 1973–75 that Ramirez wrote *To Bury Our Fathers* (original title: *¿Te dio miedo la* *sangre?*); when it was published in 1977, Ramirez was publicly calling for a broad alliance of the masses against the beleaguered Somoza dictatorship.

Apart from its genesis in the fires of combat, this novel can be considered a paradigm of the dialectical interaction of First World and Third World experiences. It offers an intriguing example of how the whole repertoire of modernist literary techniques—time shifts, contrapuntal arrangement of perspectives, stream-of-consciousness notation, internal monologue, and sheer naturalistic surface details—can be subtly deployed to invent a unique kind of fictional world where "the cunning of history" can be given kaleidoscopic free play.

From the vantage point of 1977, on the eve of the nationwide Sandinista uprising after sixteen years of failed attempts, Ramirez endeavors here to transcribe the *feel* or intuition of historical change in Nicaragua from 1930 to 1961—from the rise of the Somoza dynasty after Sandino's murder (the first Anastasio Somoza helped trap Sandino during peace talks in 1934) to the defeat of the first guerrilla incursions in the context of Fidel Castro's victory in Cuba in January 1959. Traversed by a series of aborted coups and inept conspiracies, this period comes alive in the individual tales of four Nicaraguans— Indio Larios, Turco Taleno, Jilguero Rosales, and Catalino Lopez—all burdened, in literal and metaphoric ways, by their own fathers and by one monolithic patriarch called *el hombre*. Repudiating normal chronology, the plot alternates and interlaces six narratives pervaded by violence and the agony of loss, torture, impotence, and death. At times poignantly tragic and sardonic, but most often wildly ironic and hilarious, this polyphonic text has struck critics as "circular" and "ritualistic," self-consciously literary and derivative; for them, it recalls Carpentier in its "baroque richness of vocabulary," Vargas Llosa in its fluid shifts in narrative voices, and Garcia Marquez in the sheer variety of character specimens. However bizarre the intricacies of time travel or confusing the cinematic montage of disparate images, most reviewers agree that the book radiates a clarity and power that come from its humane chronicling of sympathetic victims caught in a brutal civil war, from its multidimensional, cumulative portrait of a suffering and enduring people. In general the reviewers congratulate themselves in finding at last a Latin American novel whose claim to being revolutionary art does not reduce it to a polemical tract or propaganda.

How can we account for this baffled and uneasy reaction of the Western audience? I suggest that this kind of critical reflex may be understood as symptomatic of the specific sociohistorical conditioning of Western tastes and expectations. It might be useful to remind ourselves that the novel as a European literary genre originated as a secular epic of the individual caught between the disintegration of the feudal cosmos and the convulsive birth pangs of mercantile capitalism in the fifteenth and sixteenth centuries. In this epic of "a world without god," to use Lukács's phrase, the problematic hero of the novel searches for authentic values in a degraded and fragmented world, deprived of any roots in an organic community now permanently a thing of the past. In the Third World, however, such a community—less a setting than a milieu of symbolic inscriptions—still exists, although in the era of finance capitalism it becomes transmogrified by the reifying impact of the market, commodity fetishism, and the logic of exchange value. The problematic quest then assumes the form of a collective ordeal—in Ramirez's novel, several individuals try to locate themselves in a disrupted world, establishing their network of filiations by need or compulsion, tracing origins and destinations. Not solitary individuals but generations, families, and whole towns become the protagonists struggling for survival, for meaningful or fulfilling relationships, for the preservation of their humanity. In depicting these ordeals, the Third World novelist subverts the generic emphasis on the alienated individual and the moralizing interiority of consciousness—the Cartesian *cogito*—by foregrounding the dynamic conjuncture of lives, social conflicts, and global crises. Alejo Carpentier elucidates this privileged nexus which transcends individual psychology:

> While it is true that in some European countries—let's say in England or Scandinavia—literature can exist outside the political context, in Latin America this is absolutely impossible. For better or worse, in tragedy or in great moments of triumph and victory, our lives are so closely linked to politics that we cannot pluck someone out of his environment with tweezers, put him on a table and say: "I am going to study this person." Individuals must be studied in relation to their group, as a function of the praxis and attitudes of the social context. We have to look at where a person is going and what he wants, and only by placing him in this context do we get an epic novel. (1964, 37)

Ramirez's novel begins in 1957, shortly after the assassination of the first Somoza by the poet Rigoberto Lopez Perez, when the four characters already cited celebrate a grotesque reunion in a broken-down whorehouse outside Guatemala City—a scene that recurrently punctuates the unfolding text. The careers of Turco, Indio, and Jilguero converge in their kidnapping of National Guard Colonel Catalino Lopez, who is attending the funeral of the CIA-supported Guatemalan dictator Castillo Armas—a foreshadowing of the future. They stage the unmasking of the colonel in a quasi-legendary brothel, Lasinventura's. Except for Jilguero, whose grandfather and sister typify the victims of the regime's corruption and fraud, all have served in the infamous National Guard, the sole institution sanctioning despotic rule. Both Turco and Indio led revolts, were captured, and jailed; both escaped. With Jilguero and Raul, Turco leads a guerrilla column from Honduras to Nicaragua in 1959 to overthrow the oligarchy; Turco and Jilguero reap heroic martyrdom. In 1961, Indio Larios—the petty-bourgeois dreamer—dies in Guatemala; his body is secured by his son Bolivar (emblematic name of the continent's liberator) and returned to Nicaragua at the insistence of his widow. In that same year, the groundwork for the emergence of the FSLN is laid.

Looking at the complex architectonics of this novel—thirty-six sections divided into three parts and ten chapters, segmented by six narratives, one reviewer suggests that the structure replicates the "fragmentation of resistance" to tyranny in the thirty-year period (1930–61). Before the founding of the FSLN, the history of the Nicaraguan people may be said to coincide with the individualist projects of exiles described in the novel. But it is the trajectory of their return that serves as the figure for the fate of the community, more precisely that post-Sandino, pre-FSLN generation of seemingly inept conspirators, quixotic or ineffectual plotters who nonetheless settle accounts with their past (their fathers) and achieve a measure of self-respect and dignity.

The text may then be perceived as a counterplot against the domination of imperialist/patriarchal logic, hence its avoidance of linear cause-effect sequence, hierarchical ranking of various points of view, and definitive closure—tell-tale marks of classic expressive realism. Right from the beginning, when we are introduced to the Taleno family in 1932, juxtaposed with the voice from the forest announcing that "General Sandino has been through here!" we encounter a foreboding of the future:

> At another point on their trek they stumbled upon an aeroplane's ruined fuselage on a hillside. . . . A few steps further on, when the mist has lifted and they can see more clearly, they spot a skeleton dangling from a hawthorn branch, swaying limply in the breeze, green slime obscuring the US Marine uniform, a tuft of withered blond hair still clinging to the skull. Some golden, luminous worms crawl out along the fleshless limbs and drop off to the ground; the same worms glitter behind the airman's goggles pulled over sightless sockets. (Ramirez 1984, 12)

The time is ten years before Guernica, Spain; the United States then was already using planes for counterinsurgency operations against Sandino, who, in 1928, told a journalist: "We are no more bandits than was George Washington. We are protesting against invasion. The United States has meddled in Nicaragua for many years." (Rankin 1985, 457)[1] For six years, over four thousand U.S. Marines failed to catch Sandino. When the droll figure of Col. Lopez says, "*El hombre* has been a true father to all of us," he is alluding not just to customary paternalism, but to the heavy burden of the past engendered by repeated betrayals and sellouts. The image of the decaying corpse appears then to herald an eventual catharsis and vindication.

Cast out by *el hombre*'s mendacious authoritarianism, the three exiles who kidnap the colonel personify the convergence of dispersed motives, dreams, bitter resentments, frustration, and anger associated with various classes and sectors in Nicaraguan society. One line of development from this is their adventurist guerrilla incursions divorced from grassroots organizing, hence their betrayal by the schoolteacher Ofelia in a remote village of San Carlos. The survivors, Turco and Jilguero, become fugitives and cross their homeland to Costa Rica. Two years after their execution, the FSLN is formed, inspired by Sandino's example in the twenties: the circle is complete.

While Ramirez was composing this novel in exile, guerrilla actions accelerated throughout Nicaragua, leading to the intervention of troops form the United States and its Central American allies in 1973. Like the dissidents, Ramirez was performing a demolition job, exploring the cracks and fissures in what would otherwise be considered a closed, coherent, and objectified totality—the massive accumulation of traditions, usages, and codes inherited from the past. What this novel presents is not a documented "slice of life" but the process of change itself, that heterogeneous confluence of forces and tendencies that Ernst Bloch also discerned in European expressionism, previously condemned by mechanical Marxists as reactionary. Bloch's rhetorical questions are presciently applicable to our text: "Are there not dialectical links between growth and decay? Are confusion, immaturity and incomprehensibility always and in every case to be categorized as bourgeois decadence? Might they not equally—in contrast with this simplistic and surely unrevolutionary view—be part of the transition from the old world to the new? Or at least be part of the struggle leading to that transition?" (Bloch 1977, 22–23).

Of the novel's baroque texture and elaborate "Latin American" style, Carpentier has already provided the most cogent elucidation in various essays and interviews. Here I would like to focus on how the text offers a utopian vision of transcendence in history, utopian in the sense of prefiguring the people's revolutionary triumph in July 1979 and the subsequent unleashing of repressed impulses.

Interspersed in a seemingly rambling proliferation of anecdotes—somewhat approximating the effect of Bakhtin's *heteroglossia* as displayed in Rabelais—the figure of Pedro Altamirano, a general of the Sandino forces, stands out as a metonymic substitute for the rebellious subalterns. In 1930 his troops ambush the National Guard detachment in a movie house (repository of illusions); recovering from that disgrace with the astute advice of Indio, Col. Lopez climbs up the military ladder until he becomes the tyrant's most trusted aide. But all his life, the colonel would be haunted by his cowardice, an ancient demon he would try to exorcise. Not even his brutal massacre of Altamirano's forces five years later would wipe the shameful memory away. (His father's failure and the loss of the family lands would drive him further into *el hombre*'s arms.) Altamirano is ominously betrayed by his stepson—a doubling of an earlier betrayal. In the scene where the general's decapitated body is described, the narrative introduces a woman "crying without any hysterics," completely unmindful of the atrocities and havoc—emblem of intransigent, uncalled-for devotion:

> Even when I ordered the head to be completely severed from the body, and had it put in quicklime in a saddlebag she refused to be separated from the dead man. She hesitated only for a moment when she saw them carrying the head away, as she made up her mind whether to see where they were taking it or to stay with the body—but when she had chosen the head, she immediately mounted guard by the side of the saddlebag, which had been tied on my horse. . . .
> 
> For mile after mile I put up with the stench from the head bouncing around in the bag, just as I endured the woman's doglike moaning as she trotted along behind the horse, never flagging behind, never letting up with her lament, struggling to keep up with us even when out of spite we spurred our horses on faster. We never discovered whether she was his wife, his daughter or even perhaps his sister. We couldn't tell her age from her appearance, and the stepson who had betrayed his father stayed behind in Quilali to drink away his hundred pesos, without my having had the opportunity to ask him. It was not so much that I forgot, more that I was not really concerned to identify the forlorn woman who was following the dead man's

> head so faithfully, waiting for us whenever we halted, keeping watch all night outside the gates if we locked the head away in any barracks along the way, never eating or sleeping, always the same pattering of her bare feet, caked in white dust from the miles she had run.
>
> She lasted all the way to Managua, and in the yard of the Campo del Marte, where I had the head put on show the morning we arrived, she knelt beside it and set to cleaning the lime and blood from his face with a faded black cloth, somehow realizing that this yard, in a town she had never seen before, was our final destination. She tried to push his eyes closed with her fingers, but the lids were stuck open, then to smooth back his hair; in the end though she simply placed a candle on a piece of brick in front of the head. Heaven knows where she got it from. When I brought Larios to look at the head, the candle was already burning. (Ramirez 1984, 198–99)

Not only does the colonel's confession convict him for the regime's barbaric scorched-earth policy, it also indicts the dehumanized machismo of the Somocistas challenged by the woman's incredible fidelity, the antithesis to the military's nihilistic egotism and the reversal of the stepson's treachery and that of numerous characters. The woman's resistance repudiates the unheroic ambivalence pervading the whole society.

It is precisely to expose and destroy the fetish of the patriarchal ego incarnate in the almost mythical *el hombre* that the narrative stages the carnivalesque "orgy" in Lasinventura's. The brothel can be read as a metaphor for all Third World dictatorships: its surface affluence comes from official plunder of the public treasury. When its military patron falls, the people ransack the place. With the help of Turco and Jilguero, Indio Larios coaxes Col. Lopez to the brothel and submits his virility to the test—this incident serves as the epilogue right after the killing of Jilguero and Turco by the National Guard:

> Turco had begun pacing up and down the room, and Jilguero was about to say something more to him when the Colonel unexpectedly reappeared. He was shoeless, the flaps of his shirt hung down over his naked legs, and there were dribbles of vomit on his chin. He staggered into the room, then straightened up as he tried to work out where he was. The schoolgirl came in behind him, carrying his jacket and trousers. "He couldn't do it," she whispered to Turco, "the pig went and puked in the bed." (237)

The colonel fails the test; the prostitute mocks him. He is no longer worth killing. Addressing Indio, who "saved" him from public disgrace before, the colonel apologizes for *el hombre;* but immediately the claim is undercut by his impotence and helplessness:

"You were against *el hombre* because you didn't know him deep down: he's a good man at heart. He knows how to forgive people, to care for them." At this he broke into sobs, until he brought up more vomit into his mouth, managing to turn away to the wall before being sick, splashing Indio's legs as he did so.[2] (238)

Earlier, the colonel quoted *el hombre*'s jest on his loyalty resembling that of his mistress, attesting to the dictator's power to convert everyone into prostitutes. This gesture recapitulates the arbitrary will of the fathers in the novel, for example, Jose Taleno's repudiation of Turco—a public disowning of an "outlaw" for rebelling against the dictator.

Only in the case of Indio Larios does this patriarchal ascendancy suffer a displacement, his fraternization with the colonel overcoming political differences. Whereas Turco, rejecting his father's wish that he toady up to *el hombre*, deserts the National Guard, Indio settles accounts with his complicity in Sandino's murder by writing self-confessions, especially by memorializing himself in letters to his son Bolivar. The son, however, while fulfilling his duty to recover the body, throws his letters, including photographs and records of exiles' meetings, out of the speeding truck bearing his coffin. His funeral procession becomes an occasion to wipe the slate clean and allow the children to start anew. In exile, Indio makes *piñatas*—clay containers of sweets for birthday party games—that become symbolic of all the hopes and needs locked up in dreams or nightmares, just as the defiant Turco was locked up in a panther's cage in the dictator's private zoo.

The text closes with the reminiscences of Chepito, a barber, and Pastorita, only survivor of the musicians called *Los Caballeros*—the "horses" (a recurrent metaphor) have burst their bonds and won freedom. After seducing Alma Nubia Taleno, Pastorita is denounced by her father—Pastorita never sees his son, and ruminates alone with his memories. This father is left abandoned, even though the epigraph from Aristophanes suggests that a revolution is needed to provide a place for a deprived people to inter their dead, insuring that no one is left abandoned.

Weaving the threads of the recollected past from various characters' perspectives, the novel then reconstitutes Nicaraguan history as a transitional period where conservative and progressive forces coalesce.

The central protagonist involves the generation of sons who learn to reject their fathers' will (the Law of the Symbolic Order, whose proprietor is *el hombre*) and create their own paths. Believing in the people's will, Indio refuses the paternalism of *el hombre*. In effect, the claims of fatherhood are annulled. What the text seeks to bury is the *ancien régime* of the patriarch, law and order bereft of justice and barren of love.

Besides these individual gestures of refusal combined by the satiric debunking of all pretensions and masquerades, the text dramatizes the refusal of "the normal order" embodied in rational, coherent egos conforming to a centralized pattern of events; the plot is disrupted by a montage of unsynchronized scenes and episodes, by doubling of scenes from shifting perspectives, by dense verbalization of atmosphere and setting, and especially by intertextualization, that is, the use of diverse idioms (quotations, public notices, letters, obscene jokes, slang and colloquialisms, highfalutin rhetoric, etc.). One also notes the stylized and ironic focus on interiors and a full use of symbolic motifs as counterpoint to detailed catalogues and enumerations. Ramirez's text epitomizes the operations of a Third World sensibility exorcising the father's diktat, the received codes of rationality and virtue originating from Dalton's "two-headed monster" (imperialism and the native oligarchy), striving to construct a subject-position for itself freed from the past, especially from the illusions of aesthetic realism and the horrors of exploitation they try to hide. So then, let the dead bury the dead. What more fitting epitaph is there for what Marx calls "the prehistory of humankind" than this fiction of the revolutionary passage and deliverance of the "wretched of the earth"?

## NOTES

1. For some historical background, see Nearing and Freeman (1966, 151–72), Galeano (1973, 59, 109, 121–24), and Fagen (1981).
2. For the theory of the Third World novel as "national allegory," see Jameson (1986, 65–88). For a valuable interview of Sergio Ramirez, see Randall (1984, 21–40).

## BIBLIOGRAPHY

Aldaraca, Bridget, et al., eds. *Nicaragua in Revolution and at War: The People Speak.* Minneapolis: Marxist Educational Press, 1985.
Beverley, John. "Writing *from* the Revolution: Ernesto Cardenal and Roque Dalton." *Metamorfosis* (1984/85).

Bloch, Ernst. "Discussing Expressionism." In *Aesthetics and Politics*, by Ernst Bloch, 16–27. London: NLB, 1977.

Carpentier, Alejo. *Tientos y diferencias*. Mexico City: Universidad Nacional Autonoma de Mexico, 1964.

Dalton, Roque. *Poetry and Militancy in Latin America*. Williamantic, Conn.: Curbstone Press, 1981.

Fagen, Richard R. *The Nicaraguan Revolution*. Washington, D.C.: Institute for Policy Studies, 1981.

Galeano, Eduardo. *Open Veins of Latin America*. New York: Monthly Review Press, 1973.

Jameson, Fredric. "Third World Literature in the Era of Multinational Capitalism." *Social Text*, no. 15 (Fall 1986): 65–88.

Nearing, Scott, and Joseph Freeman. *Dollar Diplomacy*. New York: Monthly Review Press, 1966.

Ramirez, Sergio. *To Bury Our Fathers*. Translated by Nick Caistor. New York: Readers International, 1984.

Randall, Margaret. *Risking A Somersault in the Air*. San Francisco: Solidarity Publications, 1984.

Rankin, Nicholas. "Ramirez's *To Bury Our Fathers*," *Times Literary Supplement*, 26 April 1985, 457.

# Beyond Postcolonial Theorizing:
# The National-Popular in Philippine Writing

> ... *the whole nation was a great group*
> *The component parts of which remained individual and distinct*
> *Like the blades of wheat in the sheaf*
> *And the Nation could thus express itself*
> *In a form at once genuine and universal.*
>
> —Hugh MacDiarmid

Inaugurated by the United Nations' bombing of Iraq for occupying the territory of another nation (Kuwait), the post–Cold War era we inhabit today may be as far removed from the Enlightenment vision of a cosmopolitan world culture (expressed, for example, in Goethe's notion of a *Weltliteratur*) as the years when this century opened with the Boer Wars in South Africa, the Boxer rebellion against foreign incursions in China, and the Spanish-American War. Our postmodern conjuncture is in fact distinguished by ethnic particularisms and by the valorization of the aleatory, contingent, and heterogeneous. Indeed, the ideal of internationalism presupposes a plurality of nation-states asymmetrically ranked in a conflict-ridden global market. It thrives on national differences since "world interdependence has diffused balance of power considerations and transformed them into a balance of terror" (Smith, 1979, 196). As long as the ethnic archive persists amid the homogenizing secular ideals of modernization and liberal individualism that subtend the policies of most states, an order grounded on exchange value and the logic of capital accumulation, nationalism will remain a major if not decisive force shaping the economic, political, and ideological contours of the "New World Order."

Nationalism as a world phenomenon is thus a historically determinate process of group-identity formation with diverse manifestations and ramifications. How is writing as a cultural practice and *habitus* (Bourdieu) configured in this dialectic of identity and difference in the Philippines?

When the United States occupied the Philippines by military force from 1898 to 1903, a Filipino nation had already been germinating in over two hundred revolts against Spanish colonialism. Filipino intellectuals of the Propaganda Movement (1872-1896) had already implanted the Enlightenment principles of rationality, civic humanism, and autonomy (sovereignty of all citizens) in the program of the revolutionary forces of the Katipunan and the first Philippine Republic. At the outset, the Propagandists—Jose Rizal, Marcelo H. Del Pilar, Graciano Lopez Jaena, and others—used the Spanish language to appeal to an enlightened local and European audience in demanding reforms. With the aim of conscientization, Rizal's novels, *Noli Me Tangere* (1887) and *El Filibusterismo* (1891), incorporated all the resources of irony, satire, heteroglossia (inspired by Cervantes and Rabelais), and the conventions of European realism to criticize the abuses of the Church and arouse the spirit of self-reliance and sense of dignity in the subjugated natives. For his subversive and heretical imagination, Rizal was executed—a sacrifice that serves as the foundational event for all Filipino writing.

Although a whole generation of insurrectionist writers (the most distinguished is Claro Recto) created a "minor" literature in Spanish, only Rizal registered in the minds of Spaniards like Miguel de Unamuno. In effect, Hispanization failed. In 1985, when I visited Havana, Cuba, I found Rizal's two novels newly reprinted and avidly read—a cross-cultural recuperation, it seems, of a popular memory shared by two peoples inhabiting two distant continents but victimized by the same Western powers.

Just as a Filipino nation was being born, harnessing the vernacular speech of peasants and workers, U.S. imperial hubris intervened. Its conquest of hegemony or consensual rule was literally accomplished through the deployment of English as the official medium of business, schooling, and government. This pedagogical strategy was designed to cultivate an intelligentsia, a middle stratum divorced from its roots in the plebeian masses, who would service the ideological apparatus of Anglo-Saxon supremacy. Americanization was mediated through English, sanctioned as the language of prestige and aspiration. Meanwhile, the vernacular writers (the true organic intellectuals of an emergent *populus*), who voiced the majority will for sovereignty against U.S. "Manifest Destiny," sustained the libertarian Jacobin heritage of the Propagandists. Lope K. Santos, author of the first "social realist"—more precisely, anarcho-syndicalist—novel *Banaag at Sikat* (1906), and Isabelo de los Reyes, founder of the first labor union and of the Philippine Independent Church, were both deeply influenced by Victor Hugo,

Proudhon, Bakunin, and the socialist movement inspired by Marx and Engels. As I argued in my book *Reading the West/Writing the East* (1992), "vernacular discourse articulated a process of dissolving the interiority of the coherent, unitary subject" (91) in texts that dramatized the breakdown of taboos (what Deleuze and Guattari call "territorializing" codes [1982]) and the release of Desire in the sociolibidinal economy of violence and delirium.

While U.S. imperial power preserved the tributary order via the institutionalization of patronage in all levels of society, the use of English by apprentice-writers fostered individualism through the modality of aesthetic vanguardism. Personal liberation displaced the dream of national sovereignty. The overt and subterranean influence of the "Lost Generation" (Anderson, Hemingway, Gertrude Stein) on Jose Garcia Villa and his contemporaries shaped the content and direction of Philippine writing in English from the twenties to the sixties. Internationalism in this case took the form of imitation of U.S. styles of private revolt against alienation in bourgeois society. While Villa enacted the role of the native as Prometheus and achieved a measure of recognition by U.S. New Criticism in the fifties, he has never been included in the U.S. literary canon (Lopez 1976, 11). In encyclopedias and directories, Villa has always been identified as a "Filipino" writer. Interred in the pantheon of formalist mannerism, his ethnic signature survives only in his name.

A breakthrough occurred in the thirties. It was the global crisis of capitalism and the intense peasant dissidence throughout the islands that impelled Salvador P. Lopez, Teodoro Agoncillo, and others to mount a challenge to U.S. hegemonic authority and the threat of fascism by establishing the Philippine Writers League (1939-41). For them, the nation signified the working people, the producers of social wealth, whose alignment with the antifascist insurgency in Europe and Asia invested with apocalyptic *Jetztzeit* (Walter Benjamin's term) the solidarity of all the victims of capital. For the first time, the insurrectionary legacy of 1896 was rediscovered and utilized for grassroots empowerment. We find this stance of nationalist internationalism in the fiction of Manuel Arguilla and Arturo Rotor, in the novels of Juan C. Laya, in the essays of Jose Lansang, S. P. Lopez, Angel Baking, Renato Constantino, and the massive testimonies of Carlos Bulosan. For the first time, writers in English rallied together with the vernacular artists (among others, Jose Corazon de Jesus, Faustino Aguilar, and Amado V. Hernandez) to affirm the dialectical interaction between spiritual creativity and radical mobilization, even though the protest against continuing U.S. domination had to be sublimated into the worldwide united front against fascism.

The praxis of Filipino national allegory was thus born in the conjuncture of what was desired and what was exigent. It was conceived in this hiatus between the project of liberating the homeland (from Japanese invaders) and the defense of popular democracy everywhere. Consequently, it sublated nineteenth-century bourgeois nationalism in the heuristic trope of what came to be known as the "national democratic revolution."

The exemplary practitioner of this allegorical mode was Carlos Bulosan, a worker-exile in the United States from the early Depression to the beginning of the Cold War. His now classic ethnobiography, *America Is in the Heart* (1948), synthesized the indigenous tradition of antifeudal revolt in the Philippines with the multiracial workers' uprising in the West Coast and Hawaii against racist exploitation. Bulosan's art expressed his partisanship for popular/radical democracy. It demonstrated his faith in the intelligence of people of color—Reason's cunning, in the old adage—rooted in cooperative labor. His sympathy with Republican Spain beleaguered by fascism coincided with his union organizing against racist violence in the United States and Japanese militarism ravaging his homeland. Because Bulosan's sensibility was deeply anchored in the proletarian struggles of his time, he was able to capture the latent transformative impulses in his milieu as well as the emancipatory resonance of the realist-populist genealogy in U.S. literature: from Whitman to Twain, Dreiser to Richard Wright. The prime exhibit here is Bulosan's novel *The Power of the People* (1972), whose thematic burden was to render in concrete incidents the reciprocal dynamics between the Huk uprising in the fifties against U.S. imperialism and its comprador allies, and the farmworkers' agitation in the United States for equality and justice. In contrast, the aesthetes who emulated Villa could only gesture toward, or parody, U.S. neoconservative styles and banalities ranging from the compromised liberalism of the welfare state to the slogans of religious fundamentalism, laissez-faire utilitarianism, and packaged postmodern fads fresh from the dream-factories of California.

Despite Bulosan's achievement, it remains the case that the vision of a nation-in-the-making sedimented in Filipino writing in English cannot be fully assayed except in antithesis to the metropolis. Since the sixties, however, the U.S.-establishment claim of truthfully representing the Filipino has entered a period of protracted crisis. For U.S. scholarship, Filipino writing in whatever language remains invisible, at best peripheral. Because Filipino writers challenging the realism of the center and the pathos of the status quo have not refused to abandon the theme of national/class emancipation, the now contested project of modernity given a subaltern inflection, they have not been so easily coopted by paternalistic praises and assimilated to the neoliberal multicultural canon. U.S. neoliberal ideology may accord formal rights to Filipino cultural identity, but does so only to deny recognition of its substantive worth. This view has even influenced oppositional trends. While theorists of postcolonial letters celebrate their difference as the part of Commonwealth/British literature that really matters, they have so far not claimed to appropriate Philippine writing in English as an illustration of what the authors of *The Empire Writes Back* call a "hybridized" or "syncretic" phenomenon (Ashcroft, Griffiths, and Tiffin 1989, 180, 196).

The reason is not far to seek: whether in the United States or in the Philippines, Filipino writers cannot escape the vocation of resistance against neocolonial (*not* postcolonial) forces gravitating around the World Bank-IMF, guarantors of transnational hegemony. They cannot shirk the task of reinventing the nation anew in a world where the eclectic pragmatism of the transnationals seeks to impose everywhere the internationalist mandate of Eurocentric supremacy. This program of reimagining the national-popular (in Gramsci's terminology), not the state which has instrumentalized the nation, is not nationalist in the vulgar sense of seeking to preserve ethnic purity or instigate a cult of linguistic uniqueness; rather, it is "nationalist" in defense of the integrity of the work-process in a specific time-place. This nationalism inheres in affirming the dignity and worth of workers and peasants that constitute the nation-people for-itself in the ultimate analysis.

Whenever U.S. experts on the Philippines pronounce judgment on our literature, the implicit standard may be seen to originate from the notion of "tutelage." In sum, U.S. knowledge-production of the truth about the "Filipino" rests in part on the organic metaphors of parent-child and tributary-stream, a figural strategy whose repetition endows U.S. representational authority with sacramental aura. In the 1969 *Area Handbook for the Philippines*, an official government baedeker, we read: "For the first two decades of the American occupation the short story suffered from a stiltedness of style when written in English, but, after the authors went through a period of practice in acquiring the idiom, excellent writing began to emerge" (Chaffee 1969, 140). This is repeated in subsequent editions, together with the citation of authors (Villa, Romulo, Nick Joaquin, N. V. M. Gonzalez) who acquired importance by being published in the United States. In addition to such marginalizing techniques, U.S. critical discourse also occluded the reality of resistance to its client regime (the Marcos dictatorship) by the tactic of omission. One evidence among others: after 1972, "themes shifted from social comment to a search for self-awareness and personal identification" (Vreeland 1976, 148). What actually happened was that "social comment" faced with government censorship either stopped, turned Aesopean, or went underground. Further, U.S. "postcolonial" policy to categorize and subjugate its clients can be illustrated by the well-intentioned but patronizing comments of Donald Keene (in a review of an anthology of modern Filipino short stories): "We are certainly fortunate that there are now Filipinos who can speak to us beautifully in our own language . . . [this collection] is an admirable testimony to the emergence of another important branch of English literature" (1962, 44).

One response to this strategy of incorporation by subsumption is the privileging of contradictions inscribed in the site of what is alter/native, the other of paranoid mastery. I submit that Philippine writing is not a "branch" of American or English literature; it is *sui generis*. This is not just a matter of "differences 'within' English writing" or embedded national traditions which Bill Ashcroft *et al.* consider "the first and most vital stage in the process of rejecting the claims of the centre to exclusivity" (Ashroft, Griffiths, and Tiffen 1989, 17). Nick Joaquin, the most acclaimed portrait-painter of the petty-bourgeois Filipino, formulates the genealogy of his maturation as a process of awakening to the exuberant rituals of the folk and the pious gentry. After describing the itinerary of his education in the reading of American and British authors (from Dickens to Willa Cather), he finally discovers the Philippine folk-Catholic milieu of ceremonies and festivals which provide the raw materials for his imagination (1989, 4–5).

While rightly denouncing the mechanical imitation of U.S. standards and styles, Joaquin seeks to locate the authenticity of Filipino creativity in a populist version of Christianity lodged in the psyche of characters resisting commodity fetishism—in *The Woman Who Had Two Navels, Portrait of the Artist as Filipino,* and *Cave and Shadows.* More problematic than this essentialist quest for an indigenous *genius loci* subordinated to Eurocentric Christianity is Joaquin's idea of tradition as a cumulative inventory of the colonial past: Rizal was produced by three hundred years of Spanish culture, Villa by four hundred years (add about one hundred years of U.S. colonial tutelage) of Westernization, a frame of reference which includes for Joaquin "Adam and Eve, Abraham, Venus, St. Peter, Cinderella and the Doce Pares" (1982, 42). So Joaquin contends that "if Philippine writing in English is to be justified at all, it will have to assert its continuity with that particular process and development" of absorbing the Western episteme and the problematic of the Cartesian ego. Rather than a radical rupture with the past, Joaquin's empiricist naïveté legitimizes a syncretic adaptation of European forms, values, knowledge—an internationalism which replicates the less subtle conditionalities of the World Bank-International Monetary Fund. Such a mimicry of colonial icons and paradigms springs from a myth of self-apprehension characterized by syncretism and hybridity, signs of *différance* so highly prized by the current theoreticians of postcolonial or minority discourse reacting to the master narratives of bourgeois freedom and progress.

But what would differentiate this axiom of syncretism from the doctrine of liberal pluralism (either post-Keynesian or post-Fordist) under which the "New World Order" of the United States, Japan, and the European Community seeks to redivide the world into their respective spheres of influence? Is nationalism, interpreted recently as a mode of "ethnic cleansing," a genuine alternative? Is ethnocentric nativism (a return to the *pasyon*, various tribal mores, and other sectarian or autarchic practices) a viable option? How has the Filipino writer succeeded in transcending the either/or dilemma of choosing between abrogation through appropriation, or unilaterally privileging the indigenous? Is Samir Amin's universalist resolution of this predicament (1989) a cogent way of breaking through the impasse?

Initiatives for a renewal of national allegory (Jameson 1986), the renaissance of the national-popular imagination, might be witnessed in a critique of what I might call instrumental or culinary nationalism—the ideology and culture of the "New Society" of the Marcos regime— drawn up by progressive intellectuals just after the February 1986 insurrection. It might be instructive to recall, in this context, how in Africa and Asia after the sixties, the triumph of elite nationalism led to the catastrophic disillusionment of writers who expected the radical transformation of society after independence. What the "passive revolution" (Chatterjee 1986) ushered in was neocolonialism, not release from the bondage to capital. During the Marcos dictatorship, pseudohistorical propaganda and self-serving kitsch which manipulated symbols of the archaic tributary/feudal past tried to project a state obsessed with "national security" and anticommunism and at the same time purvey a simulacrum of the nation's "authentic identity." This was allowed within the parameter of the Cold War. Nicanor Tiongson and others exposed the means by which the ethos of communal cooperation called *bayanihan* or *kapitbahayan* was ascribed by the state to the *barangay* (the pre-Spanish village government) as its "soul." This ethnic locus would then function as the political base for the authoritarian political party, *Kilusang Bagong Lipunan* (1986, 53).

In 1969 Imelda Marcos raided the public treasury to realize her fantasy, the aristocratic and fetishized edifice called the "Cultural Center of the Philippines," which she designated as the "Sanctuary of the Filipino Soul." These icons, symbols, and rituals of Marcos's "Filipino ideology" might have fooled his narrow circle of cronies and compradors, but it was easily grasped by most Filipinos as mystification and apologetics for corrupt oligarchic despotism as well as marks of subservience to Western and Japanese transnational interests. Lino Brocka, the leading progressive filmmaker at that time, pointed out that such "nation-building means trying to give a 'beautiful' picture of the country, trying not to disturb people, not to make them angry by depicting the truth to them" (Tiongson 1986, 57). This understanding was shared by most artists who sympathized with the platform and principles of the underground coalition, the National Democratic Front (NDF). The NDF's alter/native project of constructing a "democratic and scientific culture" via participation of the broad masses insured that nationalism of the kind that disappointed many African writers like Chinua Achebe and Ayi Kwei Armah would not be a substitute for the thoroughgoing transformation that would be brought about by a change in property relations and the redistribution of social wealth and power. Such a change would by necessity entail the assertion of national sovereignty against U.S. impositions. Above all, it would prioritize the democratic control of a circumscribed space or territory without which the Filipino people cannot make any contribution to the community of states claiming to represent nations.

Thus we come back to the paradox that the internationalism of Goethe, Condorcet, and Marx conjured: for "national one-sidedness and narrow-mindedness" (to quote the *Communist Manifesto*) to be eradicated, what is required is precisely nationalism conceived not just as a collective primordial sentiment but as a mode of organizing a community of participant citizens. It is not the concept of the nation-people that is problematic but the comprador or dependent state that manipulates the "nation" as its instrument for accumulation.

Within the Marxist tradition one finds a rich archive of inquiries into and controversies on "the national question," from Lenin, Trotsky, Luxemburg, and Otto Bauer to Mao Tse-tung, C. L. R. James, Che Guevara, Edward Kardelj, and Amilcar Cabral. Surveying this field, Michael Lowy concludes that the principle of self-determination centers on a given community's act of deciding consciously to constitute itself as a nation (1978, 157). But before judging one nationalism as legitimate and another as suspect if not reactionary, Lowy advises us to undertake "concrete analysis of each concrete situation" relative to the goal of defeating international capitalism. In his study of ethnonationalism in Britain, Tom Nairn counseled us about the enigmatic Janus-faced nature of historical nationalisms (1990). Whatever the ambiguity of this phenomenon, the idea of the nation cannot be exorcised from thought without negating the historicist temper of modernity. As noted before, nationalism and its corollary, the nation-state, are energized by a teleology of the conquest of necessity by reason, of humanity's progress toward freedom and self-fulfillment of all. This radically historicist position, as I have suggested, has been questioned by postmodern thinking. It is also questioned by Régis Debray, who believes that the idea (or ideal-type) of the nation, which for Marxists will be rendered obsolete by the advent of communism, is permanent and irreducible. For Debray, the idea of a nation is necessary to thwart entropy and death. It performs this function by establishing boundaries and thus generating identity through difference. Claiming to be more materialist than Marx, Debray insists that the universalizing thrust of bourgeois-analytic reason (as instanced by Amin's book, mentioned earlier, or by the messianic thrust of Frantz Fanon's Third World advocacy) ignores the reality of contemporary developments, specifically the resurgence of identity politics in the forms of ethnic separatism, nationalist or regional schisms, etc. We are witnessing "a growing interdependence of the conditions of economic production and exchange, comporting a trend towards uniformity; yet this is dialectically accompanied by a new multiplication of cultural diversity. . . . Equality is never identity. . . . What we are seeing now is indeed a growing divergence of cultural identities, a search for specificity as the other face of emerging globalism" (1977, 31).

Such a schematic mapping of the present world system, a recapitulation of the principle of "uneven and unequal development," is enabled by the very contradictions of late capitalism. In this totalizing regime of exchange value, there are multiple overdetermined antagonisms. However, the primary contradiction from the perspective of oppressed people of color is still between the advanced industrial centers negotiating alliances and compromises on the one hand, and their victims within and outside their borders. And while these victims (whole groups and populations) are heterogeneous, their commonality of sharing the collective fate of domination by mainly Western capital underpins the sociolibidinal economy of their individual quests for recognition as world-historical nations.

On the terrain of an extremely uneven social formation, writing in the Philippines displays in rhetoric and narrative an emergent popular agenda or "structure of feeling." It proceeds by refunctioning residual forms (such as the *dupluhan* and *zarzuela*, folk theatrical genres) and marginalized conventions in order to subvert the aestheticist formalism authorized by U.S. disciplinary regimes as well as by the commodified imports and imitations from Japan, Europe, and elsewhere. By the logic of opposing an exploitative and alienating force, the resistance assumes the modality of revitalizing indigenous cultural practices so as to constitute an allegorical narrative of their return with new effectivities. What distinguishes this tendency is a cosmopolitan selectiveness demonstrated not just in the adaptation of Western genres (for example, Brecht's epic distancing retooled in PETA productions like *Buwan at Baril*), or in the feminist abrogation of neocolonial/feudal patriarchy (as in Lualhati Bautista's *Bata, Bata . . . Paano Ka Ginawa?* and other vernacular experiments). Nor is it fully registered in the invention of a new style of tracking the metamorphosis of the migratory sensibility, as in Jose Dalisay, Jr.'s novel *Killing Time in a Warm Place*. Rather, it can be discerned in the process of contriving a national-popular idiom addressed not to the *Volk* (Herder, Fichte) but to a resurgent *sambayanan* (*populus*). An allegorizing strategy of storytelling is explored. Its point of departure is an alter/native sensibility rooted in acts of decolonizing intransigence, in a critique of the illusions propagated by the world system of transnational capital.

The Filipino praxis of alter/native writing interrogates the "post" in "postcolonial" theory. We observe this in the partisan texts of Emmanuel Lacaba, Estrella Consolacion, Levy Balgos de la Cruz, and Argee Guervara. They all strive to actualize what Fr. Edicio de la Torre calls "incarnation politics," a theology of liberation indivisible from the daily acts of resistance against a client state that has sacrificed the nation-people to profit making (1986; see also San Juan, Jr. 1991). This project of articulating the subject denominated as "becoming-Filipino" is not nationalist in the orthodox construal of the term. For one, it rejects a state where the nation is hostage to brokers and entrepreneurs ready to sell it to the highest bidder. Its nationalism is prophetic because it materializes in everyday acts of popular resistance. The nation appealed to here would then signify a "concrete universal" embodying solidarity with other oppressed communities engaged in fighting the same enemy; such unity with others is premised on the cultural differences of peoples, including those whose histories have not yet been written; or those whose narratives have been either preempted or interrupted by the West's "civilizing mission," otherwise known as "the white man's burden." We comprehend and appreciate differences invested with identity-drives to the extent that they can be translated for the recognition of others and our mutual enrichment. How is the Other fully recognized? By transposing the mimesis of the Self (the parasitic colonizer within) into an allegory of its own constitution and self-reproduction. What I have in mind can perhaps be suggested by Edward Said's hermeneutics of the culminating moment of the decolonization process plotted by Fanon. This is the moment of liberation—"a transformation of social consciousness beyond national consciousness" (1990, 83)— enunciated, for example, in Pablo Nerduda's materialist poetics, in Aimé Césaire's *Cahier d'un retour*, and actualized in the life of the Filipino revolutionary writer Amado V. Hernandez. Because of the general reification of social life today, we cannot as yet fully understand the dynamics of these complex mutations without the mediation of allegory: Neruda evokes through Macchu Pichu the heroic resistance of the aborigines, while Césaire's Caribbean locus evokes the promise of Negritude in utopian rhythms.

What does the Philippines offer? We have so far charted the discursive terrain where the salient contradictions of our time involving race, ethnicity, class, gender, etc. are refracted in a multilayered textuality open for interpretation, critique, and ecumenical dialogue. My intervention here should be deemed a prologue to a substantial and more nuanced inventory of the historical specificities of the Philippine social formation that would determine the various modes of cultural production and appropriation pivoting around the event called "becoming Filipino." Less ethnogenesis than alter/native *poiesis*, the goal is to convert the "state-nation" (Smith 1971, 189–90) to an evolving national-popular site of dialogue and praxis. Such a reconnaissance of a Third World people's struggle to define and validate its agency is in effect a task of reconstituting the nation and its position in the world community. In doing so, we encounter ourselves in others. We engage in a catalyzing exchange with voices from other societies using a constantly revised lexicon of "communicative reason" (to borrow Habermas's phrase), an exchange oriented toward a fusion of counterpointing horizons where all can equally participate in the creation of meaning and value.

My proposal of an alter/native poetics as a hypothetical paradigm for Third World cultures depends of course on the peculiarities of each nation's history. One last example from the Philippines may be adduced here to illustrate the dialectic of metropolis and periphery which informs the ever-changing configuration of the nation-people in the former colonies. When Arturo Rotor wrote his essay "Our Literary

Heritage" in 1940 to exhort his fellow writers to respond to the needs of the working masses, he invoked as models of committed intellectuals the names of Ralph Waldo Emerson, who publicly combated slavery, and Thomas Mann, who admonished artists to seek "Right, Good and Truth" not only in art but also in the politicosocial sphere and establish a relation between his thought and the political will of his time (Rotor 1973, 21). Rotor ended his nationalist and, by the same token, internationalist manifesto vindicating literature's *raison d'être* by quoting Maxim Gorki: "[literature] must at last embark upon its epic role, the role of an inner force which firmly welds people in the knowledge of the community of their suffering and desires, the awareness of the unity of their striving for a beautiful free life" (23). In this way, Philippine vernacular allegory may be said to harmonize its pitch and rhythm with others from North and South (now replacing East and West), speaking tongues whose intelligibility is guaranteed by our sharing common planetary needs, the political unconscious of all art.

## BIBLIOGRAPHY

Amin, Samir. *Eurocentrism.* New York: Monthly Review Press, 1989.
Ashcroft, Bill, Gareth Griffiths, and Helen Tiffin. *The Empire Writes Back.* London: Routledge, 1989.
Chaffee, Frederic, et al. *Area Handbook for the Philippines.* Washington, D.C.: U.S. Government Printing Office, 1969.
Chatterjee, Partha. *Nationalist Thought and the Colonial World.* London: Zed Books, 1986.
Debray, Régis. "Marxism and the National Question." *New Left Review* 105 (Sept.-Oct. 1977): 25–41.
de la Torre, Edicio. *The Philippines: Christians and the Politics of Liberation.* London: Catholic Institute for International Relations, 1986.
Deleuze, Gilles, and Felix Guattari. *Anti-Oedipus: Capitalism and Schizophrenia.* Minneapolis: Univ. of Minnesota Press, 1982.
Jameson, Fredric. "Third World Literature in the Era of Multinational Capitalism." *Social Text,* no. 15 (Fall 1986): 69–80.
Joaquin, Nick. "The Filipino as English Fictionist." In *Literature and Social Justice,* edited by L. Yabes. Manila: Philippine Center of PEN, 1982.
———. "The Way We Were." In *Writers and Their Milieu,* edited by Edilberto Alegre and Doreen Fernandez. Manila: De La Salle Press, 1987.
Keene, Donald. "Native Voice in Foreign Tongue." *Saturday Review of Literature,* 6 October 1962: 44.
Lopez, Salvador. "Literature and Society—A Literary Past Revisited." In *Literature and Society: Cross-Cultural Perspectives,* edited by Roger Bresnahan. Manila: U.S. Information Service, 1976.

Lowy, Michael. "Marxism and the National Question." In *Revolution and Class Struggle: A Reader in Marxist Politics*, edited by Robin Blackburn. Sussex: Harvester Press, 1978.

Nairn, Tom. *The Modern Janus: Nationalism in the Modern World.* London: Hutchinson, 1990.

Rotor, Arturo. "Our Literary Heritage." In *Literature Under the Commonwealth*, by Manuel Quezon et al. Manila: Alberto Florentino, 1973.

Said, Edward. "Yeats and Decolonization." In *Nationalism, Colonialism and Literature*, by Terry Eagleton, Fredric Jameson, and Edward W. Said, 69–95. Minneapolis: Univ. of Minnesota Press, 1990.

San Juan, E. *Writing and National Liberation.* Quezon City: Univ. of the Philippines Press, 1991.

———. *Reading the West/Writing the East.* New York: Peter Lang, 1992.

Smith, Anthony. *Theories of Nationalism.* New York: Harper & Row, 1971.

———. *Nationalism in the Twentieth Century.* New York: New York Univ. Press, 1979.

Taylor, Charles. *Multiculturalism and The Politics of Recognition.* Princeton, N.J.: Princeton Univ. Press, 1992.

Tiongson, Nicanor. "The Ideology and Culture of the New Society." In *Synthesis: Before and Beyond February 1986*, 49–66, by Nicanor Tiongson et al. Quezon City: Edgar M. Jopson Memorial Foundation, 1986.

Vreeland, Nena, et al. *Area Handbook for the Philippines.* Washington, D.C.: U.S. Government Printing Office, 1976.

# The Third World Artist in the Postmodern Age

*You taught me language, and my profit on't
Is, I know how to curse.*
— Caliban, in *The Tempest*

*If we are talking about the others, things that are others must be different, "other" and "different" are the names for the same things.*
— Plato, *Parmenides*

*The old is dying and the new cannot be born; in this interregnum there arises a great diversity of morbid symptoms.*
— Antonio Gramsci, *Prison Notebooks*

    Signaled by the blast of Tomahawk missiles and the televised videotech bombing of Baghdad and the bridges across the Tigris and Euphrates rivers, the "New World Order," or "pax Americana II," is heralded by desert storm troopers. In this transition to a post–Cold War era, we—the referent here is shadowy at the outset—confront the beginning of a strategy of U.S. military intervention in regions, especially in what is called the "Third World," where transnational capital (also called Western civilization, balance of power, law and order, etc.) has assumed a triumphalist posture. A former Sandinista Foreign Ministry official calls this the era of the U.S. "declaration of perpetual war" on the world. Eqbal Ahmad calls it the "recolonizing" of former colonies or dependencies, the underdeveloped South versus the industrialized North. In any case, events in the Middle East as well as in El Salvador, South Africa, the Philippines, the former Soviet Union, or Los Angeles—we can witness some footage of those spectacles on the six o'clock news—lend an ironic twist to what Marshall McLuhan in the early sixties called "the concretization of human fraternity" through the use of information-media technology. McLuhan intoned: "With the extension of the central nervous system by electric technology, even weaponry makes more vivid the fact of the unity of the human family" (1964, 300). McLuhan celebrated the advent of the global village and one harmonious world on the eve of the holocaust in Indochina; the urban rebellions in Detroit, Watts, Paris; the overthrow of the shah in Iran; the defeat of Allende's socialist experiment in Chile; the Sandinista victory. It was a celebration of postmodernity in terms of appearance, what Baudrillard today would call "simulacra" pervading hyperreality—the end of ideology or history or the future, for those who believe that the whole world has been transformed into a suburb of California.

What can the writer from the margins of these "simulacra" say or do that can make a difference to an audience in the metropolitan center? If erstwhile exotic artists like Tagore or Ruben Dario have yielded to "boom" performers Salman Rushdie and Gabriel Garcia Marquez and Chinua Achebe and Wole Soyinka, has the margin finally penetrated the center and erased the margin/center opposition? Do our prejudicially classificatory terms "Third World" and "postmodernity" assume premature answers to problems we have not yet delineated?

I

In what I think is the best account so far of this transition that occurred circa 1973, David Harvey's *The Condition of Postmodernity*, we learn that postmodernism is a historical response to the recent crisis of overaccumulation, a crisis that manifests itself in disorienting and cataclysmic compression of time-space periodically occurring since the decline of the Middle Ages. The symptoms of this crisis include the disintegration of the centered subject; the loss of the referent; the collapse of the linkage between moral and scientific judgments; the predominance of images over narratives, aesthetics over ethics; "ephemerality and fragmentation take precedence over eternal truths and unified politics" (1989, 328). The names of Nietzsche, Marx, and Freud encapsulate these epochal transitions. Harvey points to the voodoo economics and image-making of Ronald Reagan as the epitome of the postmodernist outlook in which homelessness, unemployment, increasing poverty, and disempowerment are justified by appeals to traditional values of self-reliance, entrepreneurial individualism, the sacred family, religion, etc. Street scenes of graffiti, urban decay, and misery become "quaint and swirling backdrop" to media spectacles (as in *Blade Runner*); poverty, urban decay, hopelessness, and despair become sources of aesthetic pleasure, or signs of Otherness and

Difference—intimations of what Jean-François Lyotard calls "the sublime." Lyotard is the philosopher *par excellence* of the postmodern condition, which he celebrates as the fulfillment of the genuine spirit of the modernist project. Arguing against Jürgen Habermas's condemnation of postmodernism as a betrayal of the Enlightenment ideals of objective science, universal morality and law, and autonomous art, Lyotard rejects the Hegelian-inspired totalizing worldview that he believes leads to a transcendental illusion of organic wholeness imposed by state violence. Modernity equals terrorism over the individual. Given the heterogeneous language-games of ethics, politics, and cognition, it is necessary, insists Lyotard, to do away with the notion of a self-identical subject or a unitary end of history and uphold instead a Nietzschean nihilism or perspectivism. Or, better yet, a neo-Kantian aesthetic of the sublime that would present the unpresentable, allude "to the conceivable which cannot be presented." Refusing the nostalgia for "the whole and the one, the reconciliation of the concept and the sensible," Lyotard issues a battle-cry: "Let us wage a war on totality; let us be witnesses to the unpresentable; let us activate the differences and save the honor of the name" (1984, 82). To whom is this call addressed?

While the media broadcasted daily what became commonplace scenes of the bombing of Iraq, and all kinds of experts were totalizing this experience of the most sophisticated electronic destruction of people on a massive scale in the planet's history, I happened to read an interview with Ghassan Abdullah, president of the Palestinian Writers Union. He was imprisoned by the Israeli authorities for six months in Answar III in the Negev desert. His crime was engaging in cooperative work with Israeli writers in a committee, formed after the 1982 invasion of Lebanon, called Writers Against Discrimination and the Occupation. Numerous Palestinian writers and artists before and after the *intifada* (circa 1987), the popular uprising in the occupied territories, have been detained for writing poems, short stories, essays, or nationalist songs. In memoirs that resemble those of George Jackson or militants of the ANC in apartheid jails, Ghassan Abdullah narrates the collective efforts of his fellow prisoners to continue to develop a culture of resistance in those desert camps where even prisoners praying together have been attacked with gas. He vividly describes how he would collect paper from wrappings, cigarette packs, and cartons, so that he could have something to write on; how the prisoners organized all kinds of activities to continue the teaching/learning process: lectures and discussions, carving, drawing, games, reading and writing classes, producing a rich harvest of poems, short stories, and essays. They survived, he writes, "because of our deep belief that culture is a main part of our identity and it is more easy to reach a permanent just solution with educated and cultured people than to reach it with ignorant ones" (1991, 70; see Rushdie 1988). Here it seems that the concept (autonomy, freedom) could not be reconciled with the sensible, as Lyotard hopes, for the simple reason that state terror exists.

What can a Filipino intellectual like myself, exiled in the metropolis, do in the face of this ongoing suppression of a whole people? In the Philippines, where constitutional democracy obtains, Amnesty International reports hundreds of political prisoners, not to speak of thousands of refugees in militarized zones, in the same situation as Ghassan Abdullah, some tortured and brutalized by a military equipped and subsidized by the U.S. government. Committed writers, those whose consciousness was developed by years of resistance against the Marcos dictatorship, are silenced by fear, by the threat of vigilante or paramilitary assassination. If they cannot speak, who will speak for them?

I venture the following speculations: the Third World artist may be the specter of a postfeudal "Sublime" haunting the margins of the computerized supermalls only in the sense that as a group artists exist in what Fanon once called "zones of occult instability": resisting the representations enforced on them by the oppressor/colonizer, they are wrestling with the means of expression, how to invent them or construct them from what is given by their specific circumstances, how to wield and control them. A nation's culture is struggling to be born. There are three stages in this process of cultural ethnogenesis, according to Fanon: the first is the slavish copying of the conqueror's paradigm, the mimicry of the Shakespearean sonnet, Racine's classic style, etc. Then comes a revulsion from everything foreign leading to nativism, a worship of the indigenous and a nostalgia for origins; Negritude and the vernaculars of the Harlem Renaissance come to mind. In the third stage, the "fighting phase" associated with revolution, a new self-aware culture rooted but not coinciding with the indigenous tradition emerges in which the artist becomes "the mouthpiece of the new reality in action." The Sandinista writer-combatants like Tomas Borge, Omar Cabezas, and Sergio Ramirez belong to this third phase of metamorphosis. Ghassan Abdullah has observed that Palestinian literature underwent a metamorphosis analogous to Fanon's schema during the *intifada:* it liquidated the fetish for suffering and symbolism, it encountered in folklore the idea of sacrificing for the collective's liberty, it discovered individual Palestinian heroes—the child hurling "the holy stone" (Murphy 67–68). In the time-space compression of the *intifada,* the Palestinians reawakened to "the extreme importance of the cultural form of resistance" that, for Ghassan Kanafani, "is no less valuable than the armed struggle itself."  Writer, critic, and militant of the Popular Front for the Liberation of Palestine, Kanafani has written a novella, *All That's Left to You* (1990), which may be conceived as an antipostmodern mimesis of the condition of the victims in the process of synthesizing the past (the tragedy of 1948), the present (the process of quest for the mother, the land of Palestine), and the future (the recovery of some continuity with the past mediated by the struggle). We find this theme in practically all writings by exiles, expatriates, uprooted migrants, exported bodies, which comprise the artifacts of a new diaspora. What is interesting in Kanafani's "language-game" (to borrow Wittgenstein's term) is the montage of the consciousness of three characters (together with time and the desert as two other protagonists) where simultaneity of diverse time-segments is achieved in the process of a relentless linear unfolding. Fragmentation—the Palestinian deracination—is symbolized by the clock ticking in the bedroom, where his sister is trapped with her lover Zakaria, and the watch which Hamid discards:

> As I did so, I came to realize how insignificant a watch is when compared to the absolutes of light and dark. In the infinite expanse of this desert night, my watch appeared to represent a temporal fetter which engendered terror and anxiety. . . . I felt more at ease when I remained alone with the night. Without the contrived semblance of time, the barrier collapsed, and we became equals in the confrontation of a real and honorable struggle, with equal weapons. The black expanse before me was a series of steps no longer measured against the two small hands of a watch. (20)

Clocktime introduced by the social division of labor at the advent of mercantile capitalism is not vanquished but sublated to the pulse of the desert's body, which becomes that of a loved one, hot and exciting, mysterious and powerful. Time-space compression brought about by Israeli colonialism is defused by an act of transgressing boundaries both physical and psychic. We still find here the problematic of inwardness, not a self-referential image but a syntagmatic chain gesturing toward a lost wholeness which is finally dramatized by the deadly struggle between Hamid and the armed Israeli border guard—an allegory of the interlocked fates of two peoples—as Hamid seeks to cross the boundary between the occupied territories (Gaza) and Jordan. We find modernist modes of representation harnessed to convey a uniquely postmodern experience of dispossession and disinheritance.

I see this same recuperation of the antipostmodern project for an emancipated subject-position—no longer an essentialized human nature—in another Third World narrative, ... *y no se lo trago la tierra* (... and the earth did not devour him). Here in the manipulation of dispersed time and the allegorical rendering of fragmentation, the text can be found guilty of the "imitative fallacy." Although there is a frame story to suture the acausal and syncopated episodes together, the twelve sections of the novel present the seasonal incidents in the life of a migrant child through a stream-of-consciousness mode which Ramon Saldivar calls a "chronotopic point" [after Bakhtin] around which the collective subjective experiences of Rivera's Texas-Mexican farmworkers coalesce, forming a communal oral history (Saldivar, 1990, 75). Unlike the Palestinians, the Chicanos (as Rivera suggests) encountered the shock of a military defeat (the Mexican-American War of 1848 and after) and so they need the educational growing-up experience to drain out the trauma, a catharsis which doubles as a gradual initiation into the reality of subjugation.

Saldivar contends that Rivera's experimental technique reflects the "fragmenting effects of contemporary postmodern life" in the Texas-Mexican border just after World War II. I think Saldivar has confused historical periods: while the novel was published in 1971, the sociohistorical milieu of Chicano labor exploitation in the Southwest has an overdetermined time-configuration on which realism (with appropriate modifications) can be deployed to register effectively the Chicano community's lived experience. While conceding that the novel's proletarian milieu resembles that of the folkloric *corrido* and its socially symbolic acts of resistance, Saldivar insists that the nonsequential mode puts into question the category of an unproblematic individual identity by using "the representation of personal alienation" (85). Ultimately the "subject" becomes the fluid, nonsubjectified character of *la raza*, whose consciousness is (in Lukács's words) the "self-consciousness of the commodity ... the self-revelation of capitalist society founded upon the production and exchange of commodities" (90). The Third World deconstructive critic is caught in a dilemma where the notion of the decentered subject, the subject under erasure, is projected onto the idea of an orthodox *homo economicus* that would "recuperate historical experience" by undermining the binary oppositions of bourgeois society through the "differential structure" of the Chicano narrative. Postmodernist theory has overtaken the praxis of national self-determination. It is here perhaps that Hegel's chapter on the dialectic of master and slave in *Phenomenology of the Spirit* can be useful in safeguarding us from a premature derealization of the subject-position the Chicano people are trying to construct. It is also at this juncture where Habermas's theory of "modernity" may have residual (but qualified) resonance for activists of national liberation struggles whose concept still has no adequate presentation. What I am suggesting here is a more critical appropriation of poststructuralist theory for counterhegemonic ends to curb their recuperative and co-optative effects.

II

How should a subaltern intellectual from the periphery view Habermas's controversial thesis stated in his manifesto "Modernity—An Incomplete Project"? With suspicion if not reservation.

Those of us who went through a radicalizing apprenticeship in the sixties understand Habermas's rear-guard defense of the Enlightenment project to release the cognitive potential of the domains of science, morality, and art for the enrichment and "rational organization of everyday social life." To exorcise the curse of reification engendered by the dynamics of commodification and the imperatives of techno-bureaucratic administration, what is needed (according to Habermas) is "the unconstrained interaction of the cognitive with the moral-practical and the aesthetic-expressive elements" (11–12). Habermas envisions history progressing toward the synthesis of truth, beauty, and justice—substantive reason (the transmission of cultural tradition, social integration of the various specialized spheres) is recovered through communicative rationality pervading the praxis of everyday life. In other words, workers through art education can connect with the whole of European history and remedy their alienation. The orthodox canons are useful after all. Habermas denounces the cabal of postmodern prophets from Bataille to Derrida via Foucault who apotheosize decentered subjectivity and in a Manichean manner oppose to instrumental reason an archaic principle, either the will to power (Nietzsche), Being's sovereignty (Heidegger), or "the Dionysiac force of the poetical" (14). For all those "hewers of wood and drawers of water," past and present, who have been victimized by what I would call "actually existing modernism," transnational or multinational capital as a world-system, it is difficult not to suspect Habermas of "bad faith" since his teachers Adorno and Horkheimer, in *Dialectics of Enlightenment*, already demonstrated the internal contradictions in the Enlightenment project, in particular its harboring the seeds of future imperialist genocidal and fascist violence. We are still living in the terror of a neo-Hobbesian liberalism where life in the suburbs may be nasty, boring, and brutish, but long.

This is not to dismiss Habermas's valid criticism of neoconservative antimodernism and his profound knowledge of the historical dialectic underlying ideological and cultural practices. Unlike the postmodernists suspended in the void of a self-contained "superstructure," Habermas is in complete agreement with the anthropologist Eric Wolf's thesis that "the peoples without history" cannot but endorse: "The construction and maintenance of a body of ideological communications is therefore a social process and cannot be explained merely as the formal working out of an internal cultural logic" (388). Culture alone is not to blame. In his article "Marxism and Postmodernism," Fredric Jameson himself has revised his early quasi-formalist view of postmodernism as "the cultural logic of late capitalism" by stressing the concept of totality or cognitive mapping as a theoretical necessity without which it is virtually impossible to articulate the nature of decisive social transformations and their historical trajectories, especially as this relates to the reciprocal linkage between Europe and "the peoples without history." The role of Third World intellectuals is to keep reminding the postmodernist dissidents of the simple truth that we live in the same world where power excludes and includes so that the quality of life is not the same for everyone. Roberto Fernandez Retamar's *Caliban* is one such reminder.

For peoples who are victims of the "modernist project" of mastery over nature and all "others" outside Europe, it is less a matter of figuring out whether or not postmodernist styles can represent their lived experience as one of defining first their collective predicament as nonrepresented or unrepresentable in the present global dispensation. Victims have to seize the means, the occasions, to invent their own self-presentations. The key lies in the nature of the modalities of representation in the global system of capital. In an astute comment on Habermas's position, Anthony Giddens points out that the dissolution of avant-garde culture (from Baudelaire to the surrealists) was not triggered by an internal aporia; rather it arose from the commodification of time-space with the formation of industrial capitalism. As Marx first explained, in capitalism time acquires its quantified form in articulating class relations within the labor process; that is to say, surplus value is generated through the medium of quantified time because, unlike the direct appropriation of productive labor in agrarian society, this value has to be exploited through the commodity whose double existence—substance or concrete qualities/abstract form of exchange value—spells what Lukács calls the "reification" characterizing the totality of everyday life in business society. The problematic of ideology comes into play. Commodification of time and space inscribes a hiatus or difference in each; their doubling into quantified time—labor-power disciplined in the workplace; division of life into routine work and "free time," private and public spheres—and quantified space severs humans from nature, tradition, the past. Against this all-encompassing change in the experience of time-space (which Harvey attributes to the operations of ascertainable socioeconomic determinants), the avant-garde project that continues to inspire postmodernism tried "to recover a rational basis for the normative character of everyday life" which has suffered the mystifying power of the commodity. It tried to sublate the object world (commodified time-space), to elucidate and resolve what Giddens calls "the asymmetry of substance and form"; the enterprise failed because it failed to grasp the historical significance of the commodification of time and space as the fundamental reproductive logic of capital.

I do not have the space here—alas, we cannot escape this commodification business—to elaborate on how the emancipatory project of Gabriel Garcia Marquez in *One Hundred Years of Solitude* or Salman Rushdie in *Shame*, for example, can be conceived as a version of the avant-garde attempt to demystify the doubling of time and space when colonial intervention takes place in regions overdetermined by archaic and tributary modes of production.

In the social formation explored by Garcia Marquez in *Love in the Time of Cholera*, we can see clearly the layering of time scales and tempos in which the resistance to imperial capital (internalized in ironic ways) assumes the form of reinstating antithetical or alternative existential forms of time, a "magical realism" which projects the axis of diachrony onto that of synchrony, where poetic metaphor incessantly seeks to neutralize metonymy and mimesis. Suffice it to mention one asymmetry staged by the montage of recollected events. You will recall how the whole society, including the formidable enemy of time Florentino Ariza, was shocked when the first prize in the traditional Poetic Festival of the Antilles was won by a descendant of Chinese immigrants, railroad workers who fled the yellow fever epidemic in Panama—the good Chinese in the laundries, heirs of a sacred knowledge. When this Chinese contestant read his poem, no one understood him. You can see in the long paragraph Garcia Marquez devotes to this incident an allegorical translation of how European knowledge production operates to subdue and domesticate the unrepresentable, to transform the unknown into the negative/other:

> No one understood him. But when the new round of jeers and whistles was over, an impassive Fermina Daza read it again, in

her hoarse, suggestive voice, and amazement reigned after the first line. It was a perfect sonnet in the purest Parnassian tradition, and through it there wafted a breath of inspiration that revealed the involvement of a master hand. The only possible explanation was that one of the great poets had devised the joke in order to ridicule the Poetic Festival, and that the Chinese had been a party to it and was determined to keep the secret until the day he died. *The Commercial Daily*, our traditional newspaper, tried to save our civic honor with an erudite and rather confused essay concerning the antiquity and cultural influence of the Chinese in the Caribbean, and the right they had earned to participate in Poetic Festivals. The author of the essay did not doubt that the writer of the sonnet was in fact who he said he was, and he defended him in a straightforward manner, beginning with the title itself: "All Chinese Are Poets." The instigators of the plot, if there was one, rotted in their graves along with the secret. For his part, the Chinese who had won died without confession at an Oriental age and was buried with the Golden Orchid in his coffin, but also with the bitterness of never having achieved the only thing he wanted in his life, which was recognition as a poet. On his death, the press recalled the forgotten incident of the Poetic Festival and reprinted the sonnet with a Modernist vignette of fleshy maidens and gold cornucopias, and the guardian angels of poetry took advantage of the opportunity to clarify matters: the sonnet seemed so bad to the younger generation that no one could doubt any longer that it had, in fact, been composed by the dead Chinese. (1988, 194–95)

Ignoring the historical subtext of the migration of labor power in the period of turn-of-the-century capitalist modernization, we could construe this episode as a parable of the universality of genius, or the ubiquity of prejudice (insiders versus outsiders), and so forth. A symptom of sheer reduction to form, indeed.

The allusion to the "modernist vignette of fleshy maidens and gold cornucopias," which capture cultural overlayering, could be to Ruben Dario's *modernismo*, a term that would be misleading if it were not historicized. Now historicizing does not mean relativism. To historicize is not to flatten everything so that the value of all experiences as measured by a general equivalent form of value (money, gold) can be made interchangeable (such homologous transformations are reprised by Jean-Joseph Goux [1990]). Historicizing or historical specifying means providing the context for cultural production, demarcating in their motion through concrete time-space the limits and possibilities of certain forms of expression and representation. As an instructive example, I can only refer you to the historical analysis given by John Beverley and Marc Zimmerman (1990) to the mutations of value in any cultural production—whether Dario's modernism or Ernesto Cardenal's poetics of *exteriorismo*—in the overdetermined social formations of Central America where various signifying systems interpenetrate in nonsynchronous correspondence with changes in the class alignment of specific societies.

The lesson I can gather here is that the question of modernism versus postmodernism, Lyotard versus Habermas, is misleading in its rigid dualism and false symmetrical opposition even though one may grant the heuristic value of posited cultural dominants. This is because in the Third World context the Althusserian insight of overdetermination (which is not reducible to syncretism or hybridity) finds its nearly perfect structural embodiment. It approximates to the materialization of a concept that sometimes reverses the stereotypes of Western knowledge, sometimes inflects them in parodic unpredictable ways, or reworks them in mirages of affinity or resemblance only to find that what you think you know, what you think looks intelligible, turns out to be another of Borges's accidental collocations of odds and ends—but this time converted into media images or information easily absorbed by the Western academy as a species of the postmodernist pastiche.

One illustration caught in the polarity of two discourses is found in those unforgettable photographs of Central America by Susan Meiselas: photographs of dead bodies, mutilated beyond recognition, piled up or scattered in the streets. Apropos of their impact, the Cuban media specialist Edmundo Desnoes reflects on the disparity between the self-referential and form-centered artifacts of the West and the historical and social reference of the photos taken by an American on the basis of the incommensurable gap between two milieux:

> The United States is a fragmented society, a society where people are encouraged to live centrifugally. The parts never make a whole. The whole is removed by the subtle mechanisms of advanced capitalism and its multiple ways of escape and dispersion. In Latin America everything is centripetal, everything is striving after unity and an axis. These discourses are in conflict due to economic and political differences; it is not a matter of temperament. (1985, 38)

In the light of the two aspects of the commodity sketched earlier, I think Desnoes's disjunctions are too clear-cut—think of those straddling "free trade zones" in South Korea and elsewhere, the amphibious lives of people parasitic on U.S. bases, the enlargement of the public/private divide corresponding to the encroachment of the commodity into archaic and feudal spaces, and so on. But his point is unarguable. Humanity is still separated by all kinds of cleavages, ruptures, discontinuities inherited from the past and being reproduced daily by the unequal division of international labor and distribution of resources. In spite of media flattening, the six o'clock news cannot conceal those discontinuities. Those bodies in Meiselas's photos contemplated by affluent viewers—*hypocrite lecteur! mon semblable!*—in the art galleries of New York City and Los Angeles are pregnant evidences. They do not exist in art, Desnoes insists; they "are rescued—if such a monstrous survival is possible—by society. 'If we do not believe in God,' as Jose Marti wrote and lived, 'we believe in history'" (41–42). It is in this site of how history is conceived and narrated that the conflict between Third World heterogeneity and First World postmodernism takes place.

How trivial and irrelevant to engage in this postmodern hobby of a semiotic decoding of those bodies, Desnoes reflects. But for almost everyone in Western consumer society subjected to the commodity system, the consumption of images seems to have conditioned the public to accept the boredom of a universalized sameness induced by the mass media and academic textbooks even though, in rare moments, one sometimes hears the cry of anarchists, marginalized individualists, grotesques from behind the props and facades. Should we, can we, abolish these images? Some cry: Free, save immediate Desire! Do away with mediations and representations! In fact, not only the images but also the bodies have been done away with in Argentina and Chile, in Central America, the Philippines, and elsewhere. As for the ethico-political implication of these "disappearances," Jean Franco observes that with the rise of the internal security state funded by the West (IMF-World Bank), all hitherto immune spaces in the underdeveloped countries —church, family as refuge and shelter—are gone; they have been occupied by the deterritorializing and decoding machine of advanced capitalism. She notes the unprecedented sacrilege committed by U.S.-sponsored "low-intensity warfare" in the destruction of utopian or sacred space, specifically the oppositional potentialities of female territories, and the immunity once accorded to nuns, priests, women, and children. The "disappeared" no longer occupy a space but have inaugurated a place which neither postmodernist radicals or neoconservatives can put "under erasure": "the smell of the cadaver will not be dispelled by the commodity culture, a debt-ridden economy and the forms of restored political democracy" (1985, 420). Compensation for such a loss cannot be made by a hundred deconstructive or schizoanalytic readings of Kipling, H. Rider Haggard, Forster, Conrad, or Malraux.

Let me enter a parenthesis here concerning Malraux, a culture-hero of European modernism. It is interesting to recall how in December 1923 Malraux was caught plundering the magnificent sculptures in Banteay Srei, part of the Angkor temples, in Cambodia; his plea of innocence was that those treasures were not officially "protected." On this parasitic adventure of European modernism into the colonial frontiers, Jan Myrdal comments:

> That Malraux was young and foolish is one thing. . . . What is less self-evident is why the intellectual left wing in France should have backed Malraux up. André Breton said it was absurd to send someone to prison for raping two or three stone dancers. This radical support for Malraux concealed a profound, if hidden, chauvinistic scorn for [non-Western] culture. Would they have rallied to the defense of a young Cambodian poet who got himself arrested for collecting stone figures in the Parthenon to repair *his* finances? (1971, 44)

We are back to the central issue of the postmodernist affirmation of the unrepresentable *differend* vis-à-vis the need to exercise a totalizing vision in order to cognitively map the relationship implied by the unequal relations between margin and center, metropolis and periphery. The situation of Latin American intellectuals and artists reflects the uneven and combined development all Third World countries have experienced, thus making postmodernism almost a positivist dream of isomorphic correspondence between thought and reality.

If Desnoes and Garcia Marquez question the universal claims of Western rationality and its metaphysics of reification, the Peruvian novelist Mario Vargas Llosa, the darling of New York liberal intellectuals, advocates a return to the philosophy of the Austrian Karl Popper. In an essay entitled "Updating Karl Popper" (1990), Llosa recycles banalities and clichés from Popper's Cold War repertoire of the "open" versus "closed" (Marxist totalitarian) societies. Llosa updates Popper in condemning most, if not all, Third World societies that have not integrated scientific rationality as closed, tribal, and therefore backward, lacking the critical spirit and freedom prized in the West. Evolutionary Darwinism is resurrected from the dustbin. The source of all evil is historicism. The guilty purveyors of this evil include Plato, Hegel,

Comte, Marx, Machiavelli, Vico, Spengler, Toynbee, and their followers. They believe history has a logic or order which can be understood when, according to Popper's teaching, history is "a lively chaos," a "vertiginous totality of human activity that always overflows rational and intellectual attempts at apprehension"; and this activity mainly consists of power politics, "the history of international crime and mass murder" (1022–23).

Not only is history one damned thing after another, as the empiricist would have it, but it also surprisingly betrays a Nietzschean scenario: "vertigo, pandemonium, immeasurable absurdity, bottomless chaos, multiple disorder," and so on. And this frightening spectacle of freedom for Llosa can be tamed only by the artist, the novelist. So in a backhanded way, Llosa excuses art for its convivial liaison with the diabolic party of historicists, the totalitarian tyrants, the dogmatic believers. Postmodernism in the Third World surfaces here in Llosa's aestheticizing agenda that proclaims how the model for Latin America's progress from the tribal swamp, from the kingdom of magic and taboo, should proceed by way of the "third world" of spiritual creation, of culture as exemplified by the authors and books he cites as testaments of the "sovereign individual": "These constructs, in which free will—imaginary acts of disobedience against the limits imposed by the human condition: a symbolic deicide—is radically exercised, secretly constitute (as do Herodotus's nine *Books of History*, Michelet's *History of the French Revolution*, and Gibbon's *Decline and Fall of the Roman Empire*—prodigies of erudition, ambition, good prose, and fantasy) testimonies to the panicked fear instilled in us by the suspicion that our fate is a "feat of freedom'" (1024–25). Or in the words of Jose Garcia Villa, the Filipino modernist poet, who has disappeared in the bowels of Greenwich Village: the "Parthenogenesis of Genius" may "break, the,genetic,economy, / Springing,the,I,Absolute, / In,a,time-land, of,decimals:/Immaculate,conception, / Beyond,physiology— / The,Protagonist,of,the,age, / Mirrored,only,in,mirage" (1958, 114).

Paradoxically, Llosa's evolutionary history premised on Popper's scientism echoes the Enlightenment project endorsed by Habermas: both elide the viewpoint of its victims, the colonized, women, etc. Did Llosa fail to see the "feat of freedom" in the bodies textualized by Meiselas's camera? What kind of freedom and sense of the sovereign individual has Occidentalism brought to Peru when Llosa, during his recent campaign for the presidency, ingratiated himself with the most reactionary tribal forces of the native elite whose dogmatism, racist bigotry, and antidemocratic excesses would have made Popper blush in his grave?

## III

The postmodern Third World artist looks askance at the glorious benefits supposedly granted by the West's civilizing mission to the subalterns. For all its humanist critique of colonialism, Joseph Conrad's *Heart of Darkness* is considered racist by Chinua Achebe. While appreciative of the autonomy of bourgeois civil society and its accompanying concepts of modern democracy and social science, the Egyptian thinker Samir Amin points out how Eurocentrism—the racist ideology of domination over other cultures—reveals the fatal inadequacy of Western (Greco-Roman, Judaeo-Christian) universalism: "For Eurocentrism has brought with it the destruction of peoples and civilizations who have resisted its spread" (1989, 114). But Amin dissociates himself from the Third World assertion of a cultural identity opposed to modernization (Westernization), calling this path a "nationalist culturalist retreat" that mimics Eurocentric fundamentalism: "the affirmation of irreducible 'unique' traits that determine the course of history, or more exactly the course of individual, incommensurable histories" (135). Samir Amin believes "culturalist nationalism" leads to an impasse. It cannot substitute for the universal vocation of Marxism, the hegemony of a socialist universalism signalled by "a national popular democratic advance."

Like most theoreticians of postcolonial culture, Amin privileges a totalizing approach that will negate any notion of the incommensurability of cultures and lead to what Marx calls the realization of the "species-being" in each person. This prophetic marker in Amin's treatise on Eurocentrism seems to connote a deeply rooted impulse of Enlightenment idealism which elides the fact of uneven development, scarcity, and the mediating role of the nation. The terms of the debate are replicated in the exchange between Fredric Jameson and Aijaz Ahmad on "Third World Literature in the Era of Multinational Capitalism."

In his commentary, Ahmad refuses to accept Jameson's theory of national allegory as the distinctive literary form for indigenous narratives because he wants to preserve the uniqueness, the incalculable difference of each country's cultural configuration, some of which may not go through a "national" phase (in Urdu literature, for Ahmad, the moment of national independence was overtaken by the "gigantic fratricide conducted by Hindu, Muslim and Sikh communalists" (1987, 21–22). Ahmad's objection to a putative unitary determination in Jameson's concept of "third world" and "national allegory" recalls the postmodernist anathema on totalization. But his anxious insistence that one take into account the multiple determinations at work in any text, specifying and historicizing them in order to grasp the ideological complexity of any cultural artifact, forgets the inescapability of mediations in terms of categories like class, nation, etc. How else can one read Ngugi's *Devil on the Cross* or Nadine Gordimer's *July's People*, for instance? Jameson's stress on a recurrent tendency to allegorize in some selected Third World literatures is sensitive to this doubling process in any individual act of narration as well as to the "mode of production" in which all practices are inscribed. Ahmad's caveat focuses less on the application of nonessentialist Marxism which nonetheless takes cognizance of the single conflict between capital and labor that defines the global system for Ahmad and more on a paranoid suspicion that others will take the interlocutors (Ahmad and Jameson) as "each other's civilizational Others"; that is, as stereotypical and one-dimensional representatives of each other's societies.

What becomes clear in the course of his exposition is that Ahmad claims multiple belongingness predicated on his own *will*—a futile gesture of protest against commodifying society. But this liquidates precisely the relational dynamics of subject-position and its structural determinants (race, class, gender) with which he claims he is overconcerned for the sake of a subjective, arbitrary plurality of selves. (See analogous debates summarized in Connor 1989, 231–37). Ahmad can say anything he likes—but does it make a difference? to whom? for whose sake? I see nothing gained by ignoring how the dominant racializing ethos of U.S. society—Western society in general—has historically defined a person like Ahmad and using that as a point of departure. This, I take it, is the rationale of Jameson's method of "establishing radical *situational* difference in cultural production of meanings" so that the categories of Identity and Difference, instead of being fixed and eternal opposites (the way Amin postulates Eurocentrism versus cultural nationalism), frozen in empirical duality or sheer random difference, are set in motion "so that the inevitable starting point is ultimately transformed beyond recognition" (26–27). We graduate to another level of contradictions which sublate (cancel/preserve) the previous stages of the argument.

On the whole, I think the exchange between Ahmad and Jameson is instructive in many ways. It not only reflects certain theoretical differences in conceiving the positionality of texts (including practices) and their effects and the degree of historical specification needed to formulate a hypothetical generalization; it also epitomizes the equivocal problematic of postmodernism understood and assessed by a Third World sensibility. (I plead guilty to the totalization of Third World as a rubric for the typical colonial experience described by Fanon, Memmi,

Lu Hsun, Rizal, Rigoberta Menchu.) On another level of confrontation, I can contrive a parallel to that exchange by registering my reservation to the peremptory tone and substance of these concluding remarks by the Australian authors of *The Empire Writes Back*:

> Postcolonial culture is inevitably a hybridized phenomenon involving a dialectical relationship between the 'grafted' European cultural systems and an indigenous ontology, with its impulse to create or recreate an independent local identity. ... It is not possible to return or to rediscover an absolute precolonial cultural purity, nor is it possible to create national or regional formations entirely independent of their historical implication in the European colonial enterprise. Thus the rereading and rewriting of the European historical and fictional record is a vital and inescapable task at the heart of the postcolonial enterprise. These subversive maneuvers, rather than the construction of *essentially* national or regional alternatives, are the characteristic features of the postcolonial text. Postcolonial literatures/cultures are constituted in counterdiscursive rather than homologous practices. (Ashcroft, Griffiths, and Tiffin 1989, 195–96)

Based on these exclusive stipulations, the entire research-program of writers like Zora Neale Hurston, Scott Momaday, Leslie Marmon Silko, Jan Carew, and others can be pronounced utterly misguided. Carew, for example, describes how African and Amerindian folk myths in Guyana fused and generated "homologous" texts comprising an authentically indigenous culture free from Western contamination (1988, 69–88).

Nor can one avoid feeling that this one-sided prescription of our Australian colleagues makes a mockery of the prison writings of Ghassan Abdullah and his compatriots, of Ngugi's project for a genuinely independent Kenyan creativity, of the Negritude production of texts by Aimé Césaire and others. It dismisses what Wole Soyinka calls the project of "race retrieval":

> It involves, very simply, the conscious activity of recovering what has been hidden, lost, repressed, denigrated, or indeed simply denied by ourselves—yes, by ourselves also—but definitely by the conquerors of our peoples and their Eurocentric bias of thought and relationships. ... For a people to develop, they must have constant recourse to their own history. Not uncritical recourse but definitely a recourse. To deny them the existence of

> this therefore has a purpose, for it makes them neutered objects on whose *tabula rasa*, that clean slate of the mind, the text of the master race—cultural, economic, religious, and so on—can be inscribed. A logical resistance counterstrategy therefore develops; true nationalists find themselves, at one stage or the other and on varying levels, confronted with a need to address the recovery of their history and culture, to retrieve the fount and tributaries of their race—to plot the meanderings, drought patches, and fertile watersheds; the bewildering trick of disappearance into earth and the near-magical resurgence in a distant and differentiated epoch, potent with irrigation powers, breeding a newly aware humanity equipped with the strategies of the experience-laden journey from its beginnings to the present. (1990, 114)

Thus it is not enough simply to adduce the authority of Roland Barthes in deciphering the duplicity of "African Grammar" (103–9), or cite the authority of recent self-referential ethnography, which is what postcolonial scholars would prescribe. What Soyinka exhorts is "a retrieval of the authentic history of the struggle" against colonial oppression (such as that instanced by the Mau Mau uprising against the British in Kenya), a history indissociable from the geography of the land and the processes of collective labor. This program merges the second and third stages of Fanon's process of cultural liberation.

"National liberation" is the phrase I used earlier to counterpoint transnational postmodernity. Why can we in the Third World not skip this stage since "nation" and "nationalism" have acquired dangerous, pejorative implications in the West? Because it sutures the fragments of colonized lives in collective mobilization and so creates the historic agency for change. Otherwise, there is no collective transformation, only individual conversions. Its negativity possesses a positive side: it restores what Bakhtin calls "the dialogical principle" as the matrix of social practices. Soyinka, Ngugi, Achebe, and others, who share pan-Africanist ideals with such precursors as Dubois and Fanon, all address the priority of national liberation. In praising Aimé Césaire's poetic homage to Patrice Lumumba as capturing "the rapture of the creative soul within the convulsions of nation building," Soyinka describes the song as being transmitted "through the lips, the adze, the dance motions, the textures and designs of our fabrics, the wall paintings; it is the community song of arms and feet in the organic labor of erecting shelter, planting and harvesting the earth. It is the heroic hymn of the producers of our history and culture, in the never-ending process of development" (120)—in other words, the national allegory of the African peoples.

It is impossible to elide the national and geopolitical moment in Third World cultural struggles, as the whole life of C. L. R. James (recounted by Paul Buhle in his biography of James) would testify. The exponent of world socialist revolution and later of Pan-Africanism, James would return to the Caribbean homeland and discover the untapped revolutionary power of reggae music and the influence of the Rastafarians on the West Indian formation as well as on the diaspora in Britain as demonstrated in the 1981 urban uprisings. The Rastafari is not a hybrid or syncretic phenomenon, James writes: "They do not suffer from any form of angst. . . . The insanities of the Rastafari are consciously motivated by their acute consciousness of the filth in which they live, their conscious refusal to accept the fictions that pour in upon them from every side. . . . These passions and forces are the 'classic human virtues'" (Buhle 1988, 160). Nonetheless, this former disciple of Trotsky expressed faith in an evolving world culture, a socialist universality such as that entertained by Samir Amin, Said, and others. James believed in history—literary, political—as fashioned by outsiders: Swift, Rimbaud, the proletariat. Buhle sums up James's trajectory: "Without renouncing those [Marxist] insights, James followed the evidence which was thrown in relief by colonial revolution back to the point where he had begun his own creative literary and political thought. The proletariat had become the people (largely, peasants or just-removed peasants) and the great artists became those who could grasp the subject just emerging upon the horizon. Toussaint led to Lenin, but Lenin also led to Toussaint" (161). New situations, new subjects. As a liminal or threshold figure in the passage from New World to Old, from South to North, James's career may furnish one paradigm for sublimating the antithesis of Identity and Difference to another plane, a synthesizing labor which Gramsci reserved for organic intellectuals of classes or sectors aspiring to hegemonic leadership over a whole society, articulating the multifarious interests of the masses into the national form.

### IV

In reviewing the self-defeating revolt of the avant-garde against commodified bourgeois ethos, Habermas made a passing reference to Walter Benjamin's notion of the Now-time, *Jetztzeit*, which designates the present as a moment of revelation, a time in which "splinters of Messianic presence are enmeshed." Seizure of this moment by art creates the break with historicism. This "Messianic" or revolutionary presence can insinuate itself into a national-popular form of organizing. To blast the continuum of Western imperial history, to free us from the burdensome nightmare of Euro-American history (which Marx discounts as "prehistory" since it is more a fatalism than a consciously guided process), is the goal of Third World artistic practice, one of whose most uncompromising partisans is the Puerto Rican writer and painter Elizam Escobar, who is serving a prison term of sixty-eight years for seditious conspiracy.

Escobar was captured on 4 April 1980, together with other men and women comrades fighting for the liberation of Puerto Rico. Accused of belonging to the FALN (Puerto Rican Armed Forces for National Liberation), they immediately declared themselves combatants in an anticolonial war against the U.S. government, which they believe illegally occupies their homeland. Claiming the status of prisoners of war, they rejected the authority of U.S. courts; they refused to participate in their trials, which tried to criminalize them for their struggle for self-determination of their nation. Tried in absentia, they were convicted in spite of the lack of substantive evidence. Classified as maximum security prisoners, fourteen Puerto Rican prisoners of war have been subjected now to fourteen years of harassment, assault, isolation, and castigation in spite of their exemplary conduct. At the Federal Correctional Institution in Wisconsin, Escobar produced paintings that supporters in Chicago exhibited in a tour called "Art as an Act of Liberation" in November 1986. As a result, the Bureau of Prisons retaliated and transferred Escobar to El Reno, Oklahoma, where he was further punished by the denial of materials so that he was unable to paint for a whole year. Because of massive pressure on the prison authorities by the art community and the independence movement, Escobar was permitted to paint and write again in December 1987.

In a moving testimony entitled "Art of Liberation: A Vision of Freedom," Escobar traces four stages of his development as an artist-activist that to some extent modify Fanon's schematic: from the personal to the political, direct to the professional-personal, to his fourth stage in prison, the visionary role of the artist. This role is dictated by the power of the imagination to demystify and counter the State's "structures of simulation," simulations of equal opportunity, cultural democracy, freedom of difference, and so on. To counter this culture of fear, the politics of art is needed "to bring out the real aspects of the human condition in particular and specific contexts or experiences," and also "to create a symbolic relationship between those who participate, the artwork, and the concrete world" (1990, 88–89). Following Jean Baudrillard, Escobar rejects the formal theory of communication comprised of a linear path from transmitter to message to receiver which excludes the "ambivalence of exchange." Nonetheless, Escobar opts for a counterhegemonic strategy of disarticulation and renegotiation of signs and meanings from within the discursive modes available: "The ironic dilemma is that we have to make use of this code though we realize that it reduces and abstracts the irreducible experience of that which we call 'liberation.' . . . There is a brutal difference between 'freedom' as exchange-sign-value, or a slogan of ideologies and abstractions, and the real freedom of experience—one that is as necessary as it is terrible" (91). Escobar invokes the inventive power of art to deride and betray censorship, but he doesn't elevate art to the paramount cure since, for one, the reality of prison life for peoples of color who are also political prisoners always reminds him that the dehumanized and dehumanizing system symbolized by prison suppresses art as "the necessity of freedom." Escobar believes that his own conception of art as an act of liberation is strategic in its intent of emancipating art and people "from the dictatorship of the logic, politics, and metaphysics of the sign" (93). By "sign," he means the entire network of representations and codes—the commodity system we have encountered before—that deceives us, preventing us from comprehending "the internal relationship between human desires and aspirations and human necessity" needed to build from the ruins of the present "transitional alternatives." Escobar's recent paintings, a fusion of stark realistic details in a surrealist, dreamlike environment, may be viewed as an effort to concretize this dialectical principle: "To me, art is the best argument for talking about freedom and about necessity when one does not separate the body from the spirit" (93).

Escobar questions the pretended rupture in the fragmented totality of U.S. society between the elite status quo and open-ended democratic pluralism effected by "firstworldist occidentalism." Behind postmodernist simulacrum lies, Escobar believes, occidentalism's "moribundity, its resentment, its despair, its cultural, social, political, economic and ideological bankruptcy" whereby the ruling class projects its own decay on everyone. We should beware of being taken in by the irony and reflexiveness of postmodernism. Escobar argues that the postmodernist revolt against reification, an ambiguous one which reflects "a new historical moment" of cultural imperialism, is "the last intent of occidentalist firstworldist's self-perpetuation" (1991, 28).

Like Ghassan, Fanon, and others, Escobar emphasizes the

imperative of linking body and spirit in a milieu of alienation and dispersal. This is the challenge that I think postmodernist theory evades in its guerrilla war against the commodity masquerading in one aspect as the simulacrum, the image or spectacle. I do not know whether to laugh or be outraged when Baudrillard, in his famous essay "The Precession of Simulacra," uses the Filipino tribal group known as "Tasadays" (which the Marcos dictatorship had invented for its commercial and publicity needs) for his virtuoso ruminations. When the Marcos government for a time supposedly returned the Tasadays to "their primitive state," this withdrawal (according to Baudrillard) afforded ethnology "a simulated sacrifice of its object in order to save its reality principle." The postmodern shaman performs his own totalizing magical number here: "The Indian thereby driven back into the ghetto, into the glass coffin of virgin forest, becomes the simulation model for all conceivable Indians *before ethnology*. . . . Thus ethnology, now freed from its object, will no longer be circumscribed as an objective science but is applied to all living things and becomes invisible, like an omnipresent fourth dimension, that of the simulacrum. *We are all Tasaday*" (1984, 257–58).

The irony here is that the hoax perpetrated by the Marcos regime, by elite bureaucrats, and the military (not by ethnologists) who stand to gain by driving the Manobos (members of whom were forced to pose as a Stone-Age tribe) from their mineral-rich homeland, was actually processed into a commodity form by the *National Geographic* and other Western media, plus a gallery of spectators including Gina Lollobrigida, relatives of General Francisco Franco invited by Elizalde and Imelda Marcos, and other celebrities to which Baudrillard ascribes a tremendous mana-power of transforming all reality into simulation. But this item is not a simulation: one of those who testified in an international conference in 1986 to expose this hoax, Elizir Bon, was killed in September 1987 by paramilitary men near the Marcos-declared Tasaday reservation (Berreman, 1990, 3), while the rest of the "Tasadays" have been silenced by a machinery of terror that Baudrillard would rather ignore.

At the least, postmodernist theory in complicity with Western rationality occludes the "Indians" (the Manobos are indiscriminately dissolved into this erroneous generic classification) by depriving them of their history, their embeddedness in a specific sociocultural setting, in short, their integrity as humans. This is the textualizing revenge of imperial knowledge on the world that dares claim precedence over it. How can one recognize the Other not just as a distorted projection of all the negativity and lack in one's Self? Is the Tasaday case of victimage reducible to a parable on postmodern simulacra?

V

In the postmodern problematic, the question of the Other—alterity conjugated and declined in infinite ways—has displaced the question of the Subject and now occupies the foreground of North-South (formerly East-West) encounters. In a critique of Said's *Orientalism*, the postmodernizing anthropologist James Clifford faults Said's Foucauldian strategy by contending that it lacks a "developed theory of culture as a differentiating and expressive ensemble rather than as simply hegemonic and disciplinary" (1988, 263). Is the Other reducible to a field of representations produced by discourse? Is the genealogy of a discursive formation generating knowledge of the Other enough to legitimize Said's "fables of suppressed authenticity"? How does one represent the Other without totalizing control? Instead of a cosmopolitan humanism ascribed to Said, Clifford offers a concept of culture as a negotiated process with a differential plurality affording the subject with local resources to construct his or her discourse. His alternative, however, assigns the burden to the non-Western Other whom the anthropologist interrogates: "What does it mean . . . to speak like Aimé Césaire of a 'native land'? . . . Must the intellectual at least, in a literate global situation, construct a native land by writing like Césaire the notebook of a return?" (275).

Before discussing Said's response, I would like to invoke briefly two answers to the question of knowing the Other by the Belgian philosopher Emmanuel Levinas and the Russian critic Mikhail Bakhtin. Levinas seeks to make up for the bankruptcy of liberalism's valorization of freedom and sovereign reason—Popper's and Llosa's cult objects—by accentuating "moral consciousness" before the "face of the Other" which limits the ego's freedom. "Going beyond the self, hostage to the other, responsibility is a transcendence of my freedom from above." Levinas doubts the mandate of Western liberal ideology in securing authentic dignity for the human subject. Instead he looks to an ethics founded on the "infinite transcendence of the other" which can check power and discipline the spontaneous, autonomous self of Cartesian reason. This responsibility for the other, Levinas contends, "this transcendence of my self toward the other, is a movement more fundamental than freedom" (quoted in Davidson 1990, 45).

From the perspective of postmodern theory, Levinas has just proposed resuscitating a master-narrative familiar to all, the Kantian imperative supplemented by an existentialist or Kierkegaardian concern for my Christian brothers. But it is precisely this Western narrative of enlightenment and emancipation that Fanon has indicted as so much tawdry apology for the brutalization of the colonial masses. One can raise the question here whether or not the fusion of hermeneutic horizons proposed by Gadamer and Heidegger, an orientation informing Levinas's transcendence through the other, has been able to illuminate the concrete historical complicity of Western power in exploiting the hermeneutic circle for its benefit (see Longxi 1988). As an alternative, I would rather recommend Bakhtin's reflections on the constitutive function of alterity for a critical understanding of one's self:

> I become myself only by revealing myself to another, through another and with another's help. . . . *To be* means to *communicate*. . . . To be means to be for the other, and through him, for oneself. Man has no internal sovereign territory; he is all and always on the boundary; looking within himself, he looks *in the eyes of the other* or *through the eyes of the other*. . . . I cannot do without the other; I cannot become myself without the other; I must find myself in the other, finding the other in me (in mutual reflection and perception). Justification cannot be justification of *oneself*, confession cannot be confession of *oneself*. I receive my name from the other, and this name exists for the other (to name oneself is to engage in usurpation). Self-love is equally impossible. (Todorov, 1984, 96)

Of course, it remains to be seen how the "I" and the "Other" are fleshed in specific circumstances where the determinants of gender, sexuality, race, class, religion, and so forth begin to complicate and disturb the lines of transnational communication.

For his part, Edward Said, the engaged Palestinian intellectual and partisan of Third World liberation movements, suggests his own universalizing resolution of the Third World–postmodernism polarity: a more inclusive counternarrative of liberation in which the antagonism between self and other can be displaced. Faulting Lyotard for separating Western postmodernism from the destructive consequences of European modernism in the colonized world and thus freeing it from its own history in the unequal division of labor, depoliticization of knowledge, and so on, Said diagnoses the crisis of modernism and the postmodernist impasse as one stemming from the onset of the twentieth century when Europe was being asked to take the Other (natives, women, sexual eccentrics) seriously (1989). Neither Albert Camus, Lyotard, Baudrillard, nor Bourdieu ever takes into account the fact of colonialism, how the Others have been historically constituted by their imperial subjugation and exploitation. What is important is to foreground the dialectic of relations between the opposites and transgress the fixed, artificial boundary between the Self and Other. In *Orientalism* (1978), Said has cogently shown how the Western epistemological construction of Others in the various disciplines serves the goal of asserting the supremacy of Western culture. The modalities of the West's representation of other peoples do not furnish objective knowledge; instead they fulfill the historical agenda of confirming the ascendant identity of the British, the French, the European in general, over against non-Western/non-Christian peoples. In a recent article, Said elaborates the relational problematic of his approach and offers a qualified postmodern scenario for resolving the contradictions between Habermas and Lyotard, between those who uphold difference as an unsurpassable existential condition and those who conceive it as a process of contingent and alterable relations:

> Despite its bitterness and violence, the whole point of Fanon's work is to force the European metropolis to think its history *together with* the history of colonies awakening from the cruel stupor and abused immobility of imperial domination, in Aimé Césaire's phrase, "measured by the compass of suffering." . . . With Césaire and C. L. R. James, Fanon's model for the postimperial world depended on the idea of a collective as well as a plural destiny for mankind, Western and non-Western alike. . . . Cultures may then be represented as zones of control or abandonment, of recollection and of forgetting, of force or of dependence, of exclusiveness or of sharing, all taking place in the global history that is our element. (1989, 223–25).

Said's vision with its eloquent utopian-sounding promise might vindicate the truth of Ghassan Abdullah's honor and possibly rescue Elizam Escobar from being trapped in "the belly of the beast"—if it did not sound like Borges's enchanting heterotopia. Meanwhile the production of *Miss Saigon* and new electronically sophisticated versions of *Madama Butterfly* will continue, Puerto Rico will continue to be the last intractable colony of the United States, and the Kurds and Palestinians will continue their struggle for a national homeland—national because, as Régis Debray urges us, while the nation is a historically determined mode of existence, yet it remains a primary determinant, an invariable fact: "the cultural organization of the human collectivity in question," a materializing mediation through which the life of homo sapiens "is rendered untouchable or sacred" (1977, 26). Whatever the status of this sacralization of life, I agree to some extent with Debray, especially in his suggestion that the concept of nation curbs the voluntarism, idealism, and vanguardism that afflict intellectuals, especially cosmopolitan avant-garde postmodernists, North or South. On the other hand, we should guard against the neonationalism of Japanese postmodernism, for example, whose basic axiomatic is the presumed synthesis of Western universalism and Japanese uniqueness (Mitsuhiro 1989, 20–25). Again Bakhtin's principle of exotopy should warn us of the seductive route of the aesthetics of identification which offers an easy way of conflating opposites under the rubric of "human brotherhood," "colorblind folkish togetherness," hybrid or syncretic homogenizing only to tighten the chains around us. Neither empathy nor sentimental solidarity then. Others are needed—not the Others who are simply victims of imperial conquest—but the others who, though victimized, resist closure of the unfinished project of articulating their narrative of struggle for recognition, for collective affirmation, of which these remarks are fragments and marginalia.

### BIBLIOGRAPHY

Abdullah, Ghassan. "Culture Behind the Bars." *Left Curve* 15 (1991): 68–70.
Achebe, Chinua. "An Image of Africa." *Massachusetts Review* (Winter 1977): 782–94.
Ahmad, Aijaz. "Jameson's Rhetoric of Otherness and the National Allegory." *Social Text*, no. 17 (Fall 1987): 3–27.
Amin, Samir. *Eurocentrism*. New York: Monthly Review Press, 1989.
Ashcroft, Bill, Gareth Griffiths, and Helen Tiffin. *The Empire Writes Back*. New York: Routledge, 1989.
Barthes, Roland. *The Eiffel Tower and Other Mythologies*. New York: Hill and Wang, 1979.
Baudrillard, Jean. "The Precession of Simulacra." In *Art After Modernism*, edited by Brian Wallis, 254–81. New York: Museum of Contemporary Art, 1984.
Berreman, Gerald. "The Incredible 'Tasaday': Deconstructing the Myth of the 'Stone-Age' People." *Cultural Survival Quarterly* 15, no.1 (1990): 3–25.
Beverley, John, and Marc Zimmerman. *Literature and Politics in the Central American Revolutions*. Austin: Univ. of Texas Press, 1990.
Buhle, Paul. *C. L. R. James: The Artist as Revolutionary*. London: Verso, 1988.
Carew, Jan. *Fulcrums of Change*. Trenton, N.J.: Africa World Press, 1988.
Clifford, James. *The Predicament of Culture*. Berkeley: Univ. of California Press, 1988.
Connor, Steven. *Postmodern Culture*. New York: Blackwell, 1989.
Davidson, Arnold. "1933–34 Thoughts on National Socialism." *Critical Inquiry* 17 (Autumn 1990): 48–52.

Debray, Régis. "Marxism and the National Question." *New Left Review* 105 (Sept.-Oct. 1977): 25–41.

Desnoes, Edmundo. "The Death System." In *On Signs*, edited by Marshall Blonsky, 39–42. Baltimore: Johns Hopkins Univ. Press, 1985.

Escobar, Elizam. "Art of Liberation: A Vision of Freedom." In *Reimaging America*, edited by Mark O'Brien and Craig Little, 86–93. Philadelphia: New Society Publishers, 1990.

———. "The Stealing of Nothingness." *Left Curve* 15 (1991): 23–28.

Franco, Jean. "Killing Priests, Nuns, Women, Children." In *On Signs*, edited by Marshall Blonsky, 414–20. Baltimore: Johns Hopkins Univ. Press, 1985.

Garcia Marquez, Gabriel. *Love in the Time of Cholera.* New York: Penguin, 1988.

Giddens, Anthony. "Modernism and Postmodernism." *New German Critique* 22 (Winter 1981): 15–18.

Goux, Jean-Joseph. *Symbolic economies: After Marx and Freud.* Ithaca, N.Y.: Cornell Univ. Press, 1990.

Habermas, Jürgen. "Modernity—An Incomplete Project." In *The Anti-Aesthetic*, edited by Hal Foster, 3–15. Port Townsend, Wash.: Bay Press, 1983.

Harvey, David. *The Condition of Postmodernity.* Cambridge, Mass.: Blackwell, 1989.

Jameson, Fredric. "Postmodernism, or the Cultural Logic of Late Capitalism." *New Left Review* 146 (1984): 53–92.

———. "Third World Literature in the Era of Multinational Capitalism." *Social Text*, no. 15 (1986): 65–88.

———. "Marxism and Postmodernism." *New Left Review* 176 (July-Aug. 1989): 31–45.

Kanafani, Ghassan. *All That's Left to You: A Novella and Other Stories.* Austin, Tex.: Center for Middle Eastern Studies, Univ. of Texas at Austin, 1990.

Llosa, Mario Vargas. "Updating Karl Popper." *PMLA* 105, no. 5 (Oct. 1990): 1018–25.

Longxi, Zhang. "The Myth of the Other: China in the Eyes of the West." *Critical Inquiry* 15 (Autumn 1988): 108–31.

Lyotard, Jean François. *The Postmodern Condition: A Report on Knowledge.* Minneapolis: Univ. of Minnesota Press, 1984.

McLuhan, Marshall. *Understanding Media.* New York: New American Library, 1964.

Mitsuhiro, Yoshimoto. "The Postmodern and Mass Images in Japan." *Public Culture* 1, no. 2 (Spring 1989): 8–25.

Murphy, Jay. "Ghassan Abdullah and Palestinian Culture of the Intifada." *Left Curve* 15 (1991): 66–68.

Myrdal, Jan, and Gun Kesle. *Angkor.* New York: Vintage, 1971.

Rivera, Tomas. *. . . y no se lo trago la tierra [ . . . and the earth did not devour him]* Houston: Arte Publico Press, 1987.

Rushdie, Salman. "Edward Said: On Palestinian Identity." *North Star Review* (Fall 1988): 2–9.

Said, Edward. *Orientalism*. New York: Pantheon Books, 1978.
———. "Representing the Colonized: Anthropology's Interlocutors." *Cultural Inquiry* 15 (Winter 1989): 205–25.
Saldivar, Ramon. *Chicano Narrative*. Madison: Univ. of Wisconsin Press, 1990.
Soyinka, Wole. "Twice Bitten: The Fate of Africa's Culture Producers." *PMLA* 105, no. 1 (Jan. 1990): 110–20.
Todorov, Tzvetan. *Mikhail Bakhtin: The Dialogical Principle*. Minneapolis: Univ. of Minnesota Press, 1984.
Villa, Jose Garcia. *Selected Poems and New*. New York: McDowell Obolensky, 1958.
Wolf, Eric. *Europe and the People Without History*. Berkeley: Univ. of California Press, 1982.

# Toward Socialism: In Solidarity with the Cuban Revolution

*Let me say, with the risk of appearing ridiculous, that the true revolutionary is guided by strong feelings of love.*
—Che Guevara, "Man and Socialism in Cuba" (1965)

*What is the history of Cuba if not the history of Latin America? and what is the history of Latin America if not the history of Asia, Africa and Oceania? And what is the history of all these peoples if not the history of the cruelest and most pitiless exploitation dealt by imperialism throughout the world? . . .*

*Our people can feel proud that they have contributed in some measure to the historical withdrawal of North American imperialism by showing that only ninety miles away a small country, with no force other than the moral resolve to resist even unto death itself and the solidarity of international revolution, was capable of confronting the imperialist attack of the greatest oppressor in the history of humanity.*
—Second Declaration of Havana (1962)

Every Filipino has read of how our patriot Jose Rizal, unable to find a safe asylum in the islands after his exile in Dapitan, in the southernmost island of Mindanao, volunteered to serve as an army surgeon in Cuba at the height of the Cuban people's revolution against Spain. Whatever his hidden motives were, Rizal never made it. The blood of the *Katipunan* (the native revolutionary association that spearheaded the anticolonial revolt) insurgents saved him from what could have been, in the public view, an ironic complicity with his executioners.

I was able to make it to Cuba—for three weeks, in June–July 1985. I was a member of a collective of fifteen North American scholars invited by the Cuban Ministry of Culture. Led by the distinguished U.S. Marxist intellectual Fredric Jameson, the group was interested not only in finding out answers to questions about the Cuban path to socialism but also how to help fight the ongoing U.S. blockade. We were interested in sharing experiences. We held warm, frank exchanges with Cuban intellectuals at the Casa de las Americas, with individual workers and farmers in the surrounding countryside near Havana, with members of the Committee for the Defense of the Revolution, with responsible officials of People's Power at various levels. On the whole, everyone found our stay extremely enlightening, often intensely moving.

My understanding of this *apertura* is this: the Cuban comrades in the cultural field were interested in conducting a friendly dialogue with North Americans (including, in this case, a Venezuelan woman, one expatriate from El Salvador, and one from the Philippines) on such topics as poststructuralist semiotics, psychoanalysis, deconstruction, and other recent trends, in their interface with Marxism. We met with the Minister of Culture Armando Hart, who confessed that U.S. imperialism's most formidable weapon is music—Havana can get all the radio/televison broadcasts emanating from Florida. I recall in particular the long lines of people waiting to get into two or three movie houses screening *Flashdance*. We had memorable dialogues with Ambassador Alarcon, Roberto Fernandez Retamar, Ambrosio Fornet, Pablo Armando Fernandez, and other artists. I also recall my conversation with the revered poet Eliseo Diego in the Haydee Santamaria Art Gallery on Rizal and the Spanish influence in the Philippines.

We were also treated to a special viewing of the controversial film *Lejania* at the Cuban Film Institute, where the director Jesus Diaz spoke and answered questions, proving once more that Cuban cinema is performing its vanguard role in world cinematography.

My short visit has personally been inspiring. For my generation, one of the strongest influences in our political education—long before Ho Chi Minh and the Chinese cultural revolution—was the Argentine Che Guevara. Discussing Che's speech "Man and Socialism" and his guerrilla diaries, despite their romantic excess, became a transformative experience for many Filipinos about to discover the rich treasury of socialist art and thought (now a part of humanity's achievement) that today's local anticommunist demonology would seek to quarantine and stigmatize. It was only much later that we would read Marti's essays, Fidel Castro's classic "Words to the Intellectuals," the writings of Nicolas Guillen, Carpentier, Retamar; the now classic film *Memories of Underdevelopment*, and its successors *Lucia*, *Portrait of Teresa*, and others. I remember, in 1967, the popular slogan of youthful activists in "the belly of the beast" was one taken from the "General Declaration" of the first conference in Havana of the Organization for Latin American Solidarity (OLAS): "The duty of every revolutionary is to make the revolution." Fidel Castro's speech, "The Road to Revolution," where the triumph of revolutionary ideas was particularly stressed as "absolutely necessary," excited students as much as Che's legendary heroism.

What accounts for this powerful and persisting appeal of the Cuban revolution to Third World intellectuals and to Filipinos in particular who are engaged in the cultural frontline, in the battle of ideas and values?

Like the Philippines, Cuba has a long tradition of revolutionary struggle against colonialism and imperialism. This dates from the two episodes of insurrection against Spain in the nineteenth century to the victorious struggle against the Batista dictatorship in 1959. The 1933 revolution against Machado is often described as a popular revolution of workers and the middle strata (including intellectuals). Castro sums up this tradition in his statement: "The right to rebellion lies at the very roots of Cuba's existence as a nation." Cuba experienced profound social upheavals every twenty-five years, the most pivotal of which is the 1959 revolution that laid the foundation for socialist reconstruction. We in the Philippines have had our victory against Spain wrested away by U.S. colonizing forces that continue to suppress the national identity—from Sakay and the Sakdalistas to the Huks and today's activists. We are still forging forward to our 1959, and we can learn something from the Cuban example.

Every revolution is characterized by a profound mutation of values and ideas parallel to, or in consonance with, the necessary radical changes in the political and economic institutions of a particular society. This is true of our uprising against Spain, an armed struggle first enacted in the minds of propagandists like Rizal and M. H. del Pilar, and eventually realized in the collective projects of Bonifacio, Aguinaldo, and Mabini. This is not true at all of the February 1986 EDSA insurrection, as everyday developments confirm. You need only remember how, soon after Castro's July 26th Movement won, a thoroughgoing Agrarian Reform Law was passed in May 1959 that, according to Castro, "was the first law that really established the break between the revolution and the country's richest, most privileged sectors, and the break with the United States and the transnational corporations." These steps toward instituting popular democracy—from the rent reduction law of 1959 to the establishment of *poder popular* in 1974—trace their roots to what I would call the Cuban libertarian sensibility, one of whose prime documents is Castro's speech in defense of his 1953 attack on the Moncada barracks, "History Will Absolve Me." If there is any figure that dominates the Cuban intellectual milieu today and helped to shape its radically democratic sensibility, it is unquestionably Jose Marti. Marti's populist democratic thinking derives from the whole Western tradition (including the U.S. transcendentalists Emerson and Whitman), but is inflected radically by his response to the Haymarket Square Riots of 1886. It was Marti who said: "The path to progress in Latin America lies in the redistribution of land." Having lived "in the bowels of the monster," in the New York slums, Marti was provoked by experiences of violent racism, firing up his militancy: "you take your rights, you do not beg for them; you do not get them with tears but with blood. . . . I will stake my fate on the poor of the earth." One can observe the roots of Castro's strategy (to articulate the national-popular will, to assert the moral-intellectual leadership or hegemony of the working masses, and his sharp political intelligence vis-à-vis sectarian and dogmatist tendencies) in Marti's synthesis of *patria* and *humanidad*. Cuba's well-known internationalism rests on this affirmation of *patria* as *humanidad*. Integrating thought and action, Marti, the art critic, reader of Henry James and Marx, lived fourteen years of his life in exile in the United States but returned to Cuba to fight and die for the ideals of freedom and national independence that the revolution has continued to incarnate in everyday practice.

In Cuba perhaps more than in other countries where socialism or a noncapitalist formation is being built within historically specific parameters, the majority of writers and cultural activists—from Marti to women poets like Nancy Morejon and Belkis Cuza Malé—have been actively involved in mass struggles against colonial tyranny and capitalist exploitation. We can mention thinkers like Miguel Bravo Senties, Diego Vicente Tejeres, Carlos Loveira; the editor of *Juventud* Julio Antonio Mella; the poet Ruben Martinez Villena, among others. In Cuba, where racist oppression dates back to the Spanish extermination of the Indians, Afro-Cuban intellectuals like Nicolas Guillen and Juan Marinello have fused their anger with analytic irony and prophetic vision. Now president of the Union of Writers and Artists of Cuba, Guillen has an internationally acclaimed, solid body of work unique in concretizing the dialectic of *patria/humanidad* and the age-old problematic of racism to which Marx, Engels, and Western Marxism in general were blind. A concept of united front from below, mediated in the process of struggle, may be grasped from Guillen's poem "It's All Right" ("Esta Bien"):

It's all right that you sing when you cry, Negro brother,
Crucified Negro of the South;
All right your spirituals,
Your banners,
Your marches, and the allegations
Of your lawyers.
It's all fine.
It's all right that you try that icy surface
In pursuit of justice.
—Oh, that innocent skater who went
Drinking the breeze from Chicago to Washington—!
It's all right that you protest in the papers,
All right that you ready your fists,
And Lincoln there in his portrait,
It's all fine.

It's all right that you preach in dynamited temples,
Fine that you heroically persist
In mixing with the whites
Because the law—law?—proclaims
Equality to all Americans.
     it's all right,
     Fine,
     God damned great.
But, my crucified Southern brother,
Remember John Brown
Who wasn't a Negro, but defended you with a gun.

*Gun: a portable firearm*
(so reads the dictionary)
*Used by soldiers to shoot with.*
It must be added that *the gun*
*Was also the firearm used by slaves in their defense.*

But, in case, my brother,
Should it be the case that you
Don't have a gun, you can
Then
I don't know—
Get something
A hammer, a stick,
A stone, something that hurts,

Something sharp that wounds,
Hits, draws blood,
Something.

(Translated by Anita Whitney Romeo
from *Cuban Poetry 1959–66*, Havana, 1967)

Guillen celebrated the Agrarian Reform Law with a poem entitled "Land in the Sierra and Below" ("Tierra en la Sierra y El Llano"), where he addresses the property-owners: "Together with Fidel / Green-garbed and burgeoning Fidel / I shall come to draw your fangs / Take back what is mine / You'll have to reckon with me. / My life is nobody's but mine."

In that brief sojourn in Havana, I recall wandering around the Vedado district by myself, near the office of the *Tricontinental*, where I had a useful exchange with the editors; finding myself in a park where ordinary people were drinking beer. I conversed with some Afro-Cubans who expressed curiosity about the Philippine struggle. One refrain that I vividly carried with me after was the remark: "Here there is no racism, unlike the U.S." In contrast, my white colleagues were not so sensitive to this because they were going around Havana's bookstores checking out if there were titles by Althusser, Derrida, Foucault, etc. They didn't find any, nor were they able to encounter any by Gramsci, Lukács, or Luxemburg, among the publications imported from the Soviet Union and other East European countries. Perhaps those books were unconscionable luxuries.

What is available, however, makes up for such a lack: more than seventy-four volumes of Marti's collected writings; texts by Marx, Engels, Lenin; and an immense archive of literature in Spanish from everywhere. Nothing in this milieu is wanting (I said to myself) when it is electrified by Fidel's unending dialogue with the masses of workers, peasants, ordinary Cubans from all walks of life. Sparked by the sagacity and intelligence of this charismatic leader, the life of the mind in Cuba is not divorced from reality in the way that the psyche of intellectuals (even Marxist ones) in late capitalism is, lacking roots in a mass socialist movement. In Cuba, ideas, thought, and feeling flourish with the rhythm of everyday life, embedded in the practices of millions constructing the foundation for a socialist future not just in the Caribbean but in all of Latin America.

Cuba is indeed blessed with the presence of this charismatic revolutionary (Fidel Castro) whose discriminating mind, tact, political acumen, and sagacity may be seen in a recent collection of revealing interviews with Brazilian priest Frei Betto in a book entitled *Fidel and Religion*. Virtually a life-history of the Cuban intellectual transformed into a Marxist-Leninist, this book demonstrates again the imperative of creating a mass, national-popular practice of socialism completely opposed to the party sectarianism of an elite of cadres. This specifically Cuban practice of socialism is now being institutionalized by the system of people's power assemblies, an unprecedented innovation that seems to renew the model of the *soviets* in Lenin's time, or the factory councils in Gramsci's Turin of August 1917. (One other achievement that I cannot elaborate on here is the 1974 Family Code, which, theoretically, is the most advanced legislation of its kind in the whole world.)

In the course of explaining certain inadequacies in the relation between the Communist Party of Cuba and nonparty Christian believers, Castro comments that "this isn't just a question of principles or ethics anymore; in a sense it's a matter of aesthetics. Aesthetics in what sense? I think the revolution is a work that should be constantly improved; moreover, it's a work of art." For Castro, making a revolution doesn't just simply mean socialization of the means of production or the restructuring of property relations, including the production and distribution of wealth. Of course, that is needed, but basically it means a spiritual commitment:

> Those who don't understand that morale is a fundamental factor in a revolution are lost, defeated. . . . Values and morale are man's spiritual weapons. As you know, regardless of his beliefs, we don't inspire a revolutionary fighter with the idea that he'll be rewarded in the next world or will be eternally happy if he dies. Those men were ready to die—even those who were nonbelievers—because there were values for which they believed it was worth giving their lives, even though their lives were all they had. How can you get a man to do this if not on the basis of specific values?

Given this intense concern for transformative ideas and humanizing values that inform not just Marxist philosophy but Cuba's national consensus, where what is moral is always closely linked with morale, the continuing cultural revolution in Cuba may be a harbinger of humanity's final deliverance from the curse of alienation and commodity fetishism. Speaking on the twentieth anniversary of the death of Che Guevara, Castro reaffirmed that money or material incentive cannot be the prime motivation, that emphasis must be actively given to conscience and morals: "The building of socialism and communism is not only a production and redistribution of wealth but also the concept that totally rejects capitalist ideals that have been grafted onto some socialist systems."

Arriving in Havana one sultry June morning after a 4-A.M. flight from Miami, Florida, we were bussed to a hotel in the oldest section of Havana which uncannily resembles the old Intramuros, the Walled City of Manila. Havana is surprisingly a city without beggars or slums, without all the ugly symptoms of underdevelopment that once marked "the brothel of the Caribbean." There are no longer any glittering Cadillacs whizzing down the fashionable avenues while in the countryside only one out of ten peasants drank milk, where barely four percent ate meat, and most lived in substandard conditions. It is impossible here to enumerate all the achievements of the revolution—Cuba now ranks first in the Third World in the area of public health, with life expectancy raised from fifty four (pre-1959) to seventy. This would not have been possible if the expropriators were not expropriated. Eduardo Galeano, author of *Open Veins of Latin America,* reminds us that "the brigade that landed at the Bay of Pigs in April 1961 was not only made up of former Batista soldiers and policemen, but also of the previous owners of more than 370,000 hectares of land, nearly 10,000 buildings, 70 factories, 10 sugarmills, 3 banks, 5 mines, and 12 cabarets."

Reading the signs in Havana—the socialist tolerance of Tropicana (where before "luscious starlets modulated to the rhythms of Lecuona's famous band") and Hollywood box-office hits, the influx of European cultural groups and personalities competing with Cuban ballet and the audacious music of Sylvio Rodriguez and Pablo Millanes, the cosmopolitan worldliness of Cuban art (cinema and painting, for example)—one cannot help but wonder if Cuba, representing Third World socialist battlefields, has not become the center of a new, heterogeneous world-culture being born in the womb of revolutionary cataclysms and upheavals; a womb surrounded by interdicting warships and missiles. Cuba, a socialist future just an hour's flight from the imperialist metropolis.

I can never forget the imposing palatial homes, with antique marble bathrooms, of wealthy landlords and compradors around Havana, which have now been converted to public offices or *casas de cultura* (houses of culture) for the working people. This is a miracle I would like to see happen here in Metro Manila, in those guarded quarters of the native oligarchy and the transnational elite—enclaves of loot and plunder recalling the old Havana of Batista's times. This image was soon disrupted by a subsequent visit to Manila in August 1985 where extremes of poverty and wealth haunted one's conscience day and night. A contradiction looms here between the past and the present—our future, between the hell of imperialism (what the Black poet Amiri Baraka calls "the superstructure of filth that people in the United States call their way of life" in a society "impossibly deformed") and the catalyzing challenge of building a society free from exploitation, untrammelled by racism, released from the bondage of poverty and degradation that millions of Filipinos experience everyday in a neocolonial appendage of the U.S. empire. While "people power" overthrew the Marcos regime in February 1986, the economic and social conditions remain the same—nay, in fact have worsened, with intense racial, gender, and class conflicts pervading all sectors of the present conjuncture.

I submit that without a profound alteration of the economic and political structures, such as what the Cuban revolutionaries have carried out immediately after their seizure of state power, Third World peoples cannot regain the pride and dignity wrested from them by centuries of colonial barbarity and imperialist oppression. Only the experience of a complex, tortuous revolutionary process in one's society, contextualized in the worldwide struggle of other oppressed peoples against imperialism, can liberate the masses from the deadening nightmare of the past; from daily suffering, futility, humiliation and hopelessness that still grip us in these islands. In Havana that July 1985, reflecting on how painful and difficult our struggle has been and will continue to be, I was most pleasantly surprised to find Rizal's two novels *Noli Me Tangere* (1886) and *El Filibusterismo* (1891) newly republished, read avidly by millions of Cubans. Oh yes, Rizal made it after all.

And so it is that in that future I rediscovered the past, in that rupture called Cuba where the festival of the oppressed, the celebrations of hope and beauty and freedom by the "wretched of the earth," is just beginning its seductive adventure.

Text of an address given at the Cultural Center of the Philippines on 23 October 1987 on the occasion of Cuban Cultural Week.

# Afterword

Against the background of the continuing war led by the United States against Iraq (with Libya and Iran looming behind) and the unprecedented upheavals in regions formerly known as the Soviet Union and Yugoslavia rapidly making obsolete any ongoing academic pontification, reflections on the twin fates of freedom and progress in dependent formations are bound to assume greater urgency and resonance than before. In particular, what is the fate of culture in these contested territories? The bulk (at least two-thirds) of the world's population inhabiting the periphery exerts an incalculable force on sovereign nation-states and transnational corporate policy decisions in the industrialized metropolis (now comprising three centers: the European Community, Japan and its satellites, and North America). The logic of capital requires a hierarchical division of labor throughout the world that constantly reproduces its own condition of existence. In a world system dominated by the messiahs of the "free market" hard on the tracks of fleeing Kurds, Palestinians, and millions of refugees from Eastern Europe and elsewhere, the inauguration of a "New World Order" opens up the space for rethinking cherished beliefs and received notions rendered anachronistic by the turn of events.

In both the Middle East and Eastern Europe, the talismanic shibboleth of "democracy" broadcast by the Western media claims to promise nothing short of absolute redemption. "Free World" triumphalism for now—despite quandaries in Somalia and Haiti—preempts all dissent, criticism, refusal.[1] Meanwhile, in El Salvador, South Africa, the Philippines, and other presumed democratic polities, the problems of poverty, social injustice, military brutality, ecological disasters, and so on continue to confound the technocratic experts of the International Monetary Fund and the World Bank. The new status quo is volatile and unpredictable. But, as everyone knows, the worry of Western governments concerns not the plight of impoverished citizens but rather the gigantic debts of countries like Brazil, Mexico, Argentina, and a dozen others in Africa and Asia—debts whose foreclosure might precipitate a global financial crisis worse (in the minds of the corporate elite) than a nuclear war. We hear this uncanny whispering behind: Never question the legitimacy of this new dispensation—the same old thing, unequal exchange on a world scale—lest you unleash the barbarism of Prospero and Ariel against Caliban's hordes. In such a scenario, the significations of "postcolonial" literature and "postmodern" art, including the rubric "Third World," again become the site of struggle for redefinition, revaluation, and reappropriation (Buchanan 1974).

In retrospect, Peter Worsley's inaugural text *The Third World* (1964) is one of the first cognitive mappings of the world system—its differential political economies, its "actual infinity," as it were—which privileged the Third World as a challenge to both late capitalism and communism. He quotes Frantz Fanon's assertion that the Third World's singular task "consists in reintroducing Man into the world, man in his totality" (275). Peter Weiss concurs by rejecting the derogatory connotation of "third" and insists that by reintroducing "human dignity," these exploited and poor countries are really the actually developed ones (quoted in Gugelberger 1991, 522). In short, to echo the fabled inversion, the last is really first. What is at stake here, however, is not the revival of Renaissance humanism or biblical eschatology but the concept of a world society in which problems of poverty, ecology, and genocide implicate every human across nation-state boundaries. This idea of a planetary ethics has long been anticipated by Marxist thought and its stress on the centrality of labor as life/species activity, work which fashions the world as an expression of self-conscious, universalizing species-power. But it would not have been possible without the sequence of events that signalled the advent of a late-modern "givenness" some years after the onset of the Cold War: Ghana's independence (1957), Fidel Castro's victory in Cuba (1959), Lumumba's murder (1961), the vicissitudes of the Algerian revolution (1957–62), and the instructive lessons of U.S. involvement in Indochina.

After the 1973 military coup in Chile against the socialist Allende, the U.S. debacle in Vietnam, and the maturing of crisis in South Africa and in Central America, the quest for an internationalist ethics moved to a qualitatively new stage. The phrases "national liberation struggle" and "people's war" began to acquire substantive weight in academic exchange. The anthropologist Sidney Mintz reminds us of the original *problematique*, the interdiscursive field of our inquiry: "the uneven and multiplex relationship between the capitalist heartland and the societies and peoples on which that heartland has fed" (1976, 377). To demystify "third worldism" as contrived by the New Left, Mintz introduces Wallerstein's "theme of a worldwide capitalism transcending national and continental boundaries and encompassing forms of labor in no way reducible to a single proletarian model." In another context, Samir Amin introduces plurality within the "concrete universal" of liberation: "A development that is not merely development of underdevelopment will therefore be both national, popular-democratic, and socialist, by virtue of the world project of which it forms a part" (1977, 383). Across the spectrum of usages and references, the term "Third World" releases its force as an operational and situational signifier rather than an analytic ontological category; thus we see the ironic unfolding of its heterogeneity in Gerard Chaliand's *Revolution in the Third World* (1978), contemporaneous with Mintz's essay, in which disillusionment with Utopia (now synonymous with all those transitional experiments Chaliand used to extoll) becomes a pretext for valorizing the key "Western" ideas of freedom and equality.

It seems that the messianic vision of Fanon's *Wretched of the Earth* has become simply a Third World Imaginary, an erstwhile heresy now reduced to superstition. Before the waning of third-worldism into the eclectic cosmopolitanism of postcoloniality, I want to enter a personal digression here to frame my subsequent remarks. In June, 1981, I organized a seminar on "Revolutionary Third World Culture: Theory and Literature" for the Inter-University Centre of Postgraduate Studies in Dubrovnik, Yugoslavia, an extension of my years of teaching Third World cultural practices at the University of Connecticut, Brooklyn College, and other schools. Two years before, at about the time when the Sandinistas (FSLN) overthrew the Somoza dynasty, the first chapter of this book was published in *Social Praxis*. Its abstract contained these initial propositions: "In the specific historic juncture of the late seventies, culture in the Third World has increasingly asserted itself as a form of ideological practice structurally determined by the class struggle. Literature is defined as an instance of concrete political practice which reflects the dynamic process of the national democratic revolution in the developing countries." Two years after the seminar, just after the invasion of Grenada by U.S. Marines, I attended a conference on "Marxism and the Interpretation of Culture" at the University of Illinois, Urbana-Champaign. A group of participants in Stuart Hall's class distributed a leaflet entitled "Third World Intervention" whose intent and thrust can be discerned in these passages:

> Given the new international division of labor, and given this era of the multinational economy (which characterizes the postmodern), is it any longer possible to limit questions of culture and Marxism to culture defined within the framework of the nation-state or within the framework of the western world? The

second related question regards the adequacy or applicability of theories generated in and for the first world context to the third world scene... The third world is always an implicit part of first world cultural production.

The project of anthropology, which is the locus of cultural studies par excellence in the U.S., has been to describe, codify, and systematize cultures on the margins of Western civilization. Not only has ethnographic representation entailed an imposition of synchronicity upon these other societies whereby transformation can only be seen as initiated from the outside. It also displaces the question of domination into an issue of relativized cultural logics of difference. But the ideological project of anthropological practice succeeds in assigning to those other cultures a symbolic meaning within the dominant ideological discourse of the West, a meaning of alterity which is constitutive in the construction of the identity of the subject in the West, which entails a certain deformation of the colonial subject as well.

The Third World Study Group responsible for this manifesto also speculated whether the international division of labor has not also entailed the "international division of the subject," rendering the category of "nation" suspect in the context of the dynamics of international capital and also the idea of exploitation as chiefly derivative of the capital-labor class contradiction. This instance of dissent may be taken as emblematic of the unequal distribution of interpretive power in the academy. Order is guaranteed by the "excluded middle," in this case the "absent" or "erased" labor of subjugated nationalities. In an ironic twist, the protest against unwarranted generalization by Eurocentric discourse refunctioned the poststructuralist "exorbitation" of discourse attributed to Derrida, Foucault, Lacan, etc., so that what it aimed ostensibly to deny at the start is reaffirmed in the end.

It is perhaps at this juncture that we can appreciate Aijaz Ahmad's *In Theory* (1992) as a salutary polemical intervention, clarifying in its exposition of the historical background the ambiguities and ironies of the new counterhegemonic trend. Problematizing the ethos of its adherents, Ahmad attacks the poststructuralist skepticism of postcolonial theorists, their avant-gardist stance of irony, and their rhetorics of migrancy. His rejection of nationalism (of the bourgeois comprador or *desarrollista* brand) posited as the determinate opposite of imperialism is based on a prior calculation of its role "in the determinate socialist project"; hence the struggle is not against "nations and states as such, but for different articulations of class, nation, and state." While condemning reactionary "third-worldist nationalism," Ahmad does not dismiss (like the epigones of Baudrillard and Lyotard) "the historical reality of the sedimentations which do in fact give particular collectivities of people real civilizational identities" (1992, 11). He also recognizes how "the tendential law of global accumulation" produces not greater homogenization but "greater differentiation among its various national units," hence his rejection of Fredric Jameson's hypothesis of "national allegory" (which I discuss later). Ahmad's prudent qualifications, however, do not save him from a certain leftist monumentality that has no patience with alliance or populist politics practiced in, say, South Africa today; nor do we find much latitude there for calculating and harnessing to our advantage the oppositional effects of what Ernst Bloch calls "nonsynchronicities" in the interstices of middle-strata quotidian existence. Ahmad may yet prove to be a nostalgic "postcolonial" in spite of himself.

In general I agree with Ahmad and others (for example, Mukherjee 1990) in their view that theory from the metropolis cannot escape the "specter" of insurgent "natives," of anti-imperialist resistance. But neither can we in the Third World escape its contagion. The question is: how do we negotiate the complex linkages of this ideological conjuncture and use the "weak links" of the enemy? In my judgment, the only dialectical way of mediating the capitalist world system and historically specific national formations as we examine concrete processes of cultural production is to deploy Gramsci's concept of the "national-popular," as I attempt in my essay "Beyond Postcolonial Theorizing." Following Otto Bauer's insight that "in each country, the socialist ideology merges with its peculiar cultural tradition and becomes nationally differentiated" (1971, 274–75), Gramsci emphasizes the circumstantiality of aesthetic form and cultural practice in general as shaped by varied audiences and generic conventions (1985, 117–19), local knowledges, ethnic self-construals, and other contingencies. The philosophical justification for discerning the force of a specific "national" concern and a popular orientation lies in Gramsci's historical-materialist understanding of aesthetic praxis:

> If one cannot think of the individual apart from society, and thus if one cannot think of any individual who is not historically conditioned, it is obvious that every individual, including the artist and all his activities, cannot be thought of apart from society, a specific society. Hence the artist does not write or paint—that is, he does not externalize his phantasms—just for his

own recollection, to be able to relive the moment of creation. He is an artist only insofar as he externalizes, objectifies and historicizes his phantasms. Every artist-individual, though, is such in a more or less broad and comprehensive way, he is "historical" or "social" to a greater or lesser degree. (1985, 112)

The historicity of the forms of individual consciousness, the social contradictions immanent in the language of the psyche, the dynamic interconnections of social existence registered in the flows of desire and flux of lived experience—all these axioms found in Gramsci can be used to explain the collectivist impulse behind artistic representation. In the peripheral hinterlands, this impulse is very much alive. It has escaped complete dissolution by the levelling "realism" of exchange value in the marketplace. And so far as one can calculate from this distance, the force of reification has not yet sublimated or transmogrified its inhabitants into free-floating signifiers or aleatory simulacra.

Given this unashamedly totalizing (but not essentializing) framework, we can now appreciate Jameson's cogently argued hypothesis of the characteristic Third World narrative as a kind of national allegory when a dialectical hermeneutic or metacommentary is applied on it (as he does on Lu Hsun's "Diary of a Madman" and Sembene's *Xala*). Jameson writes: "Third-world texts, even those which are seemingly private and invested with a properly libidinal dynamic, necessarily project a political dimension in the form of national allegory: *the story of the private individual destiny is always an allegory of the embattled situation of the public third-world culture and society*" (1986, 69). Note that his formulation assumes that in the West the public-private split tends to reduce everything into subjectivist or psychologized phenomena, while the radical disparity of the Third World lies in its uneven, unsynchronized milieu where subjectivity is grounded and refigured by its social context, where the metonymy/syntax of personal lived experience ultimately finds intelligible expression in the paradigmatic axis of the community (see also Beverley and Zimmerman 1990). In the Third World narrative of quotidian existence, the artist is necessarily a political intellectual since the forms of artistic expression assume political valence in all the moments of its production, circulation, and reception.[2]

At this point I can think of no better illustration of what Jameson is saying about the necessarily ethico-political function of the Third World intellectual than C. L. R. James and his massive life-long engagement in the cultural and political transformation of three continents. One can easily demonstrate how, for example, James's early story "Triumph" exemplifies the Caribbean allegory of conscientization

"Triumph" exemplifies the Caribbean allegory of conscientization originating from the intersection of sexuality, economics, and the resistance against patriarchy (1992). Suffice it to consider here briefly his dramatization of the nonsychronic and overdetermined process of Haiti's slave revolution, *The Black Jacobins*. The subtle choreography of moods, attitudes, and actions displayed by the major protagonists of the drama—Toussaint, Dessalines, and Moise—is plotted primarily to reveal the complex sensorium in which the colonial *habitus* operates and how uneven is the alignment of diverse ideological agencies in any transitional conjuncture. The defeat of the symbol of autonomy and of becoming-human, Moise, and the eclipse of the masses (symbolized by the displacement of voodoo by European music/dance) signal the way in which the force of historical necessity limits the influence of European radicalism (bourgeois individualism) as much as it suggests for us how the deformation of the Bolshevik revolution by Stalin's authoritarian diktat translates into James's quest for a new historic agency in the form of the colonized, oppressed people of color in the Third World. Nationalitarian allegory metamorphoses into a world-system parable. A note in the staging of the play betokens James's prefigurative sensibility: "Crowds say little but their presence is felt powerfully at all critical moments" (1992, 68). Certain key texts may be alluded to here as effectively demonstrating James's overarching principle that the masses of workers and peasants with their organized spontaneous energies create the decisive breaks in history (for example, the destruction of mercantilism by the slave revolt): "From Toussaint L'Ouverture to Fidel Castro," "The People of the Gold Coast," and the uncompromising testament of his faith, "Dialectical Materialism and the Fate of Humanity." Because James perceived the paradoxical and contradictory effects of capital, its progressive and regressive pressures on specific communities which triggered the astute responses of all classes and types, he was fully appreciative not only of the totalizing regime of commodity exchange where the socialist project is the only alternative but also of the concrete sites where resistance is born. Thus by attending to the configuration of events in specific arenas of struggle and its interplay with the concrete mechanisms of the world system, James embodied in his life-work the allegorizing imagination, catholicity, and rigor that distinguish Marxism as a revolutionary praxis, the name of an intractable heterogeneous desire.

Under the aegis of allegory, synecdoche writ large, the Third World presents itself as a complex of narratives juxtaposing movements of disenfranchisement and of empowerment, of ruptures and convergences. In the light of varying temporalities, "nation" is only one term for reinscribing the fusion between agency and structure; other categories are race, class, ethnicity, religion, and their permutations—all loci for the strategic affirmation of a creative Third World subjectivity. The moment/process called "nation" is easily conflated or subsumed in that of class, gender, etc. How is it that Fanon's inaugural project of the nationalitarian conquest of identity has been disparaged and disavowed by postcolonial intellectualism?

One answer lies in the worldwide hegemony of poststructuralist ideology that valorizes the primacy of exchange, pastiche, fragmentation, textuality, and difference as touchstones of critique and understanding. Repudiating myths of origin (for example, Wole Soyinka's invocation of "universal verities" contained in the worldview or "self-apprehension" of indigenous peoples) via techniques of abrogation and appropriation, the Australian authors of the influential textbook *The Empire Writes Back* proclaim that only syncretism, hybridity, and counterdiscourse can be the authentic categories of postcolonial literatures. But who authorizes this new doctrine? And what kind of rationality or will-to-power underwrites its portentous agendas? We are now indeed far removed from the time when a skilfully nuanced historicizing approach to cultural practices such as that illustrated by Umberto Melloti's *Marx and The Third World* (1977) is still a viable option. After criticizing the Eurocentric discourse of "Asiatic despotism" as well as the distortions of "bureaucratic collectivism" in transitional formations, Melotti proceeds to demarcate Third World civilizational uniqueness as an integral part of "world society":

> The different structure of the Third World has given birth to other no less important values, such as the communal ethic, the concept of a proper balance between man and nature, and the integration of the social and natural worlds, but it has never interpreted them in a truly liberating sense and has frequently carried them to a repressive conclusion. But today we are more than ever one world, and the synthesis of those values through truly socialist relations will finally permit the supersession of bourgeois individualism and repressive collectivism alike by a society where, as summed up in Marx's phrase, "The free development of each is the premise of the free development of all." (157).

At the threshold of the twenty-first century, we arrive at the crossroad of tradition and modernity in the far-flung margins of the empire. Obviously this trope of a journey insinuates a metanarrative biased against fixity and stasis, a "totalizing" figure suspect to postcolonial thinkers. But what is the alternative? Mapping the contours of the recent past may help prefigure the shape of what is to come in the controversy over the internationalization of critical (poststructuralist) theory. The impasse of technocratic development in the Third World in the last twenty-five years, since the two UNCTAD (United Nations Conference on Trade and Development) sessions in 1964 and 1968, returns us to the ineluctable questions that defy any premature forecasting of "the end of history" as touted by neoconservative pundits: Is the Enlightenment project of winning human freedom from Necessity a ruse for imperial hegemony on people of color? Is the discourse of progress a mask for oppression? Is Marxism, inheritor of Enlightenment ideals, complicit with the discourse of modernization? What original humane culture can the "natives" in the periphery offer to counter the fetishism of simulacra, pastiche, spectacle? Culture for the sake of whom, in the name of what?

We know from the historical record that the uneven and combined development of the Third World is the consequence of the lopsided and hierarchical division of international labor as well as the accumulation of capital by the industrial powers through plunder, slave trade, direct expropriation of resources and surplus value in the colonies from the sixteenth century up to the present (Wolf 1982, Rodney 1982, Weisskopf 1972). Notwithstanding the periodic realignments of nation-states today, we still persist in the reign of sameness-with-difference: commodity exchange for the sake of profit/surplus value. But the growth of productive forces and people's critical responses have altered the systemic forms of capital accumulation. From market to transnational capitalism, the pattern of imperialist exploitation of the world's labor and resources has undergone a series of mutations. When the prescription of import-substitution carried out in the fifties and sixties failed to usher in sustained, independent growth, the elite of the dependent countries resorted to export-oriented industrialization administered by the National Security State. The result? A rich harvest of massive human rights violations by U.S.-backed authoritarian regimes, systematic corruption of cultures, degradation of work through "warm body exports" (migrant labor), and unrelenting pauperization of the masses. In the Free Trade Zones, where the global assembly line generates superprofits out of cheap labor, total surveillance and draconian prohibitions prevail. Western monopoly of knowledge/information and the means of communication (mass media) become more crucial (see Schiller 1889). Empirical evidence and all kinds of testimony demonstrate that the cult of the GNP (Gross National Product) institutionalized by the disciples of W. W. Rostow's *Stages of Economic*

*Growth* and the Chicago school of monetary economics, among others, has brought with it only rampant unemployment, widespread poverty, cycles of repression and stagnation, and the destruction of cultures and environments for people of color, whose underdevelopment is reproduced daily by formulas meant to maintain archaic patronage systems and "trickle-down" philanthropy (Alavi and Shanin 1982, Woddis 1972, Amin 1977). Meanwhile, World Bank/IMF structural adjustments or conditionalities serve only to reinforce dependency. The plight of Argentina or Chile might well foreshadow the future of the Asian NICs (Newly Industrialized Countries).

In this life-and-death agon for millions, the literary conceits of undecidability and indeterminacy offer neither catharsis nor denouement, only mock-heroic distractions. Long before the failure of the reformist UN "Programme of Action on the Establishment of a New International Economic Order," Denis Goulet, in his provocative work *The Cruel Choice* (1971), had already proposed that the philosophy of development involves not just democracy in the political realm but "the basic questions about the quality of life in society, the relationship between goods and the good, and human control over change processes." He asked whether "underdeveloped" societies would become mere "consumers of technological civilization or agents of their own transformation" (260). To answer this question, we need to confront the key issue of self-determination in the realm of civil society and the public sphere: who decides and ultimately determines the goals, means, and trajectory of any development program? Can the indigenous elite who inherited the colonial state be relied upon to mobilize the masses, articulate their aspirations, and redistribute wealth/power? In short: Is the path of material progress for former colonies via dependent capitalism or popular-democratic (socialist) revolution?

There is no doubt that this mode of critical inquiry challenges conventional wisdom and official paradigms. Its criterion of social practice unsettles postcolonial ambivalence and Manichean delirium. It repudiates the bureaucratic syndrome concerned with "who gets what when" and with the economics of scarcity and supply-and-demand. In practically all orthodox thinking on modernization, private ownership of the means of production (land, technology, etc.) and "efficient resource allocation and enhanced productivity" through foreign investment and marketing strategies of elite sectors function as axiomatic givens, received "common sense." By privileging private interests and instrumental/utilitarian solutions, the explanatory model of neoclassical economics fails to take into account the historical contexts of class, ethnicity, gender, sectoral conflicts, etc. It elides the centuries-long dispute over land. It evades the question of citizen participation in political-economic decisions, a context in which (as the Philippine case demonstrates so clearly)[3] ownership of land is only one factor embroiled in the larger issue of oligarchic monopoly of wealth and power maintained by hierarchical structures, institutions, and mentalities left over from the past. Top-down bureaucratic planning ignores the overriding force of the international division of labor in the removal of economic surplus by foreign capital, a phenomenon that Paul Baran, in his classic study *The Political Economy of Growth* (1957), has thoroughly analyzed. Baran concludes:

> It is the economic strangulation of the colonial and dependent countries by the imperialist powers that stymied the development of indigenous industrial capitalism, thus preventing the overthrow of the feudal-mercantile order and assuring the rule of the comprador administrations. It is the preservation of these subservient governments, stifling economic and social development and suppressing all popular movements for social and national liberation, that makes possible at the present time the continued foreign exploitation of underdeveloped countries and their domination by the imperialist powers. (1982, 203-04)

It is not surprising to discover once again that neoliberal empiricism and its postFordist descendants cannot envisage what is really at stake in such a life-or-death matter as land reform or grassroots democracy in contested zones.

One last marker of geopolitical import should be noted. The centrality of transnational corporations in structuring power relations among nations and peoples needs no elaborate argument. Considering how today six hundred of these corporations produce twenty-five percent of everything made in the world and account for eighty to ninety percent of the exports of the United States, Japan, Britain, and Canada, no substantive appraisal of programs for democratic change can be conducted without interrogating the role and impact of such entities in the social, political, and cultural transformation of the Third World (Fitt, Faire, and Vigier 1980). This is precisely what Armand Mattelart has accomplished in his book *Transnationals and the Third World* (1983). Mattelart analyzes the logistics and ideological apparatuses engaged in the production of cultural commodities for the world market and reveals how the ethos of Western business practice, legitimized by such notions as security, freedom, efficiency, and so forth, is normalized in Third World societies through the virtually unconstrained operations of the Western-managed knowledge or consciousness industry.[4] Can the postcolonial intellect dismantle this setup? Fed to this recuperative machine of the conglomerates, the now archetypal romance of decentered alterity can only be one more consumer item for Baudrillard and Lyotard's indefatigable shopper.

The prospect, however, need not be dismaying, an occasion for intoning the mantra of certain fellow-travellers: "pessimism of the mind, optimism of the will." Against the long duration of colonial reification and fragmentation fostered by metropolitan High Culture, virtually the "prehistory" of people of color, Third World activists inspired by Fanon, Mao, Che Guevara, Malcolm X, and others have mounted offensives against the Orientalizing will-to-power of the Western Self. One can cite here Aimé Césaire's eloquent *Discourse on Colonialism*; the *testimonios* of Rigoberta Menchu and other indigenous witnesses from South America, Africa, and Oceania; *Song of Ariran*, the magnificent allegory of a revolutionary coming-of-age by the Korean Kim San (Wales and San 1941); and film-texts from the Philippines like *The Perfumed Nightmare* by Kidlat Tahimik and *Orapronobis* by Lino Brocka, not to mention the rich exemplary achievement of Cuban cinema.

In a revisionary move in the early eighties, I proposed that national allegories composed under authoritarian or military fascist regimes be designated "emergency writing" after Walter Benjamin's ever-timely exhortation: "The tradition of the oppressed teaches us that the 'state of emergency' in which we live is not the exception but the rule. We must attain to a conception of history in keeping with this insight. Then we shall clearly realize that our task is to bring about a real state of emergency" (1969, 257). The resonance of "emergency" corresponds better to the structures of feeling in the works of Ngugi, Darwish, Dalton, and others in their beleaguered positions than to terms such as "postcolonial" or "subaltern."

Symptomatic of the attenuation of Third World resistance in the eighties is the rise of postcolonial textualism. In contrast to the counter-canonical archive cited above, this new speculative trend inaugurated by Edward Said's path-breaking *Orientalism* (1978) focuses on one singular task: the demystifying interrogation of Eurocentric discourse. It seeks to dismantle the truth-claims of this discourse by exposing how its epistemic violence has fashioned the marginal, negative, subaltern Other. The problematic within which postcolonial critics like Homi Bhabha, Gayatri Spivak, Trinh T. Minh-ha, and their disciples operate is defined by what Ahmad calls "the main cultural tropes of bourgeois humanism" (Aijas Ahmad 1992, 36): the exorbitation of discourse; the poststructuralist epistemology of the unstable, schizoid, and polyvocal subject; the constitution of knowledge/power by language, by *différance*, aporia, and so on (Bhabha 1992; Spivak 1990). Such maneuvers to transcend the fate of marginality bear all the stigmata of their social-historical determinations. Where is the "Other" situated in this play of Symbolic and Imaginary registers? Benita Parry has charged postcolonial deconstructionists of erasing "the voice of the native" or else limiting "native resistance to devices circumventing and interrogating colonial authority," thereby discounting the salience of "enabling socio-economic and political institutions and other forms of social praxis" (1987, 43). Thus the "posting" of reality coincides if not sanctions the metaphysics of the West's infamous "civilizing mission" (see Callinicos 1989).

Recently, the German critic Frank Schulze-Engler (1993) has inventoried the inadequacies of this trend by commenting on how Bhabha, Spivak, and others have consistently ignored the fact that "it is the interaction of communicating people that constitutes the world for language" and in so doing they cannot account for 'subjectivity' or 'agency' except in a highly instrumental or strategic sense." The result is "epistemological necrophilia." In this carnival of shifting positionalities, amid this ludic heteroglossia inconceivable even from the standpoint of the arch-dialogist Bakhtin, the postcolonial intelligence is unable to discriminate the specific modernities found in the settler colonies (one model of a postcolonial society proposed by *The Empire Writes Back* is the United States!), the invaded/occupied domains, and assorted neocolonies. It cannot imagine such an unthinkable event as New Zealand becoming the nation of Aotearoa (see During 1987; Slemon 1987), or the new order envisaged by the Brazilian Worker's Party described by its spokesperson Luiz da Silva as "a new society founded on the values of liberty and social justice" (1993); or the commitment of Hawaiian Haunani-Kay Trask in fighting for Papahanaumoku, the Earth Mother. Could it be that these intellectuals, as Henry Louis Gates (1994) insinuates, are only sophisticated narcissists acting out the predicament of exile and dislocation? Or are they the new heroines/avatars of an apocalyptic judgment looming in the horizon?

We in the Third World certainly hope for change, not for utopia but for the chance to be in control of our lives. This can only happen under conditions not of our own making, in the shadow of "forms of life" inherited from the past. While most of the essays gathered here, responding to the circumstantial imperatives of the seventies and early eighties, evoke a conjuncture that will not be replicated again after the demise of "actually existing socialism," I believe that the examples of Ho Chi Minh, Ngugi, Dalton, Ramirez, Turki, and many others (the rich tradition of oral performances have only been alluded to here) possess a catalyzing usefulness and relevance for present and future generations. The reason for this is that the ground or substratum of manifold experience allegorized by their art persists in the Third World, manifest in the nightmare of exploited and alienated labor, of sexism and racist oppression, and latent in the gratifications of the postmodern Sublime. The historic agency of native actors/protagonists and the sensuous particularities of their resistance demand to be witnessed, not just represented, inscribed in that space once circumscribed by the colonial episteme and now multiply determined by global exchange, a stage where social identity has become world-historical in its constitution. It is in the context of an evolving planetary horizon of cultural politics that Neil Lazarus contends that postcolonial intellectuals disavow their comprador ventriloquism and instead try to revitalize the category of universality—nationalitarian, radical, liberationist— "from which it is possible to assume the burden of speaking for all humanity" (1993, 52).

We are then finally faced with the dilemma of discriminating among native informant, ethnographic construct, subaltern mimicry, and/or genuine historical agent of insurrectionary practice. We are in search of the collective speaking subject, a figure that refers to specific communities, variegated and no longer anonymous "identity groups," with all their incommensurable genealogies and dissonant traditions. They comprise the quanta of energy in the unsynchronized force field of the "national popular." They are not unitary or monadic subjects of a metaphysical nationalism sprung from Hegel's brain and privileging the telos of self-realization (Eagleton 1990). They materialize in a contradictory unity of classes and groups locked in conflict but in permanent motion (which is what "dialectic" signifies), in the uneven disarticulated sites labelled (for convenience's sake) the "Third World." In those sites, what proves efficacious is a dialectical approach which subverts the containment strategy of idealist metaphysics and allows Eqbal Ahmad (1981) and Samir Amin (1989), among others, to discern the resonance of autochtonous or aboriginal subtexts in dependent milieus, to hear a multiplicity of voices running against the grain. It also allows us to acknowledge the originality of the Palestinian *intifada*, its virtue as the "moral and mobilizable force of coordinated, intelligent courageous human action." This dialectical method of allegorizing the resistance of the subjugated is our antithesis/substitute for postcolonial scholasticism.

In July 1993, a gathering of left and progressive organizations around the world known as the Sao Paolo Foro released a declaration which makes obsolete previous UN programs. The founding vision is enunciated in this affirmation: "We urge ... the creation and implementation of development models which, expressing the interests and organized power of mass movements, move toward sustained and independent, environmentally balanced economic growth with equitable distribution of wealth, in the framework of strengthening democracy in all areas" (Pizarro 1993). Daniel Ortega of the Sandinista party in Nicaragua counseled that while integration of national economies is needed, "policies must be according to our own circumstances in our own countries." This is a view shared by Cuauhtemoc Cardenas, leader of the Revolutionary Democratic Party of Mexico, for whom policies "must be rooted in our own country's history and culture." We apprehend here not a totalizing unity but a contradictory or dialogical synthesis that heralds the advent of a new epoch for the impoverished majority of our planet. We are just beginning to witness the emergence of Third World peoples as historic agents in the shaping of their own ethnic, racial, and national histories salvaged from the hubris of Manichean politics and the specular abyss of *différance*. Amid the revolt in the hinterlands, metropolitan elites with their monopoly of knowledge and apparatuses of ideological hegemony continue to uphold and impose their supremacy over a planet where exchange value and the commodification of everything still govern our sensibilities, stultify our imagination, and limit the pleasure of use values in our everyday lives.

Historical materialism affords us insight into the present crisis of revolutionary movements in the "Third World." Changes there will come from a convergence of popular initiatives, the mediating force of the indigenous intellectuals (in the large sense defined by Gramsci) both traditional and organic, and the solidarity of progressive forces across nation-state, linguistic, and religious/ethnic borderlines. This is perhaps the moment to suggest how the absence of a democratizing impulse in mainstream development thought (soon to be absorbed in the new discipline of Cultural Studies), a characteristic of the ideology of competitive accumulation in the global marketplace, can be traced to two foundations of capitalism as a world system that Immanuel Wallerstein (1983, 75–93) denominates as racism and universalism. While racism functions as a worldwide mechanism to control the direct producers by hierarchical and differential distribution of wealth (see also Sivanandan 1982), universalism proclaims truth (in the mind of the ascendant European bourgeoisie) to inhere in technical and instrumental rationality, hence the slogan of progress and modernization justifying the predatory effects of Western cultural imperialism.

Opposing technocratic modernization sponsored by transnational conglomerates are diverse nationalisms, ethnic revivals, and a diverse coalition of communities and regions bound to be sacrificed in the name of free enterprise and consumer satisfaction. What is called for in any democratizing mandate, in any counterhegemonic project today, is critical anatomy or diagnosis of the contemporary resurgence of ethnically based or religion-oriented nationalisms and, in particular, of sharp racial antagonisms overdetermined by *ressentiment*, unaddressed grievances, and assorted libidinal investments which are currently renegotiating the boundaries of First World/Third World transactions.

The revolutionary power of native agency absent in postcolonial discourse may be encountered in the current transvaluation of traditional beliefs and archaic practices. From the perspective of liberation theology (as enunciated particularly by Asian and Latin American activists), the radically democratic aspiration of people of color in both metropolis and periphery is in essence a struggle for liberation, a process of self-empowerment. This endeavor problematizes the construction of subaltern agents in neocolonial society and releases social energies otherwise channelled to profit making and other wasteful pursuits. This process of transition involves difficult choices, antinomies, zigzags and detours, vexing ambiguities and paradoxes (Fagen 1986). Refusing to be seduced by "ethnocentric thinking of the white North," the struggle of the impoverished masses will have to choose, as Goulet puts it, between two principles of social organization: one which values efficiency and social control, the other social justice and "the creation of a new man." While the rhetoric of that statement is oppositional, disjunctive, and even utopian, the emancipatory thrust of grassroots organizing among workers and peasants in many developing countries is unequivocal. Meanwhile, in the industrialized nations, both fetishisms of technology and of untamed nature (advocated by some ecology groups) rule out the attainment of social justice and the shaping of new alternative forms of life, collective goals which Raymond Williams (1983, 175–217) foresees as the real challenge of the twenty-first century. The spirit of national-popular liberation celebrated by Third World allegories encompasses both order and freedom, discipline and social justice.

What is at stake in this initiative of reconceptualizing popular agency and foregrounding the transgressive potential of the national-popular imagination? Precisely the answer to the questions introduced earlier: Growth for whom? Progress for what?

Opposing the chauvinist elitism of Western planners and advisers, *The People's Development Agenda* (1990) drawn up by the Council for

People's Development in the Philippines presents an alternative. It sums up the lessons of half a century of mass struggles for popular democracy and national liberation: development "refers to the struggle to advance the socioeconomic rights of the poor majority, to strengthen their capacity to gain control of production resources, to improve their capability to meet basic needs, and to create the means towards their sustained development. It is an integral part of the process of transferring political and socioeconomic power from the elite to the majority who are poor." This Filipino desideratum of "democratic participation of the people in development processes" echoes the sentiment of Third World self-determination crystallized in "The Pastoral Letter from the Third World" issued by fifteen Latin American bishops headed by Dom Helder Camara in 1968. It takes up the message of the Cocoyoc (Mexico) Declaration formulated in 1974 by the participants of the Symposium on Models of Resources Utilization: A Strategy for the Environment and Development organized by UNCTAD and UNPE (United Programs for the Environment). This declaration affirms the primacy of self-reliance even as it valorizes the solidarity of peoples: "reliance on the capacity of people themselves to invent and generate new resources and techniques, . . . to take a measure of command over the economy, and to generate their own way of life." It upholds production for equitable use, not for profit or power, to satisfy basic human needs (which include self-fulfillment, participation, togetherness, conviviality). It also calls for affirming the first principle of human dignity, "namely that human beings as well as their culture need to be treated by others with due respect, for their own sakes and on their own terms." Surpassing the demand for formal civil rights, this principle of reciprocity/integrity rejects outright the canonical methodology of technocratic development and assigns priority to the task of preserving and enriching indigenous, national/popular culture as "an integral whole of accumulated resources, both material and non-material, which they [the Calibans of transnational capital] utilize, transform and transmit in order to satisfy their needs, assert their identity and give meaning to their lives" (Mattelart 1983, 25).

A decade after the UN call for a New International Economic Order, Samir Amin (1985) reprised the major contradiction in the world-system arena: "between the pressures of globalization (or 'transnationalization') imposed by the predominance of capital, and the aspirations of working classes, peoples and nations for some autonomous space." To remedy the disarticulating effects of the new "electronic revolution" resulting in drastic time-space compression (Harvey 1989) and various forms of coercive displacements, constituencies in the

Third World have invented an arsenal of novel techniques of resistance, transgression, and self-recovery. Unity of opposites thus gives way to antagonism and subject-formation. Witness (to cite only the most well-known instances) the 1986 "people power" insurrection in the Philippines, the student rebellions in South Korea, the revival of revolutionary opposition in Brazil after decades of military rule, and the inexhaustible resourcefulness of Mandela's African National Congress faced with the vicious terrorism of the apartheid State. Sparks of hope in the wasteland of the global megamall? Perhaps. This intervention of new historical subjects—the spiritually dispossessed "hewers of wood and drawers of water" carving out a zone of nomadic, perverse energies which then explode and circulate across the East-West ideological divide—is a protean and self-renewing movement that may bridge the gulf between North and South, between rich and poor nations, between the past and the future.

Of late some activists in the United States have claimed that the Brundtland UN Report of 1987 on Environment and Development focusing on the theme of "sustainable development" can serve as a basis for a political-ethical alliance between North and South. Resource depletion, environmental injury, burgeoning human populations, oppression—these are surely urgent concerns with universal appeal. But can the project of participatory democracy and self-reliance survive the "New World Order" born from a war propelled by racist exterminism and commercial greed? There are in fact several wars raging today in every continent (one can cite offhand those in East Timor, in Kurdistan, in the Philippines). With the demise of Soviet and East European "socialism" as a counterbalance to the domination of the transcendental commodity and the omnipotent market, increased rivalry among the European states, the United States, and Japan is bound to complicate interstate relations, notwithstanding the establishment of free trade linkages and respective spheres of influence. Local surrogate wars (targeting recalcitrant states such as Iran, North Korea, or Cuba) will be tomorrow's scenarios. Some observers (Petras 1991) predict that the compradorization of Eastern Europe and the refeudalization of other regions as a result of the weakening and fragmentation of state structures will open up new markets of cheap labor and capital. This will occur in the wake of revitalized racisms and ethnocentrisms, along with the recrudescence of sexist, chauvinist, and religious intolerance of all sorts.

What is the alternative? In a lecture delivered at Tribhuvan University, Kathmandu, Nepal, Sam Noumoff, director of the Center for Developing Area Studies at McGill University, sketched the dismal prospect of development in the Third World: greater penetration of these societies by transnational market's control of the production process (knowledge-intensive industries), loss of leverage with the decline of the need for raw materials, decrease of agricultural earnings due to Western protectionism, the traps of the "green revolution" and debt (this last administered by the IMF/World Bank prevents indigenous capital formation), export-led growth insuring permanent dependency through import of capital-intensive technology, the rule of comparative advantage freezing the Third World in a dual economy, and so on (1991). Among other countermeasures, Noumoff suggested regional cooperation in research to break the North's technological monopoly, integrated training in joint ventures to break the MNC marketing monopoly, and internal diffusion of technology throughout society.

In retrospect, Noumoff's proposal evokes the ideal of self-reliance affirmed by the 1974 Coyoyoc Declaration, the theme of empowerment in the Filipino "people's agenda," and the prophetic passion of the Latin American theology of liberation: "One must institute a program which uses as a measure of development the most deprived in the society. The measure of a developed society is not how the best live; the measure of a society is what is the state of the poorest person, and one must start there. . . . It is through internal strength and empowerment at the local level that self-sustained development will occur which will be the basis of the prosperity of this country [Nepal]." Only in that way, I think, will the antinomy of postcolonial democracy and capitalist modernization inscribed in the history of the world system be transmuted by those whom Fanon designated as "the wretched of the earth" into the protracted process of liberation and empowerment of the majority—workers, women, peasants, the poor in general—that will also guarantee the preservation of the earth's biosphere. Against the leviathan of commodification marching on the ruins of Baghdad and the Kremlin, one can oppose the solidarity of peoples of color, their history of creativity and resourcefulness, their heterogeneous cultures of resistance, their commitment to the dignity and freedom of specific communities, as the best hope of humankind's survival and regeneration in the next millennium.

## NOTES

1. A *Newsweek* article (9 September 1991, 37) entitled "How the West Can Win the New World Order" registers this Establishment triumphalism in a mass media style.

2. As validation, see the ingenious commentary on the Angolan writer Manuel Rui's short story by Wlad Godzich's (1988), who argues for the inclusion of "emergent literature" in the field of comparative literature.
3. A succinct background to the problems of land reform and social inequality, and to the prospect of popular democracy, in the Philippines may be found in Canlas, Miranda, and Putzel (1988).
4. For a brilliant specimen of deconstructive analysis dealing with asymmetrical North/South encounters, and also epitomizing the dialectic of an exploitative modernity and popular resistance, see Buck-Morss (1987).

BIBLIOGRAPHY

Ahmad, Aijaz. *In Theory*. London: Verso, 1992.
Ahmad, Eqbal. "The Contemporary Crisis of the Third World." *Monthly Review* 32 (1981): 1–11.
Alavi, Hamza, and Theodor Shanin, eds. *Introduction to the Sociology of Developing Societies*." New York: Monthly Review Press, 1982.
Amin, Samir. *Imperialism and Unequal Development*. New York: Monthly Review Press, 1977.
———. "The Crisis, the Third World, and North-South, East-West Relations." In *Rethinking Marxism*, edited by Stephen Resnick and Richard Wolff, 1–8. New York: Autonomedia, 1985.
———. *Eurocentrism*. New York: Monthly Review Press, 1989.
Ashcroft, Bill, Gareth Griffiths, and Helen Tiffin. *The Empire Writes Back*. New York: Routledge, 1989.
Baran, Paul. *Political Economy of Growth*. New York: Monthly Review Press, 1957.
———. "A Morphology of Backwardness." In *Introduction to the Sociology of "Developing Societies,"* 195–204. New York: Monthly Review Press, 1982.
Bauer, Otto. "National Character and the Idea of the Nation." In *Essential Works of Socialism*, edited by Irving Howe, 267–78. New York: Bantam Books, 1971.
Benjamin, Walter. *Illuminations*. New York: Schocken, 1969.
Beverley, John, and Marc Zimmerman. *Literature and Politics in the Central American Revolutions*. Austin: Univ. of Texas Press, 1990.
Bhabha, Homi K. "Postcolonial Criticism." In *Redrawing the Boundaries*, edited by Stephen Greenblatt and Giles Gunn, 437–65. New York: Modern Language Association of America, 1992.
Buchanan, Keith. "Reflections on a 'Dirty Word.'" *Dissent* 31 (Summer 1974): 25–31. Reprinted in *Radical Geography*, edited by Richard Peet. Chicago: Maaroufa Press, 1977.
Buck-Morss, Susan. "Semiotic Boundaries and the Politics of Meaning: Modernity on Tour—A Village in Transition." In *New Ways of Knowing*, edited by Marcus G. Raskin and Herbert J. Bernstein, 200–236. Totowa, N.J.: Rowman & Littlefield, 1987.

Callinicos, Alex. *Against Postmodernism*. New York: St. Martin's Press, 1989.
Canlas, Mamerto, Mariano Miranda, and James Putzel. *Land, Poverty and Politics in the Philippines*. London: Catholic Institute for International Relations, 1988.
Césaire, Aimé. *Discourse on Colonialism*. New York: Monthly Review Press, 1972.
Chaliand, Gerard. *Revolution in the Third World*. New York: Penguin Books, 1978.
Council for People's Development. *People's Development Agenda*. Manila: Council for People's Development, 1990.
During, Simon. "Postmodernism or Post-colonialism Today." *Textual Practice* (1987): 32–47.
Eagleton, Terry. "Nationalism: Irony and Commitment." In *Nationalism, Colonialism, and Literature*, by Terry Eagleton, Frederic Jameson, and Edward W. Said, 23–42. Minneapolis: Univ. of Minnesota Press, 1990.
Fagen, Richard R. "The Politics of Transition." In *Transition and Development*, edited by Richard Fagen, Carmen Diana Deere, and Jose Luis Coraggio. New York: Monthly Review Press, 1986.
Fitt, Yann, Alexandre Faire, and Jean-Pierre Vigier. *The World Economic Crisis*. London: Zed Press, 1980.
Gates, Henry Louis, Jr. "Critical Fanonism." In *Contemporary Literary Criticism*, edited by Robert Con Davis and Ronald Schleifer, 132–43. New York: Longman, 1994.
Godzich, Wlad. "Emergent Literature and the Field of Comparative Literature." In *The Comparative Perspective on Literature*, edited by Clayton Koelb and Susan Noakes, 18–36. Ithaca: Cornell Univ. Press, 1988.
Goulet, Denis. *The Cruel Choice*. New York: Atheneum, 1971.
Gramsci, Antonio. *Selections from Cultural Writings*. Cambridge, Mass.: Harvard Univ. Press, 1985.
Gugelberger, Georg. "Decolonizing the Canon: Considerations of Third World Literature." *New Literary History* 22 (Summer 1991): 505–24.
Harvey, David. *The Condition of Postmodernity*. Oxford: Basil Blackwell, 1989.
James, C. L. R. *The C. L. R. James Reader*. New York: Blackwell, 1992.
Jameson, Fredric. "Third-World Literature in the Era of Multinational Capitalism." *Social Text*, no. 15 (1986): 65–88.
Lazarus, Neil. "National Consciousness and the Specificity of (Post)Colonial Intellectualism." 1993. Unpublished typescript.
Mattelart, Armand. *Transnationals and the Third World: The Struggle for Culture*. South Hadley, Mass.: Bergin & Garvey, 1983.
Melotti, Umberto. *Marx and the Third World*. London: Macmillan, 1977.
Mintz, Sidney. "On the Concept of a Third World." *Dialectical Anthropology* 1 (1976): 377–82.
Mukherjee, Arun. "Whose Post-Colonialism and Whose Postmodernism?" *World Literature Written in English* 30 (1990): 1–9.

Noumoff, Sam J. "The New International Order as an Impediment to Third World Development." Lecture delivered at the Centre for Nepal and Asian Studies, Tribhuvan Univ., Kathmandu, Nepal, 11 June 1991. 20 pages.

Parry, Benita. "Problems in Current Theories of Colonial Discourse." *Oxford Literary Review* 9 (1987): 27–58.

Petras, James. "World Transformations: The Challenges for the Left." *Against the Current*, No. 34 (Sept.-Oct. 1991): 17–22.

Pizarro, Rafael. "The Regrouping of the Latin American Left." *Corresponder* 2 (Aug.-Sept. 1993): 22.

Rodney, Walter. *How Europe Underdeveloped Africa*. Washington D.C.: Howard Univ. Press, 1982.

Said, Edward. *Orientalism*. New York: Pantheon Books, 1978.

Schiller, Herbert. *Culture, Inc.* New York: Oxford Univ. Press, 1989.

Schulze-Engler, Frank. "Universalism with a Difference: The Politics of Post-Colonial Theory." Paper read at Karl-Franzens Univ., Graz, 18 May 1993.

Silva, Luiz da. "The Transformations Must Be Deep and Global." In *Global Visions*, edited by Jeremy Brecher et al., 171–74. Boston: South End Press, 1993.

Sivanandan, A. *A Different Hunger*. London: Pluto Press, 1982.

Slemon, Stephen. "Monuments of Empire: Allegory/Counter-Discourse/Post-Colonial Writing." *Kunapipi* 9 (1987): 1–16.

Spivak, Gayatri Chakravorty. *The Post-Colonial Critic*. New York: Routledge, 1990.

Wales, Nym, and Kim San. *Song of Ariran*. San Francisco: Ramparts Press, 1941.

Wallerstein, Immanuel. *Historical Capitalism*. London: Verso, 1983.

Weisskopf, Thomas E. "Capitalism and Underdevelopment in the Modern World." In *The Capitalist System*, by Richard C. Edwards, Michael Reich, and Thomas E. Weiskopf, 442–57. Englewood Cliffs, N.J.: Prentice-Hall, 1972.

Williams, Raymond. *The Year 2000*. New York: Pantheon Books, 1983.

Woddis, Jack. *Introduction to Neo-Colonialism*. New York: International Publishers, 1972.

Wolf, Eric. *Europe and the People Without History*. Berkeley: Univ. of California Press, 1982.

Worsley, Peter. *The Third World*. Chicago: Univ. of Chicago Press, 1964.

# NAME INDEX

**A**
Abdo, Nahla, 73
Abdullah, Ghassan, 135, 136, 149, 153, 157
Achebe, Chinua, 11, 22, 40, 85, 126, 134, 147, 150
Adorno, Theodor, 139
Agoncillo, Teodoro, 121
Aguilar, Faustino, 121
Aguinaldo, Emilio, 163
Ahmad, Aijaz, 147–48, 174–75
Ahmad, Eqbal, 133, 184
Alarcon, Roberto, 162
al-Hout, Shafiq, 68
Alighieri, Dante, 87
Allende, Salvador, 134, 172
Althusser, Louis, 38, 86, 143, 166
Amin, Samir, 125, 127, 147, 148, 151, 173, 184, 187
Anderson, Sherwood, 121
Arafat, Yasir, 63, 67
Arguilla, Manuel, 46, 121
Aristophanes, 116
Armah, Ayi Kwei, 126
Arnold, Matthew, 23
Ashcroft, Bill, 52, 124
Asturias, Miguel, 23
Awoonor, Kofi, 22

**B**
Bakhtin, Mikhail, 43, 48, 114, 138, 150, 155, 156, 158, 183
Baking, Angel, 49, 121
Bakunin, Mikhail, 121
Balagtas, Francisco, 45
Baraka, Amiri, 169
Baran, Paul, 181
Barros, Maria Lorena, 16, 66

Barthes, Roland, 150
Bataille, George, 139
Baudelaire, Charles, 140
Baudrillard, Jean, 134, 153–54, 156, 175, 182
Bauer, Otto, 126, 175
Bautista, Lualhati, 128
Beckett, Samuel, 83
Benjamin, Walter, 53, 121, 151, 182
Betto, Frei, 167
Beverley, John, 49, 108, 143
Bhabha, Homi, 182, 183
Blanco, Hugo, 11
Bloch, Ernst, 52, 53, 74, 113, 175
Blount, James, 37
Borge, Tomas, 136
Borges, Jorge Luis, 81, 143, 157
Bourdieu, Pierre, 119, 156
Brathwaite, Edward, 40
Brecht, Bertolt, 86, 97, 104, 128, 133
Breton, André, 109, 145
Brocka, Lino, 49, 126, 182
Brown, John, 165
Brutus, Dennis, 25
Buhle, Paul, 151
Bui, Hien, 89
Bulosan, Carlos, 44, 49, 121, 122
Bunyan, John, 27
Buscayno, Bernabe, 49

**C**
Cabezas, Omar, 136
Cabral, Amilcar, 12, 30, 51, 61, 78, 85, 126
Cage, John, 86
Camara, Dom Helder, 187

# NAME INDEX

Camus, Albert, 60, 156
Cardenal, Ernesto, 5, 11, 49, 108, 109, 143
Cardenas, Cuauhtemoc, 185
Carew, Jan, 149
Carpentier, Alejo, 109, 110, 111, 113, 162
Castillo, Otto Rene, 28, 66, 104
Castro, Fidel, 89, 110, 162, 163, 164, 167, 166, 172
Cather, Willa, 124
Cervantes, Miguel de, 87, 120
Césaire, Aimé, 21, 23, 81, 129, 149, 150, 155, 157, 182
Chaliand, Gerard, 173
Chomsky, Noam, 69
Chungara, Domitila Barrios de, 52
Clifford, James, 155
Coleridge, Samuel, 23
Comte, Auguste, 146
Condorcet, Marquis de, 126
Confucius, 30
Conrad, Joseph, 25, 145, 147
Constantino, Renato, 39, 121
Crisologo, Mena Pecson, 47

## D

Dalisay, Jose, 128
Dalton, Roque, 11, 103–09, 117, 182, 183
Dario, Ruben, 49, 134, 142, 143
Darwish, Mahmoud, 68, 73, 74, 88, 182
De Jesus, Jose Corazon, 121
De la Torre, Edicio, 44, 49, 128
Dean, Vera Micheles, 27
Debray, Regis, 127, 157, 158
Del Pilar, Marcelo, 45, 120, 163
Deleuze, Gilles, 41, 121
Depestre, René, 28
Derrida, Jacques, 14, 139, 166, 174
Desnoes, Edmundo, 143, 144, 145
Diaz, Jesus, 162
Dickens, Charles, 124

Diego, Eliseo, 162
Ding Ling, 5, 12
Diop, David, 28
Dostoevsky, Feodor, 25
Dreiser, Theodore, 122
Dubois, W.E.B., 150

## E

Eliot, T.S., 11, 12, 24, 27
Emerson, Ralph Waldo, 130, 164
Empson, William, 11
Engels, Friedrich, 15, 77, 121, 166
Enriquez, Virgilio, 41
Escobar, Elizam, 152–53, 157
Estrada, Joseph, 49

## F

Fanon, Frantz, 10, 20, 21, 23, 51, 72, 82, 127, 129, 136, 148, 150, 152–53, 156, 157, 172, 173, 178, 182
Faulkner, William, 24
Fichte, Johann, 128
Fitzgerald, F. Scott, 60
Flaubert, Gustave, 24
Forbes, William Cameron, 36
Fornet, Ambrosio, 162
Forster, E. M., 145
Foucault, Michel, 47, 139, 166, 174
Franco, Jean, 144
Freud, Sigmund, 134
Friend, Theodore, 36
Frye, Northrop, 27
Fuentes, Carlos, 23, 82, 84

## G

Gadamer, Hans-Georg, 156
Galeano, Eduardo, 168
Gandhi, Mahatma, 20
Garaudy, Roger, 108
Garcia Marquez, Gabriel, 14, 23, 110, 134, 141, 145
Gaspar, Karl, 45
Gates, Henry Louis, 183
Giddens, Anthony, 140, 141

Ginsberg, Allen, 16
Godelier, Maurice, 39
Goethe, Johann Wolfgang, 87, 119, 126
Gonzalez, Andrew, 42–43, 45
Gordimer, Nadine, 148
Gorki, Maxim, 130
Goulet, Denis, 180, 186
Goux, Jean Joseph, 142
Gramsci, Antonio, 38, 53, 86, 106, 123, 151, 166–67, 175–76, 185
Guattari, Felix, 41, 121
Guevara, Ernesto "Che," 12, 51, 82, 126, 161, 162, 163, 167, 182
Guillen, Nicolas, 12, 27, 82, 162, 164, 166

## H

Habash, George, 70
Habermas, Jürgen, 129, 135, 139–40, 143, 146, 151, 157
Haggard, H. Rider, 145
Haley, Alex, 30
Hall, Stuart, 173
Hao, Jan, 23
Hardy, Thomas, 16
Harlow, Barbara, 72, 73
Harris, Wilson, 40
Hart, Armando, 162
Harvey, David, 134, 141
Hawatmeh, Nayef, 70
Hayden, Joseph, 36
Heidegger, Martin, 139, 156
Hegel, Friedrich, 14, 105, 145, 184
Hemingway, Ernest, 121
Herder, Johann, 128
Hernandez, Amado, 49, 85, 121, 129
Hikmet, Nazim, 31–33, 66, 84
Ho Chi Minh, 20, 93–102, 162, 183
Hobbes, Thomas, 139

Horace, 106
Horkheimer, Max, 139
Hugo, Victor, 120
Hulme, T. E., 11
Hurston, Zora Neale, 149

## J

Jabra, Ibrahim Jabra, 73
Jackson, George, 51, 135
Jaena, Graciano Lopez, 120
Jakobson, Roman, 42
James, C. L. R., 9, 12, 51, 126, 151, 157, 176, 177
James, Henry, 24, 164
Jameson, Fredric, 48, 125, 140, 147–48, 161, 175, 176
Javellana, Stevan, 44
Joaquin, Nick, 44, 124–25
Joyce, James, 103

## K

Kafka, Franz, 25
Kanafani, Ghassan, 73, 137
Kant, Immanuel, 23, 103, 155
Kardelj, Edward, 126
Karnow, Stanley, 36, 37, 50
Keene, Donald, 124
Kenyatta, Jomo, 61
Khoury, Elias, 71
Kierkegaard, Soren, 156
Kim Chi Ha, 19
Kim Il Sung, 80
Kim San, 182
Kipling, Rudyard, 145
Kosinski, Jerzy, 83–84
Kunene, Mazisi, 22

## L

La Guma, Alex, 25
Lacan, Jacques, 14, 174
Lansang, Jose, 121
Larson, Charles, 24–25, 27
Laya, Juan, 44, 121
Lazarus, Neil, 184
Le Corbusier, 86

# 196 NAME INDEX

Leonard, John, 19
Lenin, Vladimir, 15, 20, 66, 70, 78, 86, 100, 126. 166
Levinas, Emmanuel, 155
Lopez, Salvador, 121
Loti, Pierre, 30–31
L'Ouverture, Toussaint, 151
Lowy, Michael, 126
Lucretius, 27
Lu Hsun, 12, 17, 51, 149, 176
Lumumba, Patrice, 20, 50, 172
Lukács, Georg, 86, 107, 111, 138, 140, 166
Lyotard, Jean Francois, 135, 136, 143, 156, 157, 175, 182

## M

Mabini, Apolinario, 163
MacDiarmid, Hugh, 16, 119
McKinley, William, 38
McLuhan, Marshall, 133–34
Machiavelli, Niccolo, 146
Mailer, Norman, 86
Malcolm X, 182
Malé, Belkis Cusa, 164
Malraux, Andre, 25, 145
Mandela, Nelson, 188
Mann, Thomas, 130
Mao Tse-tung, 20, 23, 85, 87, 88, 93, 126, 182
Marcos, Ferdinand, 19, 35, 36, 125, 136
Marcos, Imelda, 126, 154
Marcuse, Herbert, 83
Marinello, Juan, 164
Markandaya, Kamala, 81
Marquez-Benitez, Paz, 38
Marti, Jose, 144, 164, 166
Mattelart, Armand, 181
Marx, Karl, 12, 15, 30, 77, 107, 117, 121, 126, 134, 146, 147, 152, 164, 166, 172, 177–79
Mayakovsky, Vladimir, 104
Meiselas, Susan, 143, 144, 146
Mellotti, Umberto, 178
Memmi, Albert, 148

Menchu, Rigoberta, 11, 52, 149, 182
Mihardja, Achdiat, 12
Millanes, Pablo, 168
Miller, Stuart Creighton, 37
Milton, John, 87
Miner, Earl, 48
Mintz, Sidney, 172, 173
Momaday, Scott, 149
Morejon, Nancy, 164
Mustafa, Yusuf, 71
Myrdal, Jan, 145

## N

Nabokov, Vladimir, 83
Nairn, Tom, 127
Neruda, Pablo, 15, 28, 82, 129
Ngugi, Wa Thiong'o (James), 19, 23, 24, 40, 57–62, 66, 148, 149, 150, 182, 183
Nietzsche, Friedrich, 51, 134, 135, 139, 146
Nkosi, Lewis, 81
Nogenda, John, 81
Noumoff, Sam, 188–89

## O

Ortega, Daniel, 185
Oyono, Ferdinand, 23

## P

Parra, Ramona, 82
Parry, Benita, 183
Perez, Rigoberto Lopez, 112
Perkins, David, 29
Plato, 107, 145
Plekhanov, Georgi, 86
Popper, Karl, 145–46
Pound, Ezra, 11, 12, 24, 26, 103
Pratt, Mary Louise, 48
Protacio-Marcelino, Elizabeth, 42
Proudhon, Pierre Joseph, 121
Proust, Marcel, 24

## R

Rabelais, Francois, 114, 120

# NAME INDEX

Rabin, Yitzhak, 67
Rao, Raja, 23, 40
Ramirez, Sergio, 106, 136, 183
Recto, Claro, 120
Retamar, Roberto Fernandez, 140, 162
Reyes, Isabelo de los, 120
Reyes, Severino, 47, 109–117
Richards, I. A., 23
Rimbaud, Arthur, 151
Rivera, Tomas, 138
Rizal, Jose, 45, 120, 124, 149, 161, 163, 169
Robbe-Grillet, Alain, 86
Rodriguez, Sylvio, 168
Rossi-Landi, Ferruccio, 42
Rostow, W.W., 179–80
Rotor, Arturo, 121, 129–30
Rushdie, Salman, 134, 141

S
Said, Edward, 68, 72, 74, 129, 154, 155, 156, 182
Saldivar, Ramon, 138
Sandino, Augusto Cesar, 113, 116
Santos, Lope K., 120
Sartre, Jean Paul, 86
Saussure, Ferdinand, 48
Schulze-Engler, Frank, 183
Sembene, Ousmane, 11, 23, 176
Senghor, Leopold, 20, 81
Shakespeare, William, 87
Silko, Leslie Marmon, 149
Silva, Luis da, 183
Sison, Jose Maria, 44, 49
Sitwell, Edith, 81
Somoza, Anastasio, 110
Soto, Vicente, 42
Soyinka, Wole, 134, 149, 150, 178
Spengler, Oswald, 146
Spinoza, Benedict, 51
Stalin, Joseph, 177
Stanley, Peter, 36, 37, 38
Stauffer, Robert, 37–38
Stein, Gertrude, 81, 121
Steinberg, David, 36

Sukarno, 20
Swift, Jonathan, 151

T
Taft, William Howard, 39
Tagore, Rabindranath, 12, 82, 134
Tahimik, Kidlat, 49, 182
Tarr, Peter, 38
Tavera, T. H. Pardo de, 40
Taylor, George, 36
Tiongson, Nicanor, 47, 49, 125
Tolstoy, Leo, 101
Toynbee, Arnold, 146
Trask, Haunani-Kay, 183
Trotsky, Leon, 126
Turki, Fawaz, 30, 63–67, 70, 71, 73, 183
Twain, Mark, 122

U
Unamuno, Miguel de, 120

V
Valdez, Luis, 82
Vallejo, Cesar, 11
Vargas Llosa, Mario, 110, 145–46
Vasquez, Adolfo Sanchez, 51
Vico, Giambattista, 146
Vien, Nguyen Khac, 29
Villa, Jose Garcia, 38, 45, 49, 81, 121, 122, 124, 146

W
Wallerstein, Immanuel, 172, 185
Weiss, Peter, 88, 172
Whitman, Walt, 61, 122, 164
Williams, Raymond, 186
Wittgenstein, Ludwig, 137
Wolf, Eric, 140
Wolff, Leon, 37
Worsley, Peter, 172
Wright, Richard, 122

Y
Yeats, William Butler, 24

Z
Zimmerman, Marc, 49, 143